PENGUIN BOOKS

WRITERS AT WORK

SECOND SERIES

The Paris Review, founded in 1953 by a group of young Americans including Peter Matthiessen, Harold L. Humes, George Plimpton, Thomas Guinzburg, and Donald Hall, has survived for twenty-seven years—a rarity in the literary-magazine field, where publications traditionally last for a few issues and then cease. While the emphasis of *The Paris Review*'s editors was on publishing creative work rather than nonfiction (among writers who published their first short stories there were Philip Roth, Terry Southern, Evan S. Connell, Samuel Beckett), part of the magazine's success can be attributed to the public interest in its continuing series of interviews on the craft of writing. Reasoning that it would be preferable to replace the traditional scholarly essay on a given author's work with an interview conducted with the author himself, the editors found a form which attracted considerable comment—from the very first interview, with E. M. Forster, which appeared in the initial issue, in which the distinguished author, then considered the greatest novelist in the English language, divulged why he had not been able to complete a novel since 1926. Since that early interview the magazine has continued to complement its fiction and poetry selection with interviews from a wide range of literary personages, which in sum constitute an authentic and invaluable contribution to the literary history of the past few decades.

D0051352

WRITERS AT WORK

The *Paris Review* Interviews

FIRST SERIES

Edited, and with an Introduction, by MALCOLM COWLEY

E. M. Forster	Frank O'Connor
François Mauriac	Robert Penn Warren
Joyce Cary	Alberto Moravia
Dorothy Parker	Nelson Algren
James Thurber	Angus Wilson
Thornton Wilder	William Styron
William Faulkner	Truman Capote
Georges Simenon	Françoise Sagan

THIRD SERIES

Edited by GEORGE PLIMPTON and introduced by ALFRED KAZIN

William Carlos Williams	Saul Bellow
Blaise Cendrars	Arthur Miller
Jean Cocteau	James Jones
Louis-Ferdinand Céline	Norman Mailer
Evelyn Waugh	Allen Ginsberg
Lillian Hellman	Edward Albee
William Burroughs	Harold Pinter

FOURTH SERIES

Edited by GEORGE PLIMPTON and introduced by WILFRID SHEED

Isak Dinesen	Christopher Isherwood
Conrad Aiken	W. H. Auden
Robert Graves	Eudora Welty
John Dos Passos	John Berryman
Vladimir Nabokov	Anthony Burgess
Jorge Luis Borges	Jack Kerouac
George Seferis	Anne Sexton
John Steinbeck	John Updike

FIFTH SERIES
Edited by George Plimpton and introduced by
Francine du Plessix Gray

P. G. Wodehouse

Archibald MacLeish

Pablo Neruda

Isaac Bashevis Singer

Henry Green

John Cheever

Irwin Shaw

Kingsley Amis

James Dickey

Joseph Heller

William Gass

Gore Vidal

Jerzy Kosinski

Joan Didion

Joyce Carol Oates

Writers at Work

The Paris Review Interviews

SECOND SERIES

Edited by George Plimpton
Introduced by Van Wyck Brooks

PENGUIN BOOKS

Penguin Books Ltd, Harmondsworth,
Middlesex, England
Penguin Books, 625 Madison Avenue,
New York, New York 10022, U.S.A.
Penguin Books Australia Ltd, Ringwood,
Victoria, Australia
Penguin Books Canada Limited, 2801 John Street,
Markham, Ontario, Canada L3R 1B4
Penguin Books (N.Z.) Ltd, 182–190 Wairau Road,
Auckland 10, New Zealand

First published in the United States of America by
The Viking Press 1963
First published in Great Britain by
Martin Secker & Warburg Ltd 1963
Viking Compass Edition published 1965
Reprinted 1965, 1966, 1968, 1969, 1972, 1974
Published in Penguin Books 1977
Reprinted 1979, 1982

Copyright © The Paris Review, Inc., 1963
Copyright in all countries of the International Copyright Union
All rights reserved

LIBRARY OF CONGRESS CATALOGING IN PUBLICATION DATA
Main entry under title:
Writers at work.
1. Authors—Interviews.   I. Plimpton, George.
II. The Paris review.
[PN453.P3 1977]   809   77-7033
ISBN 0 14 00.4541 4

Printed in the United States of America by
The Murray Printing Company, Westford, Massachusetts
Set in Linotype Electra

The interviews and biographical notes in this volume have
been prepared for book publication by George Plimpton.

Except in the United States of America,
this book is sold subject to the condition
that it shall not, by way of trade or otherwise,
be lent, re-sold, hired out, or otherwise circulated
without the publisher's prior consent in any form of
binding or cover other than that in which it is
published and without a similar condition
including this condition being imposed
on the subsequent purchaser

Contents

WRITERS AT WORK

Second Series

Introduction

Unlike the first collection of interviews from *The Paris Review*, all of which dealt entirely with novelists, this volume deals with several kinds of writers. There are at least five poets, Robert Frost, Eliot and Pound, Marianne Moore and Robert Lowell, with essayists like Mary McCarthy who also writes novels, the humorist S. J. Perelman, and Henry Miller. They are individualists, one and all, diverse in their talents as in their kinds, but one generalization seems quite clear, that there is little difference any longer between the American mind and the European. When one thinks of the prewar world and the authors who were outstanding then, Rudyard Kipling, Henrik Ibsen, and Anatole France—all redolent of their countries and so unlike—most of the writers who have lived through the world wars seem to have been denationalized in quality and type. There is nothing local in their points of view, nothing in any way provincial. While they are unique in the outlook of each and the surroundings of their lives, they seem, in these well-prepared interviews, to represent the one world toward which the modern mind is aiming.

Where these writers spend their lives seems to be immaterial, Hemingway in Cuba, Aldous Huxley in California, Eliot in England, Lawrence Durrell in Cyprus and Greece. For everybody lives everywhere at present. But while the motives they exhibit are common to the whole Western world, there are still plenty of other differences among these individuals—for example, between Hemingway, so much a child of the twenties in Paris, and Katherine Anne Porter, who was in Mexico then. To her, everything in Paris in the twenties was "shallow, trivial, and silly" and

1

Scott Fitzgerald was anything but a great writer. She is happy rather to have been involved in the Obregón Revolution. Everyone was talking of the renaissance in Mexico, and she had a marvelous experience in the midst of that.

These writers all have intense convictions and high animal spirits, but after they had passed their adolescence and found their own direction they never belonged to any group. "You are more alone," Hemingway says, "because that is how you must work and the time is shorter all the time." Henry Miller is "against groups and sets and sects and cults and isms," and, always a lone wolf, he never met Gertrude Stein in Paris or any of the set that followed her. Not even a friend of George Orwell, who was "down and out in Paris" at about that time, Miller likes only what is alien and has felt an alien wherever he was, in Paris or at Big Sur. Finding America hostile, he has always had better contact with Europeans, and he feels that America is essentially against the artist who stands for individuality and creativeness. "America," he says, "is the most mechanized and robotized of countries," yet he feels "a hundred per cent American, and I know it more and more every day." Lawrence Durrell says he feels in England like a sort of refugee. Everyone there is worried to death about moral uplift and moral downfall, and everyone feels separated from the artist, whereas in France he feels "on a par with a good cheese or a bad one." That is why, he says, it is so vitally important to identify oneself more and more with Europe. "As for me, I have joined the Common Market, as it were." When Robert Frost was living in England, "my instinct," he says, "was not to belong to any gang," and he adds, "I don't 'belong' here, either." Yet Ezra Pound says, "A man who fits in his milieu, as Frost does, is to be considered a happy man." Pound himself, for whom Italy was disappointing when he returned there from St. Elizabeth's Hospital, has moments when he would "like very much to live in America." He feels "more American all the time," and he would like at least to spend a month or two a year in the United States.

While most of these writers had wished from the first to be writers—like Lawrence Durrell, "madly scribbling . . . since the age of eight"—they usually seem glad to talk of anything but the business of writing. Robert Lowell is the exception. He not only revises "endlessly" but he likes to dwell on technique. On the other hand, Henry Miller says, "I know what I want to write about, but I'm not concerned too much with how I say it"; and Ezra Pound, who has replaced his interest in form with an interest in content, says, "The *what* is so much more important than *how*." Hemingway thinks it is "bad for a writer to talk about how he writes"; he feels that ideas on writing should remain unexpressed. One trait all these writers show is a great exactness of thought and speech but, whether they find writing difficult or easy, they prefer to discuss their subjects rather than their form. "I never think about form at all," Katherine Anne Porter says, nor has she ever taken or adopted a symbol. Henry Miller even feels that "It's bad to think . . . a writer shouldn't think too much," as if the process of cogitation inhibited the natural flow of feeling. "A writer is a man who has antennae, . . . knows how to hook up the currents which are in the atmosphere." He believes one should dive into the unconscious, follow one's impulses of the heart or the guts. He is still working on a project laid out in 1927 that covers everything he has done since then.

One might suppose that Marianne Moore and Robert Frost had little in common, and in fact on one matter they disagree totally. Marianne Moore is interested in mechanical things, in, as she puts it, machines in general, and one remembers the episode of the Ford Company and how Miss Moore was asked to find a name for the new car. Frost, on his part, actively dislikes machines, detests them as much as Willa Cather did, and he says that people "like to hear me say nasty things about machines." But both are equally interested in science, the "greatest adventure of man," says Frost, "the adventure of penetrating into matter, into the material universe." It seems to Marianne Moore that the poet and the scientist work analogously, that both are attentive to clues and strive for precision, though she says, "What I write could only be called poetry because there is no other category in which to put it." Frost is especially interested in astronomy. He is able to name twenty of his poems that have astronomy in them, and he says that a book on astronomy was one of the first he read when he began to read a book through. Henry Miller thinks that the scientists, not the artists, are at present ahead of their time. "The artist is lagging behind," he says. "His imagination is not keeping pace with the men of science."

On the best time of day for writing, on politics, on teaching, several of these writers have interesting things to say. They agree that morning is best for work, although Henry Miller at one time wrote from midnight until dawn. Aldous Huxley works in the morning, three or four hours a day, while he writes everything many times over, and Hemingway writes, or wrote, early after the first light and continued usually until noon, when he went for a swim. "There is no one to disturb you," he says, "and it is cool or cold and you come to your work and warm as you write." Katherine Anne Porter, who works "whenever I'm let," used to do the day's housework and then write at night; "but I prefer," she says, "to get up very early," when there is perfect silence, and work "until the vein is out." This is the way she worked on *Ship of Fools* during the three years she spent in Connecticut. In fact, as compared with certain writers of the past, there is something oddly "normal" about these twentieth-century writers. They do not seem to depend on opium, as Coleridge and De Quincey did, or the fifty thousand cups of strong coffee that enabled Balzac to do his work, nor do they live, like Proust, in cork-lined bedrooms.

About teaching, for writers, there is a certain agreement that it makes them more cautious and makes them write less. Robert Lowell says, "It means a lot to me as a human being, though the danger is that it's much too close to what you're doing." Ezra Pound says, "A man's got to get his rent somehow," and Hemingway's main doubt is that it might limit one's growth in knowledge of the world. Eliot believes he would have been handicapped if he hadn't had to bother about earning a living. Exercising activities other than writing and reading prevented him from writing too much rather than concentrating on and perfecting smaller amounts. As for politics, Henry Miller feels the political world is foul and rotten, and about the work of politically minded writers Hemingway is sure that one must skip the politics when one reads them. But Mary McCarthy was deeply involved in politics at the time she was swept into the Trotskyite movement; and politics has been important in the life of Ezra Pound. Robert Lowell thinks that social credit and Fascism were a tremendous gain to Pound; for even when they were bad beliefs, and sometimes they were terrible, they brought him closer to life. Hemingway thought that Pound should be released from St. Elizabeth's on an understanding by him to abstain from politics, and Robert Frost, who helped to have him released, thought that Pound was "*very* foolish in what he bet on." Pound himself, who says, "I may have been completely nuts," feels that he was not committing treason. He believed that he was fighting an "internal question of constitutional government." But most of these writers seem to be politically passive. In the atomic age, political issues have become at once too simple and too massive, beyond the scope of writers and literary thinking.

In these interviews there is much autobiography, an account of the meeting, for instance, between Pound and Frost in England. Pound wrote the first favorable review of Frost's work, and he gave Frost a lesson in jiu-jitsu at a restaurant in Soho. He grabbed Frost's hand, tipped backward, and threw Frost over his head. Pound had gone to London, he said, because he thought Yeats knew more about poetry than anybody else, and he spent his evenings with Yeats and his afternoons with Ford Madox Hueffer. His great friends were Gaudier-Brzeska and Hueffer, or Ford, until he heard that a young man was arriving from Harvard and presently fell in with T. S. Eliot. Pound's father was in charge of a government land office in Idaho, where his grandfather had built a railroad and where he spent his first eighteen months, but he had grown up in suburban Philadelphia. There his father was connected with the mint. Later, Pound felt that monetary reform was the key to good government and his interest in coinage had begun with his father's work. He had seen the smelting room and been told that he could take away a large bag of gold—if he could lift it. In England a Confucian, in contrast to Eliot, he won the disapproval of Wyndham Lewis, for Lewis said that Pound never noticed how wicked, what "S.O.B.'s," people were. "I wasn't interested," Pound says, "in the vices of my friends, but in their intelligence." Henry Miller, who began to write when he was working for the Western Union, tried to do a book on D. H. Lawrence, but after being in Lawrence's grip he became bewildered and ceased to be able to place Lawrence amid all his contradictions. Miller loves Lewis Carroll and would give his right arm to have written Lewis Carroll's books. As for Lawrence, Aldous Huxley, who knew him well, quite agrees with Miller about the contradictions. In *The Plumed Serpent*, on one page, he glorifies the Indians with their "dark life of the blood," and later he damns the lazy natives like a British colonel of the days of Kipling. Huxley could not make out what Lawrence was driving at, but Huxley's first wife, a Belgian, who typed the manuscript of *Lady Chatterley's Lover*, seemed to understand him. In fact, Lawrence died in her arms. But Lawrence had been profoundly shocked when, not knowing English well, she used in conversation some of his four-letter words.

There are odds and ends of autobiography that now and then bring these authors together. Henry Miller wrote *The Colossus of Maroussi* after he had visited Lawrence Durrell in Greece. Ralph Ellison learned from reading Hemingway how to shoot a bird on the wing, and there was a time when he and his brother hunted and sold game in Dayton for a living. The interviews read like good conversation, usually lively, often gay and always penetrating, in which skillfully thought out questions bring to the surface hidden depths, and the writers draw portraits of themselves. As a rule, these portraits strikingly confirm the impressions which the writers had already created. I think, as interviews, they are the best I have ever read, certainly the most pointed and the most revealing.

VAN WYCK BROOKS

1. Robert Frost

A regional poet who has achieved international stature, Robert Frost was born in San Francisco on March 26, 1874. His father, an editor, politician, and Democrat, had gone there to escape the Republican atmosphere of New England. Sympathizing with the Southern cause, he christened his son Robert Lee Frost. When the senior Frost died, young Robert returned with his mother to New England to live with his paternal grandfather in Lawrence, Massachusetts. Here he soon began, but with little encouragement, his life-long commitment to poetry. He attended Dartmouth but could not abide the academic routine. At twenty-two he entered Harvard, specializing in Latin and Greek during his two years there. He then went to live on a farm in Derry, New Hampshire, teaching, doing occasional work for a local newspaper, and continuing to write his poems. It was a trip to England, however, in 1912, which gave his literary career its decisive push forward. There his first two books were published—A Boy's Will and North of Boston. When he returned to America in 1915, he was already well known, and his future as a poet and teacher was secure.

Mr. Frost received the Pulitzer Prize for poetry four times—in 1924, for New Hampshire; in 1931, for Collected Poems; in 1937, for A Further Range; and in 1943, for A Witness Tree. His latest collection, In the Clearing, was published in 1962.

More than any other quality in Frost, his individualism stood out. He spurned what he called "the necessary group." As in other areas of life, he believed "there are too many gangs, cliques, or coteries in poetry. Maybe that's one of the ways they have to manage it. But I'm a lone wolf."

Robert Frost died on January 29, 1963.

I only say it as worth thinking of
But loyalty in friendship and in love
In times like these mught be a different thing
From what they say they used to be O King.

I do not like the way you stuff your eyes
When you say that, the King replies.
I stand up and say it." The Vizier stood up
So suddenly he overset his cup.

Never more dangerous than when affable
The King enjoys the moment to the full
He looks from face to face all down the board
To see with whom he has or hasn't scored.

The statesman stumbled: I don't know what to talk
This argument. But would you call false-hearted
The one who from devising dissuades faction
Gave an attachment up for an attraction?"

"You stand yourself in peril of extinction.
You went bag and down in a situation. But
just what are you preparing to forsake
If you can tell us so we stay awake."

The hangers over wide awake with fear
Of what was happening to the Vizier.
Their only comfort in the thought
That they were not the traitors being caught

. . . . that shock

Manuscript page from an unpublished poem by Robert Frost.

HANS BECK

Robert Frost

Mr. Frost came into the front room of his house in Cambridge, Massachusetts, casually dressed, wearing high plaid slippers, offering greetings with a quiet, even diffident friendliness. But there was no mistaking the evidence of the enormous power of his personality. It makes you at once aware of the thick, compacted strength of his body, even now at eighty-six; it is apparent in his face, actually too alive and spontaneously expressive to be as ruggedly heroic as in his photographs.

The impression of massiveness, far exceeding his physical size, isn't separable from the public image he creates and preserves. That this image is invariably associated with popular conceptions of New England is no simple matter of his own geographical preferences. New England is of course evoked in the scenes and titles of many of his poems and, more importantly, in his Emersonian tendencies, including his habit of contradicting himself, his capacity to "unsay" through the sound of his voice what his words seem to assert. His special resemblance to New England,

9

however, is that he, like it, has managed to impose upon the world a wholly self-created image. It is not the critics who have defined him, it is Frost himself. He stood talking for a few minutes in the middle of the room, his remarkably ample, tousled white hair catching the late afternoon sun reflected off the snow in the road outside, and one wondered for a moment how he had managed over so long a life never to let his self-portrait be altered despite countless exposures to light less familiar and unintimidating. In the public world he has resisted countless chances to lose himself in some particular fashion, some movement, like the Georgians, or even in an area of his own work which, to certain critics or readers, happens for the moment to appear more exotically colorful than the whole. In one of the most revealing parts of this interview, he says of certain of his poems that he doesn't "want them out," the phrase itself, since all the poems involved have been published, offering an astonishing, even peculiar, evidence of the degree to which he feels in control of his poetic character. It indicates, too, his awareness that attempts to define him as a tragic philosophical poet of man and nature can be more constricting, because more painfully meaningful to him, than the simpler definitions they are designed to correct.

More specifically, he seemed at various points to find the most immediate threat to his freedom in the tape recorder. Naturally, for a man both voluble and often mischievous in his recollections, Frost did not like the idea of being stuck, as he necessarily would be, with attitudes expressed in two hours of conversation. As an aggravation of this, he knew that no transcript taken from the tape could catch the subtleties of voice which give life and point to many of his statements. At a pause in the interview, Mr. Robert O'Clair, a friend and colleague at Harvard who had agreed to sit in as a sort of witness, admitted that we knew very little about running a tape recorder. Frost, who'd moved from his chair to see its workings, readily agreed. "Yes, I noticed that," he laughed, "and I respect you for it," adding at once—and this is the point of the story—that "they," presumably the people "outside," "like

*to hear me say nasty things about machines." A thoroughly
supple knowledge of the ways in which the world tries to take
him and a confidence that his own ways are more just and liberating was apparent here and everywhere in the conversation.*

*Frost was seated most of the time in a blue overstuffed chair
which he had bought to write in. It had no arms, he began, and
this left him the room he needed.*

FROST: I never write except with a writing board. I've never had
a table in my life. And I use all sorts of things. Write on the sole
of my shoe.

INTERVIEWER: Why have you never liked a desk? Is it because
you've moved around so much and lived in so many places?

FROST: Even when I was younger I never had a desk. I've never
had a writing room.

INTERVIEWER: Is Cambridge your home base now pretty much?

FROST: In the winter. But I'm nearly five months in Ripton,
Vermont. I make a long summer up there. But this is my office
and business place.

INTERVIEWER: Your place in Vermont is near the Bread Loaf
School of Writing, isn't it?

FROST: Three miles away. Not so near I know it's there. I'm a
way off from it, down the mountain and up a side road. They connect me with it a good deal more than I'm there. I give a lecture
at the school and a lecture at the conference. That's about all.

INTERVIEWER: You were a co-founder of the school, weren't you?

FROST: They say that. I think I had more to do with the starting
of the conference. In a very casual way, I said to the president
[of Middlebury], "Why don't you use the place for a little socia-
bility after the school is over?" I thought of no regular business—
no pay, no nothing, just inviting literary people, a few, for a week
or two. The kitchen staff was still there. But then they started a
regular business of it.

INTERVIEWER: When you were in England from 1912 to 1915,
did you ever think you might possibly stay there?

FROST: No. No, I went over there to be poor for a while, nothing else. I didn't think of printing a book over there. I'd never offered a book to anyone here. I was thirty-eight years old, wasn't I? Something like that. And I thought the way to a book was the magazines. I hadn't too much luck with them, and nobody ever noticed me except to send me a check now and then. So I didn't think I was ready for a book. But I had written three books when I went over, the amount of three books—*A Boy's Will, North of Boston,* and part of the next [*Mountain Interval*] in a loose-leaf heap.

INTERVIEWER: What were the circumstances of your meeting Pound when you were in England?

FROST: That was through Frank Flint. The early Imagist and translator. He was a friend of Pound and belonged in that little group there. He met me in a bookstore, said, "American?" And I said, "Yes. How'd you know?" He said, "Shoes." It was the Poetry Book Shop, Harold Monro's, just being organized. He said, "Poetry?" And I said, "I accept the omen." Then he said, "You should know your fellow countryman, Ezra Pound." And I said, "I've never heard of him." And I hadn't. I'd been skipping literary magazines—I don't ever read them very much—and the gossip, you know, I never paid much attention to. So he said, "I'm going to tell him you're here." And I had a card from Pound afterwards. I didn't use it for two or three months after that.

INTERVIEWER: He saw your book—*A Boy's Will*—just before publication, didn't he? How did that come about?

FROST: The book was already in the publishers' hands, but it hadn't come out when I met Pound, three or four months after he sent me his card. I didn't like the card very well.

INTERVIEWER: What did he say on it?

FROST: Just said, "At home, sometimes." Just like Pound. So I didn't feel that that was a very warm invitation. Then one day walking past Church Walk in Kensington, I took his card out and went in to look for him. And I found him there, a little put out that I hadn't come sooner, in his Poundian way. And then he

said, "Flint tells me you have a book." And I said, "Well, I
ought to have." He said, "You haven't seen it?" And I said, "No."
He said, "What do you say we go and get a copy?" He was eager
about being the first one to talk. That's one of the best things
you can say about Pound: he wanted to be the first to jump.
Didn't call people up on the telephone to see how they were
going to jump. He was all silent with eagerness. We walked over
to my publisher; he got the book. Didn't show it to me—put it
in his pocket. We went back to his room. He said, "You don't
mind our liking this?" in his British accent, slightly. And I said,
"Oh, go ahead and like it." Pretty soon he laughed at something,
and I said I knew where that was in the book, what Pound would
laugh at. And then pretty soon he said, "You better run along
home, I'm going to review it." And I never touched it. I went
home without my book and he kept it. I'd barely seen it in his
hands.

INTERVIEWER: He wrote perhaps the first important favorable
review, didn't he?

FROST: Yes. It was printed in the States, in Chicago, but it
didn't help me much in England. The reviewing of the book there
began right away, as soon as it was out. I guess most of those who
reviewed it in England didn't know it had already been reviewed
in Chicago. It didn't sound as though they did. But his review
had something to do with the beginning of my reputation. I've
always felt a little romantic about all that—that queer adventure
he gave me. You know he had a mixed, a really curious position
over there. He was friends with Yeats, Hueffer, and a very few
others.

INTERVIEWER: Did you know Hueffer?

FROST: Yes, with him. And Yeats, with him.

INTERVIEWER: How much did you see of Yeats when you were
in England?

FROST: Oh, quite a little, with him nearly always—I guess
always.

INTERVIEWER: Did you feel when you left London to go live on a farm in Gloucestershire that you were making a choice against the kind of literary society you'd found in the city?

FROST: No, my choices had been not connected with my going to England even. My choice was almost unconscious in those days. I didn't know whether I had any position in the world at all, and I wasn't choosing positions. You see, my instinct was not to belong to any gang, and my instinct was against being confused with the—what do you call them?—they called themselves Georgians, Edwardians, something like that, the people Edward Marsh was interested in. I understand that he speaks of me in his book, but I never saw him.

INTERVIEWER: Was there much of a gang feeling among the literary people you knew in London?

FROST: Yes. Oh, yes. Funny over there. I suppose it's the same over here. I don't know. I don't "belong" here. But they'd say, "Oh, he's that fellow that writes about homely things for that crowd, for those people. Have you anybody like that in America?" As if it were set, you know. Like Masefield—they didn't know Masefield in this gang, but, "Oh, he's that fellow that does this thing, I believe, for that crowd."

INTERVIEWER: Your best friend in those years was Edward Thomas?

FROST: Yes—quite separate again from everybody his age. He was as isolated as I was. Nobody knew he wrote poetry. He didn't write poetry until he started to war, and that had something to do with my life with him. We got to be great friends. No, I had an instinct against belonging to any of those crowds. I've had friends, but very scattering, a scattering over there. You know, I could have . . . Pound had an afternoon meeting once a week with Flint and Aldington and H. D. and at one time Hulme, I think. Hulme started with them. They met every week to rewrite each other's poems.

INTERVIEWER: You saw Hulme occasionally? Was it at these rewriting sessions, or didn't you bother with them?

FROST: Yes, I knew Hulme, knew him quite well. But I never went to one of those meetings. I said to Pound, "What do you do?" He said, "Rewrite each other's poems." And I said, "Why?" He said, "To squeeze the water out of them." "That sounds like a parlor game to me," I said, "and I'm a serious artist"—kidding, you know. And he laughed and he didn't invite me any more.

INTERVIEWER: These personal associations that you had in England with Pound and Edward Thomas and what you call the Georgians—these had nothing to do with your establishing a sense of your own style, did they? You'd already written what were to be nearly the first three volumes of your poetry.

FROST: Two and a half books, you might say. There are some poems out in Huntington Library that I must have written in the nineties. The first one of mine that's still in print was in '90. It's in print still, kicking round.

INTERVIEWER: Not in *A Boy's Will*—the earliest poem published in there was written in '94, I think.

FROST: No, it's not in there. First one I ever *sold* is in there. The first one I ever had printed was the first one I wrote. I never wrote prose or verse till 1890. Before that I wrote Latin and Greek sentences.

INTERVIEWER: Some of the early critics like Garnett and Pound talk a lot about Latin and Greek poetry with reference to yours. You'd read a lot in the classics?

FROST: Probably more Latin and Greek than Pound ever did.

INTERVIEWER: Didn't you teach Latin at one time?

FROST: Yes. When I came back to college after running away, I thought I could stand it if I stuck to Greek and Latin and philosophy. That's all I did those years.

INTERVIEWER: Did you read much in the Romantic poets? Wordsworth, in particular?

FROST: No, you couldn't pin me there. Oh, I read all sorts of things. I said to some Catholic priests the other day when they asked me about reading, I said, "If you understand the word 'catholic,' I was very catholic in my taste."

INTERVIEWER: What sort of things did your mother read to you?

FROST: That I wouldn't be able to tell you. All sorts of things, not too much, but some. She was a very hard-worked person— she supported us. Born in Scotland, but grew up in Columbus, Ohio. She was a teacher in Columbus for seven years—in mathematics. She taught with my father one year after he left Harvard and before he went to California. You know they began to teach in high schools in those days right after coming out of high school themselves. I had teachers like that who didn't go to college. I had two noted teachers in Latin and Greek who weren't college women at all. They taught Fred Robinson.* I had the same teachers he had. Fritz Robinson, the old scholar. My mother was just like that. Began teaching at eighteen in the high school, then married along about twenty-five. I'm putting all this together rather lately, finding out strolling round like I do. Just dug up in Pennsylvania the date of her marriage and all that, in Lewistown, Pennsylvania.

INTERVIEWER: Your mother ran a private school in Lawrence, Massachusetts, didn't she?

FROST: Yes, she did, round Lawrence. She had a private school. And I taught in that some, as well as taking some other schools. I'd go out and teach in district schools whenever I felt like springtime.

INTERVIEWER: How old were you then?

FROST: Oh, just after I'd run away from Dartmouth, along there in '93, '4, twenty years old. Every time I'd get sick of the city I'd go out for the springtime and take school for one term. I did that I think two or three times, that same school. Little school with twelve children, about a dozen children, all barefooted. I did newspaper work in Lawrence, too. I followed my

---

* Editor of Chaucer, and formerly a professor of English at Harvard.

father and mother in that, you know. I didn't know what I wanted to do with myself to earn a living. Taught a little, worked on a paper a little, worked on farms a little, that was my own departure. But I just followed my parents in newspaper work. I edited a paper a while—a weekly paper—and then I was on a regular paper. I see its name still up there in Lawrence.

INTERVIEWER: When you started to write poetry, was there any poet that you admired very much?

FROST: I was the enemy of that theory, that idea of Stevenson's that you should play the sedulous ape to anybody. That did more harm to American education than anything ever got out.

INTERVIEWER: Did you ever feel any affinity between your work and any other poet's?

FROST: I'll leave that for somebody else to tell me. I wouldn't know.

INTERVIEWER: But when you read Robinson or Stevens, for example, do you find anything that is familiar to you from your own poetry?

FROST: Wallace Stevens? He was years after me.

INTERVIEWER: I mean in your reading of him, whether or not you felt any—

FROST: Any affinity, you mean? Oh, you couldn't say that. No. Once he said to me, "You write on subjects." And I said, "You write on bric-a-brac." And when he sent me his next book he'd written "S'more bric-a-brac" in it. Just took it good-naturedly. No, I had no affinity with him. We were friends. Oh, gee, miles away. I don't know who you'd connect me with.

INTERVIEWER: Well, you once said in my hearing that Robert Lowell had tried to connect you with Faulkner, told you you were a lot like Faulkner.

FROST: Did I say that?

INTERVIEWER: No, you said that Robert Lowell told you that you were a lot like Faulkner.

FROST: Well, you know what Robert Lowell said once? He said, "My uncle's dialect—the New England dialect, *The Biglow*

Papers—was just the same as Burns's, wasn't it?" I said, "Robert! Burns's was not a dialect, Scotch is not a dialect. It's a language." But he'd say anything, Robert, for the hell of it.

INTERVIEWER: You've never, I take it then, been aware of any particular line of preference in your reading?

FROST: Oh, I read 'em all. One of my points of departure is an anthology. I find a poet I admire, and I think, well, there must be a lot to that. Some old one—Shirley, for instance, "The glories of our blood and state"—that sort of splendid poem. I go looking for more. Nothing. Just a couple like that and that's all. I remember certain boys took an interest in certain poems with me in old times. I remember Brower one day in somebody else's class when he was a student at Amherst—Reuben Brower, afterwards the Master of Adams House at Harvard. I remember I said, "Anyone want to read that poem to me?" It was "In going to my naked bed as one that would have slept," Edwards's old poem. He read it so well I said, "I give you A for life." And that's the way we joke with each other. I never had him regularly in a class of mine. I visited other classes up at Amherst and noticed him very early. Goodness sake, the way his voice fell into those lines, the natural way he did that very difficult poem with that old quotation— "The falling out of faithful friends is the renewing of love." I'm very catholic, that's about all you can say. I've hunted. I'm not thorough like the people educated in Germany in the old days. I've none of that. I hate the idea that you ought to read the whole of anybody. But I've done a lot of looking sometimes, read quite a lot.

INTERVIEWER: When you were in England did you find yourself reading the kind of poetry Pound was reading?

FROST: No. Pound was reading the troubadours.

INTERVIEWER: Did you talk to one another about any particular poets?

FROST: He admired at that time, when I first met him, Robinson and de la Mare. He got over admiring de la Mare anyway, and I think he threw out Robinson too. We'd just bring up a couple of little poems. I was around with him quite a little for a few weeks. I was charmed with his ways. He cultivated a certain rudeness to people that he didn't like, just like Willy Whistler. I thought he'd come under the influence of Whistler. They cultivated the French style of boxing. They used to kick you in the teeth.

INTERVIEWER: With grace.

FROST: Yes. You know the song, the nasty song: "They fight with their feet—" Among other things, what Pound did was show me Bohemia.

INTERVIEWER: Was there much Bohemia to see at that time?

FROST: More than I had ever seen. I'd never had any. He'd take me to restaurants and things. Showed me jiu jitsu in a restaurant. Threw me over his head.

INTERVIEWER: Did he do that?

FROST: Wasn't ready for him at all. I was just as strong as he was. He said, "I'll show you, I'll show you. Stand up." So I stood up, gave him my hand. He grabbed my wrist, tipped over backwards and threw me over his head.

INTERVIEWER: How did you like that?

FROST: Oh, it was all right. Everybody in the restaurant stood up. He used to talk about himself as a tennis player. I never played tennis with him. And then he'd show you all these places with these people that specialized in poets that dropped their aitches and things like that. Not like the "beatniks," quite. I remember one occasion they had a poet in who had a poem in the *English Review* on Aphrodite, how he met Aphrodite at Leatherhead.* He was coming in and he was a navvy. I don't remember his name, never heard of him again—may have gone on and had

---

* Frost is thinking of a poet named John Helston, author of "Aphrodite at Leatherhead," which took up fourteen pages of the *English Review* for March 1913. Frost's recollection gives a special flavor, if one is needed, to the note appended to the poem by the editors of the magazine: "Without presuming to 'present' Mr. Helston after the manner of fashionable actors, we think it will interest the public to know that he was for years a working mechanic—turner, fitter, etc.—in electrical, locomotive, motor-car, and other workshops."

books. But he was a real navvy. Came in with his bicycle clips on. Tea party. Everybody horrified in a delighted way, you know. Horror, social horror. Red-necked, thick, heavy-built fellow, strong fellow, you know, like John L. Lewis or somebody. But he was a poet. And then I saw poets made out of whole cloth by Ezra. Ezra thought he did that. Take a fellow that had never written anything and think he could make a poet out of him. We won't go into that.

INTERVIEWER: I wonder about your reaction to such articles as the recent lead article by Karl Shapiro in the *New York Times Book Review* which praised you because presumably you're not guilty of "Modernism" as Pound and Eliot are. [*Telephone rings.*]

FROST: Is that my telephone? Just wait a second. Halt! [*Interruption. Frost leaves for phone call.*]

FROST: Where were we? Oh yes, you were trying to trace me.

INTERVIEWER: I wasn't trying to trace you. I was—

FROST: Oh, this thing about Karl Shapiro. Yeah, isn't it funny? So often they ask me—I just been all around, you know, been out West, been all around—and so often they ask me, "What is a modern poet?" I dodge it often, but I said the other night, "A modern poet must be one that speaks to modern people no matter when he lived in the world. That would be one way of describing it. And it would make him more modern, perhaps, if he were *alive* and speaking to modern people."

INTERVIEWER: Yes, but in their way of speaking, Eliot and Pound seem to many people to be writing in a tradition that is very different from yours.

FROST: Yes. I suppose Eliot's isn't as far away as Pound's. Pound seemed to me very like a troubadour, more like the troubadours or a blend of several of them, Bertrand de Born and Arnault Daniel. I never touched that. I don't know Old French. I don't like foreign languages that I haven't had. I don't read translations of things. I like to say dreadful, unpleasant things about Dante. Pound, though, he's supposed to know Old French.

INTERVIEWER: Pound was a good linguist, wasn't he?

FROST: I don't know that. There's a teacher of his down in Florida that taught him at the University of Pennsylvania. He once said to me, "Pound? I had him in Latin, and Pound never knew the difference between a declension and a conjugation." He's death on him. Old man, still death on Ezra. [*Breaks into laughter.*] Pound's gentle art of making enemies.

INTERVIEWER: Do you ever hear from Pound? Do you correspond with him now?

FROST: No. He wrote me a couple of letters when I got him out of jail last year. Very funny little letters, but they were all right.

INTERVIEWER: Whom did you speak to in Washington about that?

FROST: Just the Attorney General. Just settled it with him. I went down twice with Archie [MacLeish] and we didn't get anything done because they were of opposite parties, I think. And I don't belong to any party.

INTERVIEWER: Yes, but weren't you named Robert Lee because your father was a stanch Democrat around the time of the Civil War? That makes you a Democrat of sorts, doesn't it?

FROST: Yeah, I'm a Democrat. I was born a Democrat—and been unhappy ever since 1896. Somebody said to me, "What's the difference between that and being a Republican?" Well, I went down after we'd failed, and after Archie thought we'd failed, I just went down alone, walked into the Attorney General's office and said, "I come down here to see what your mood is about Ezra Pound." And two of them spoke up at once. "Our mood's your mood; let's get him out." Just like that, that's all. And I said, "This week?" They said, "This week if you say so. You go get a lawyer, and we'll raise no objection." So, since they were Republicans, I went over and made friends with Thurman Arnold, that good leftish person, for my lawyer. I sat up that night and wrote an appeal to the court that I threw away, and, in the morning, just before I left town, I wrote another one, a shorter one. And that's all there was to it. Ezra thanked me in a very short note that read: "Thanks for what you're doing. A little conversation would be in order." Then signed, in large letters. And then he wrote me another one, a nicer one.

INTERVIEWER: Did you see him before he left for Italy?

FROST: No, no, I didn't want to high-hat him. I wanted him to feel kind of free from me. But he feels, evidently, a little gratitude of some kind. He's not very well, you know. Some of them didn't want . . . [*What Frost was about to say here, it turned out later in the interview, not recorded, was that some friends of Pound— he mentioned Merrill Moore—felt Pound would be better off staying in St. Elizabeth's Hospital. Moore said that Pound had a room to himself and a cabana!*] Well, it's a sad business. And he's a poet. I never, I never questioned that. We've been friends all the way along, but I didn't like what he did in wartime. I only heard it second-hand, so I didn't judge it too closely. But it sounded pretty bad. He was very foolish in what he bet on and whenever anybody really loses that way, I don't want to rub it into him.

INTERVIEWER: I've been asking a lot of questions about the relationship of your poetry to other poetry, but of course there are many other non-literary things that have been equally important. You've been very much interested in science, for example.

FROST: Yes, you're influenced by the science of your time, aren't you? Somebody noticed that all through my book there's astronomy.

INTERVIEWER: Like "The Literate Farmer and the Planet Venus"?

FROST: Yes, but it's all through the book, all through the book. Many poems—I can name twenty that have astronomy in them. Somebody noticed that the other day: "Why has nobody ever seen how much you're interested in astronomy?" That's a bias, you could say. One of the earliest books I hovered over, hung around, was called *Our Place among the Infinities*, by an astronomer in England named Proctor, noted astronomer. It's a noted old book. I mention that in one of the poems: I use that expression "our place among the infinities" from that book that I must have read as soon as I read any book, thirteen or fourteen, right in there I began to read. That along with *Scottish Chiefs*. I remember that year when I first began to read a book through. I had a little sister who read everything through, lots of books, everybody's books—very young, precocious. Me, I was—they turned me out of doors for my health.

INTERVIEWER: While we're thinking about science and literature, I wonder if you have any reaction to the fact that Massachusetts Institute of Technology is beginning to offer a number of courses in literature?

FROST: I think they'd better tend to their higher mathematics and higher science. Pure science. They know I think that. I don't mean to criticize them too much. But you see it's like this: the greatest adventure of man is science, the adventure of penetrating into matter, into the material universe. But the adventure is our property, a human property, and the best description of us is the humanities. Maybe the scientists wanted to remind their students that the humanities describe you who are adventuring into science, and science adds very little to that description of you, a little tiny bit. Maybe in psychology, or in something like that, but it's awful little. And so, the scientists to remind their students of all this give them half their time over there in the humanities now. And that seems a little unnecessary. They're worried about us and the pure sciences all the time. They'd better get as far as they can into their own subject. I was over there at the beginning of this and expressed my little doubts about it. I was there with Compton one night—he was sitting on the platform beside me. "We've been short"—I turned to him before the audience—"we've been a little short in pure science, haven't we?" He said, "Perhaps—I'm afraid we may have been." I said, "I think that better be tended to." That's years ago.

INTERVIEWER: You just mentioned psychology. You once taught psychology, didn't you?

FROST: That was entirely a joke. I could teach psychology. I've been asked to join a firm of psychiatrists, you know [by Merrill Moore], and that's more serious. But I went up there to disabuse the Teacher's College of the idea that there is any immediate connection between any psychology and their classroom work, disabuse them of the notion that they could mesmerize a class if they knew enough psychology. That's what they thought.

INTERVIEWER: Weren't you interested at one time in William James?

FROST: Yes, that was partly what drew me back to Harvard. But he was away all the time I was around here. I had Santayana, Royce, and all that philosophy crowd, Munsterberg, George Herbert Palmer, the old poetical one. I had 'em all. But I was there waiting for James, and I lost interest.

INTERVIEWER: Did Santayana interest you very much at that time?

FROST: No, not particularly. Well, yes. I always wondered what he really meant, where he was headed, what it all came to. Followed that for years. I never knew him personally. I never knew anybody personally in college. I was a kind of—went my own way. But I admired him. It was a golden utterance—he was something to listen to, just like his written style. But I wondered what he really meant. I found years afterward somewhere in his words that all was illusion, of two kinds, true and false. And I decided false illusion would be the truth: two negatives make an affirmative.

INTERVIEWER: While we're on things other than poetry that you were and are interested in, we might get onto politics for a moment. I remember one evening your mentioning that Henry Wallace became somehow associated with your poem, "Provide, Provide."

FROST: People exaggerate such things. Henry Wallace was in Washington when I read the poem. Sat right down there in the first row. And when I got to the end of it where it says, "Better to go down dignified—With boughten friendship at your side— Than none at all. Provide, Provide!" I added, "Or somebody else will provide for ya." He smiled; his wife smiled. They were right down there where I could see them.

INTERVIEWER: Well, you don't have a reputation for being a New Dealer.

FROST: They think I'm no New Dealer. But really and truly I'm not, you know, all that clear on it. In "The Death of the Hired Man" that I wrote long, long ago, long before the New Deal, I put it two ways about home. One would be the manly way: "Home is the place where, when you have to go there, They have to take you in." That's the man's feeling about it. And then the wife says, "I should have called it/Something you somehow hadn't to deserve." That's the New Deal, the feminine way of it, the mother way. You don't have to deserve your mother's love. You have to deserve your father's. He's more particular. One's a Republican, one's a Democrat. The father is always a Republican toward his son, and his mother's always a Democrat. Very few have noticed that second thing; they've always noticed the sarcasm, the hardness of the male one.

INTERVIEWER: That poem is often anthologized, and I wonder if you feel that the poems of yours that appear most often in the anthologies represent you very well.

FROST: I'm always pleased when somebody digs up a new one. I don't know. I leave that in the lap of the gods, as they say.

INTERVIEWER: There are some I seldom see; for example, "A Servant to Servants" or "The Most of It" or "The Subverted Flower." All of these I noticed the other day are omitted, for instance, from Untermeyer's anthology of your poems. Strange, isn't it?

FROST: Well, he was making his own choice. I never said a word to him, never urged him. I remember he said [Edward Arlington] Robinson only did once. Robinson told him, "If you want to please an old man you won't overlook my 'Mr. Flood's Party.'" That is a beautiful poem.

INTERVIEWER: Do you feel that any particular area of your work hasn't been anthologized?

FROST: I wouldn't know that. "The Subverted Flower," for instance, nobody's ever touched. No—I guess it is; it's in Matty's [F. O. Matthiessen's] anthology. That's the one he made for the Oxford people.

INTERVIEWER: Yes, but its appearance is extremely rare in any selection of your work. It doesn't seem to fit some people's preconceptions about you. Another neglected poem, and an especially good one, is "Putting In the Seed."

FROST: That's—sure. They leave that sort of thing out; they overlook that sort of thing with me. The only person ever noticed that was a hearty old friend of mine down at the University of Pennsylvania, Cornelius Weygandt.* He said, "I know what *that's* about."

INTERVIEWER: Do you ever read that poem in public?

FROST: No, I don't bother with those. No, there are certain ones. I wouldn't read "The Subverted Flower" to anybody outside. It isn't that I'm afraid of them, but I don't want them out. I'm shy about certain things in my books, they're more— I'd rather they'd be read. A woman asked me, "What do you mean by that 'subverted flower'?" I said, "Frigidity in women." She left.

INTERVIEWER: Do you think that it was to correct the public assumption that your poetry is represented by the most anthologized pieces such as "Birches" that Lionel Trilling in his speech at your eighty-fifth birthday emphasized poems of a darker mood?

FROST: I don't know—I might run my eye over my book after Trilling, and wonder why he hadn't seen it sooner: that there's plenty to be dark about, you know. It's full of darkness.

INTERVIEWER: Do you suppose he imagined he was correcting some sort of public ignorance—some general mistake about your work?

FROST: He made the mistake himself. He was admitting he made it himself, wasn't he? He was telling what trouble he'd had to get at me. Sort of a confession, but very pleasant.

---

* Author of historical and descriptive studies of New Hampshire.

INTERVIEWER: That's true, but many admirers of yours did object to his emphasis on the "darkness" or "terror" in your poems.

FROST: Yes, well, he took me a little by surprise that night. He was standing right beside me and I had to get up right after him. Birthday party. And it took me—it didn't hurt me, but I thought at first he was attacking me. Then when he began comparing me to Sophocles and D. H. Lawrence I was completely at sea. What the two of them had to do with me, you know. Might be I might like it about Sophocles, but I'd be puzzled, oh, utterly at sea about D. H. Lawrence. It's all right, though. I had to get up and recite soon after that, and so I was a little puzzled what to recite to illustrate what he was talking about. And right there—new to me: I hadn't read his paper. I'd never read him much. I don't read criticism. You see no magazines in the house.

INTERVIEWER: Did you feel better about his talk when you read his substantiation of it in the *Partisan Review*?

FROST: I read his defense of it. Very clever, very—very interesting. Admired him. He's a very—intellectual man. But I read very little, generally, in the magazines. Hadn't read that Shapiro thing you mentioned. That's news to me what he said. Is he a friend of mine?

INTERVIEWER: Oh, yes. He's a friend of yours, but he's like many friends of yours: he chooses to see in you something more simple than your best friends see. It's a bit like J. Donald Adams, also in the *Times*, angrily defending you against Trilling, only J. Donald Adams doesn't understand you very well either.

FROST: What was Shapiro saying?

INTERVIEWER: He was saying that most modern poetry is obscure and overdifficult, that this is particularly true of Pound and Eliot, but that it isn't true of you.

FROST: Well, I don't want to be difficult. I like to fool—oh, you know, you like to be mischievous. But not in that dull way of just being dogged and doggedly obscure.

INTERVIEWER: The difficulty of your poetry is perhaps in your emphasis on variety in tones of voice. You once said that consciously or unconsciously it was tones of voice that you counted on to double the meaning of every one of your statements.

FROST: Yes, you could do that. Could unsay everything I said, nearly. Talking contraries—it's in one of the poems. Talk by contraries with people you're very close to. They know what you're talking about. This whole thing of suggestiveness and *double entendre* and hinting—comes down to the word "hinting." With people you can trust you can talk in hints and suggestiveness. Families break up when people take hints you don't intend and miss hints you do intend. You can watch that going on, as a psychologist. I don't know. No, don't . . . no don't you . . . don't think of me . . . See, I haven't led a literary life. These fellows, they *really* work away with their prose trying to describe themselves and understand themselves, and so on. I don't do that. I don't want to know too much about myself. It interests me to know that Shapiro thinks I'm not difficult. That's all right. I never wrote a review in my life, never wrote articles. I'm constantly refusing to write articles. These fellows are all literary men. I don't have hours; I don't work at it, you know. I'm not a farmer, that's no pose of mine. But I have farmed some, and I putter around. And I walk and I live with other people. Like to talk a lot. But I haven't had a very literary life, and I'm never very much with the gang. I'm vice-president, no, I'm Honorary President of the Poetry Society of America. Once in a great while I go. And I wish them well. I wish the foundations would take them all, take care of them all.

INTERVIEWER: Speaking of foundations, why do you think big business, so long the object of literary ridicule for being philistine, should now be supporting so much literary effort?

FROST: It's funny they haven't sooner, because most of them have been to college and had poetry pushed into them. About half the reading they do in all languages will be in verse. Just think of it. And so they have a kind of respect for it all and they probably don't mind the abuse they've had from our quarter.

They're people who're worried that we just don't have enough imagination—it's the lack of imagination they're afraid of in our system. If we had enough imagination we could lick the Russians. I feel like saying, "Probably we won the Civil War with Emily Dickinson." We didn't even know she was there. Poor little thing.

INTERVIEWER: Would you agree that there are probably more good prizes for poetry today than there are good poets?

FROST: I don't know. I hate to judge that. It's nice for them—it's so nice for them to be interested in us, with their foundations. You don't know what'll come of it. You know the real thing is that the sense of sacrifice and risk is one of the greatest stimuli in the world. And you take that all out of it—take that away from it so that there's no risk in being a poet, I bet you'd lose a lot of the pious spirits. They're in it for the—hell of it. Just the same as these fellows breaking through the sound barrier up there, just the same. I was once asked in public, in front of four or five hundred women, just how I found leisure to write. I said, "Confidentially—since there's only five hundred of you here, and all women—like a sneak I stole some of it, like a man I seized some of it—and I had a little in my tin cup." Sounds as if I'd been a beggar, but I've never been consciously a beggar. I've been at the mercy of . . . I've been a beneficiary around colleges and all. And this is one of the advantages to the American way: I've never had to write a word of thanks to anybody I had a cent from. The colleges came between. Poetry has always been a beggar. Scholars have also been beggars, but they delegate their begging to the president of the college to do for them.

INTERVIEWER: I was suggesting just now that perhaps the number of emoluments for poets greatly exceeds the number of people whose work deserves to be honored. Isn't this a situation in which mediocrity will necessarily be exalted? And won't this make it more rather than less difficult for people to recognize really good achievement when it does occur?

FROST: You know, I was once asked that, and I said I never knew how many disadvantages anyone needed to get anywhere in the world. And you don't know how to measure that. No psychology will ever tell you who needs a whip and who needs a spur to win races. I think the greatest thing about it with me has been this, and I wonder if others think it. I look at a poem as a performance. I look on the poet as a man of prowess, just like an athlete. He's a performer. And the things you can do in a poem are very various. You speak of figures, tones of voice varying all the time. I'm always interested, you know, when I have three or four stanzas, in the way I *lay* the sentences in them. I'd hate to have the sentences all lie the same in the stanzas. Every poem is like that: some sort of achievement in performance. Somebody has said that poetry among other things is the marrow of wit. That's probably way back somewhere—marrow of wit. There's got to be wit. And that's very, very much left out of a lot of this labored stuff. It doesn't sparkle at all. Another thing to say is that every thought, poetical or otherwise, every thought is a feat of association. They tell of old Gibbon—as he was dying he was the same Gibbon at his historical parallels. All thought is a feat of association: having what's in front of you bring up something in your mind that you almost didn't know you knew. Putting this and that together. That click.

INTERVIEWER: Can you give an example of how this feat of association—as you call it—works?

FROST: Well, one of my masques turns on one association like that. God says, "I was just showing off to the Devil, Job." Job looks puzzled about it, distressed a little. God says, "Do you mind?" And, "No, no," he says, "No," in that tone, you know, "No," and so on. That tone is everything, the way you say that "no." I noticed that—that's what made me write that. Just that one thing made that.

INTERVIEWER: Did your other masque—*Masque of Mercy*—have a similar impetus?

FROST: I noticed that the first time in the world's history when mercy is entirely the subject is in Jonah. It does say somewhere earlier in the Bible, "If ten can be found in the city, will you spare it? Ten good people?" But in Jonah there is something worse than that. Jonah is told to go and prophesy against the city —and he *knows* God will let him down. He can't trust God to be unmerciful. You can trust God to be anything but unmerciful. So he ran away and—and got into a whale. That's the point of that and nobody notices it. They miss it.

INTERVIEWER: Why do you suppose, Mr. Frost, that among religious groups the masques had their best reception among Jesuits and rabbis?

FROST: Amusing you say that—that's true. The other, the lesser sects without the law, you see, they don't get it. They're too apt to think there's rebellion in them—what they go through with their parents when they're growing up. But that isn't in them at all, you know. They're not rebellious. They're very doctrinal, very orthodox, both of them. But how'd you notice that? It's amusing to me too. You see, the rabbis have been fine to me and so have the SJ's particularly, all over the country. I've just been in Kansas City staying with them. See, the masques are full of good orthodox doctrine. One of them turns on the thought that evil shows off to good and good shows off to evil. I made a couplet out of that for them in Kansas City, just the way I often do, offhand: "It's from their having stood contrasted/That good and bad so long have lasted."

INTERVIEWER: Making couplets "offhand" is something like writing on schedule, isn't it? I know a young poet who claims he can write every morning from six to nine, presumably before class.

FROST: Well, there's more than one way to skin a cat. I don't know what that would be like, myself. When I get going on something, I don't want to just—you know . . . Very first one I wrote I was walking home from school and I began to make it—a March day—and I was making it all afternoon and making it so I was late at my grandmother's for dinner. I finished it, but it burned right up, just burned right up, you know. And what started that? What burned it? So many talk, I wonder how falsely, about what it costs them, what agony it is to write. I've often been quoted: "No tears in the writer, no tears in the reader. No surprise for the writer, no surprise for the reader." But another distinction I made is: however sad, no grievance, grief without grievance. How could I, how could anyone have a good time with what cost me too much agony, how could they? What do I want to communicate but what a *hell* of a good time I had writing it? The whole thing is performance and prowess and feats of association. Why don't critics talk about those things—what a feat it was to turn that that way, and what a feat it was to remember that, to be reminded of that by this? Why don't they talk about that? Scoring. You've got to *score*. They say not, but you've got to score, in all the realms—theology, politics, astronomy, history, and the country life around you.

INTERVIEWER: What do you think of the performances of the poets who have made your birthplace, San Francisco, into their headquarters?

FROST: Have they? Somebody said I saw a lot of them in Kansas City at the end of my audience. They said, "See that blur over there? That's whiskers." No, I don't know much about that. I'm waiting for them to say something that I can get hold of. The worse the better. I like it anyway, you know. Like you say to somebody, "Say something. Say something." And he says, "I burn."

INTERVIEWER: Do young poets send you things?

FROST: Yes, some—not much, because I don't respond. I don't write letters and all that. But I get a little, and I meet them, talk with them. I get some books. I wonder what they're at. There's one book that sounded as if it might be good, "Aw, hell." The book was called "Aw, hell." Because "aw," the way you say "aw," you know, "Aw, hell!" That might be something.

INTERVIEWER: Most of the titles are funny. One is called *Howl* and another *Gasoline*.

FROST: *Gasoline*, eh? I've seen a little of it, kicking round. I saw a bunch of nine of them in a magazine in Chicago when I was through there. They were all San Franciscans. Nothing I could talk about afterwards, though, either way. I'm always glad of anybody that says anything awful. I can use it. We're all like that. You've got to learn to enjoy a lot of things you don't like. And I'm always ready for somebody to say some outrageous thing. I feel like saying, "Hold that now, long enough for me to go away and tell on you, won't you? Don't go back on it tomorrow." Funny world.

INTERVIEWER: When you look at a new poem that might be sent to you, what is it usually that makes you want to read it all or not want to read it?

FROST: This thing of performance and prowess and feats of association—that's where it all lies. One of my ways of looking at a poem right away it's sent to me, right off, is to see if it's rhymed. Then I know just when to look at it. The rhymes come in pairs, don't they? And nine times out of ten with an ordinary writer, one of two of the terms is better than the other. One makeshift will do, and then they get another that's good, and then another makeshift, and then another one that's good. That is in the realm of performance, that's the deadly test with me. I want to be unable to tell which of those he thought of first. If there's any trick about it, putting the better one first so as to deceive me, I can tell pretty soon. That's all in the performance realm. They can belong to any school of thought they want to, Spinoza or Schopenhauer, it doesn't matter to me. A Cartesian I heard Poe called, a Cartesian philosopher, the other day . . . tsssssss . . .

INTERVIEWER: You once saw a manuscript of Dylan Thomas's where he'd put all the rhymes down first and then backed into them. That's clearly not what you mean by performance, is it?

FROST: See, that's very dreadful. It ought to be that you're thinking forward, with the feeling of strength that you're getting them good all the way, carrying out some intention more felt than thought. It begins. And what it is that guides us—what is it? Young people wonder about that, don't they? But I tell them it's just the same as when you feel a joke coming. You see somebody coming down the street that you're accustomed to abuse, and you feel it rising in you, something to say as you pass each other.

Coming over him the same way. And where do these thoughts come from? Where does a thought? Something does it to you. It's him coming toward you that gives you the animus, you know. When they want to know about inspiration, I tell them it's mostly animus.

RICHARD POIRIER

2. Ezra Pound

Ezra Pound was born in a frontier community of Idaho on October 30, 1885, and was educated at the University of Pennsylvania and at Hamilton College. His first book of poems was published in Venice in 1908, and since then he has published over ninety volumes of poetry, criticism, and translation—particularly the translation of poetry.

As a young poet, Mr. Pound lived first in London, and then in Paris during the early 1920s. Later he moved to Rapallo in Italy, where he remained until the war dislodged him. He was foreign editor for *Poetry* for several years as a young man.

For many years Pound has been intensely preoccupied with national monetary systems, which he feels to be the cornerstone of all social order. During World War II he lived in Italy and delivered radio broadcasts denouncing American participation in the war against the Axis. One of the darker footnotes in American history is the treatment Pound received when made prisoner in the spring of 1945. At the American "Disciplinary Training Center" at Pisa he was confined in a cage made of metal airstrip mats, with a concrete floor, having only blankets for a bed, a can for a toilet, and an ever-burning light. After three weeks he collapsed with partial amnesia and claustrophobia. In all he was kept in strict solitary confinement for more than six months, during which time he repeatedly suffered attacks of hysteria and terror. Afterward he was taken to Washington, tried for treason, and judged insane. Following fourteen years in Saint Elizabeth's Hospital, he returned in 1958 to Italy, where he now lives with his daughter.

Pound's major poetic work, *The Cantos*, began appearing in 1917, and the latest section of it, *Thrones*, was published in 1959. His shorter poems were collected in *Personae* (1926, enlarged edition 1950). *Love Poems of Ancient Egypt*, a translation, was published in 1962, and *From Confucius to Cummings*, an anthology of poetry edited by Pound and Marcella Spann, in 1963.

NOTE TO BASE CENSOR

The Cantos contain nothing in the nature of cypher or

intended obscurity . The present Cantos do , naturally ,contain
a number of allusions and " recalls " to matter in the
earlier 7I cantos already published , and many of these
cannot be made clear to readers unacquainted with the
earlier parts of the poem.

There is also an extreme condensation in the quotations , for
example
         " Mine eyes have " (given as mi-hine eyes hev
refers to the Battle Hymn of the Republic as heard from the
loud speaker . There is not time or place in the narrative to
give the further remarks on ⌀ seeing the glory of the lord.

In like manner citations from Homer or ████████ Sophokles
or Confucius are brief ,and serve to remind the ready reader
that we were not born yesterday.
                                 The Chinese ideograms are mainly
     translated , or commented in the english text. At any rate
they contain nothing seditious .

     The form of the poem and main progress is conditioned by
its own inner shape , but the life of the D.T.C. passing
OUTSIDE the scheme cannot but impinge ,or break into the
main flow. The proper names given are mostly those of men
on sick call seen passing my tent. A very brief allusion to
further study in names ,that is , I am interested to note that
the   prevalence of early american names ,either of whites
of the old tradition (most of the early presidents for example)
or of descendents of slaves who took the names of their
masters . Interesting in contrast to the relative scarcity of
melting-pot names.

*Typescript of an explanatory note from Ezra Pound to the censor at the Pisa Detention
Camp, where Pound was held after the war. The officer, in censoring Pound's correspondence (which included the manuscripts of verse on its way to the publisher), apparently
suspected that the Pisan Cantos were in fact coded messages. Pound is writing to explain
this is not the case.*   (Courtesy: James Laughlin)

FRANCO GENTILINI

Ezra Pound

Since his return to Italy, Ezra Pound has spent most of his time in the Tirol, staying at Castle Brunnenberg with his wife, his daughter Mary, his son-in-law Prince Boris de Rachewiltz, and his grandchildren. However, the mountains in this resort country near Merano are cold in the winter, and Mr. Pound likes the sun. The interviewer was about to leave England for Merano, at the end of February, when a telegram stopped him at the door: "Merano icebound. Come to Rome."

Pound was alone in Rome, occupying a room in the apartment of an old friend named Ugo Dadone. It was the beginning of March and exceptionally warm. The windows and shutters of Pound's corner room swung open to the noises of the Via Angelo Poliziano. The interviewer sat in a large chair while Pound shifted restlessly from another chair to a sofa and back to the chair. Pound's impression on the room consisted of two suitcases and three books: the Faber Cantos, *a Confucius, and Robinson's edition of Chaucer which he was reading again.*

In the social hours of the evening—dinner at Crispi's, a tour among the scenes of his past, ice cream at a café—Pound walked with the swaggering vigor of a young man. With his great hat, his sturdy stick, his tossed yellow scarf, and his coat, which he trailed like a cape, he was the lion of the Latin Quarter again. Then his talent for mimicry came forward, and laughter shook his gray beard.

During the daytime hours of the interview, which took three days, he spoke carefully and the questions sometimes tired him out. In the morning when the interviewer returned, Mr. Pound was eager to revise the failures of the day before.

INTERVIEWER: You are nearly through the *Cantos* now, and this sets me to wondering about their beginning. In 1916 you wrote a letter in which you talked about trying to write a version of Andreas Divus in Seafarer rhythms. This sounds like a reference to *Canto* 1. Did you begin the *Cantos* in 1916?

POUND: I began the *Cantos* about 1904, I suppose. I had various schemes, starting in 1904 or 1905. The problem was to get a form —something elastic enough to take the necessary material. It had to be a form that wouldn't exclude something merely because it didn't fit. In the first sketches, a draft of the present first *Canto* was the third.

Obviously you haven't got a nice little road map such as the middle ages possessed of Heaven. Only a musical form would take the material, and the Confucian universe as I see it is a universe of interacting strains and tensions.

INTERVIEWER: Had your interest in Confucius begun in 1904?

POUND: No, the first thing was this: you had six centuries that hadn't been packaged. It was a question of dealing with material that wasn't in the *Divina Commedia.* Hugo did a *Légende des Siècles* that wasn't an evaluative affair but just bits of history

strung together. The problem was to build up a circle of reference
—taking the modern mind to be the mediaeval mind with wash
after wash of classical culture poured over it since the Renaissance.
That was the psyche, if you like. One had to deal with one's own
subject.

INTERVIEWER: It must be thirty or thirty-five years since you
have written any poetry outside the *Cantos*, except for the Alfred
Venison poems. Why is this?

POUND: I got to the point where, apart from an occasional
lighter impulse, what I had to say fitted the general scheme. There
has been a good deal of work thrown away because one is attracted
to an historic character and then finds that he doesn't function
within my form, doesn't embody a value needed. I have tried to
make the *Cantos* historic (Vid. G. Giovannini, *re* relation history
to tragedy. Two articles ten years apart in some philological peri-
odical, not source material but relevant) but not fiction. The
material one wants to fit in doesn't always work. If the stone isn't
hard enough to maintain the form, it has to go out.

INTERVIEWER: When you write a *Canto* now, how do you plan
it? Do you follow a special course of reading for each one?

POUND: One isn't necessarily reading. One is working on the life
vouchsafed, I should think. I don't know about method. The
what is so much more important than how.

INTERVIEWER: Yet when you were a young man, your interest in
poetry concentrated on form. Your professionalism, and your devotion to technique, became proverbial. In the last thirty years, you
have traded your interest in form for an interest in content. Was
the change on principle?

POUND: I think I've covered that. Technique is the test of sincerity. If a thing isn't worth getting the technique to say, it is of
inferior value. All that must be regarded as exercise. Richter in
his *Treatise on Harmony*, you see, says, "These are the principles
of harmony and counterpoint; they have nothing whatever to do
with composition, which is quite a separate activity." The statement, which somebody made, that you couldn't write Provençal

canzoni forms in English, is false. The question of whether it was
advisable or not was another matter. When there wasn't the
criterion of natural language without inversion, those forms were
natural, and they realized them with music. In English the music
is of a limited nature. You've got Chaucer's French perfection,
you've got Shakespeare's Italian perfection, you've got Campion
and Lawes. I don't think I got around to this kind of form until I
got to the choruses in the *Trachiniae*. I don't know that I got to
anything at all, really, but I thought it was an extension of the
gamut. It may be a delusion. One was always interested in the
implication of change of pitch in the union of *motz et son*, of
the word and melody.

INTERVIEWER: Does writing the *Cantos*, now, exhaust all of your
technical interest, or does the writing of translations, like the
Trachiniae you just mentioned, satisfy you by giving you more
fingerwork?

POUND: One sees a job to be done and goes at it. The *Trachiniae*
came from reading the Fenollosa Noh plays for the new edition,
and from wanting to see what would happen to a Greek play,
given that same medium and the hope of its being performed by
the Minorou company. The sight of Cathay in Greek, looking like
poetry, stimulated crosscurrents.

INTERVIEWER: Do you think that free verse is particularly an
American form? I imagine that William Carlos Williams probably
does, and thinks of the iambic as English.

POUND: I like Eliot's sentence: "No verse is *libre* for the man
who wants to do a good job." I think the best free verse comes
from an attempt to get back to quantitative meter.

I suppose it may be *un-English* without being specifically
American. I remember Cocteau playing drums in a jazz band as
if it were a very difficult mathematical problem.

I'll tell you a thing that I think *is* an American form, and that
is the Jamesian parenthesis. You realize that the person you are
talking to hasn't got the different steps, and you go back over

them. In fact the Jamesian parenthesis has immensely increased now. That I think is something that is definitely American. The struggle that one has when one meets another man who has had a lot of experience to find the point where the two experiences touch, so that he really knows what you are talking about.

INTERVIEWER: Your work includes a great range of experience, as well as of form. What do you think is the greatest quality a poet can have? Is it formal, or is it a quality of thinking?

POUND: I don't know that you can put the needed qualities in hierarchic order, but he must have a continuous curiosity, which of course does not make him a writer, but if he hasn't got that he will wither. And the question of doing anything about it depends on a persistent energy. A man like Agassiz is never bored, never tired. The transit from the reception of stimuli to the recording, to the correlation, that is what takes the whole energy of a lifetime.

INTERVIEWER: Do you think that the modern world has changed the ways in which poetry can be written?

POUND: There is a lot of competition that never was there before. Take the serious side of Disney, the Confucian side of Disney. It's in having taken an ethos, as he does in *Perri*, that squirrel film, where you have the values of courage and tenderness asserted in a way that everybody can understand. You have got an absolute genius there. You have got a greater correlation of nature than you have had since the time of Alexander the Great. Alexander gave orders to the fishermen that if they found out anything about fish that was interesting, a specific thing, they were to tell Aristotle. And with that correlation you got ichthyology to the scientific point where it stayed for two thousand years. And now one has got with the camera an *enormous* correlation of particulars. That capacity for making contact is a tremendous challenge to literature. It throws up the question of what needs to be done and what is superfluous.

INTERVIEWER: Maybe it's an opportunity, too. When you were a young man in particular, and even through the *Cantos*, you changed your poetic style again and again. You have never been content to stick anywhere. Were you consciously looking to extend your style? Does the artist *need* to keep moving?

POUND: I think the artist *has* to keep moving. You are trying to render life in a way that won't bore people and you are trying to put down what you see.

INTERVIEWER: I wonder what you think of contemporary movements. I haven't seen remarks of yours about poets more recent than Cummings, except for Bunting and Zukovsky. Other things have occupied you, I suppose.

POUND: One can't read everything. I was trying to find out a number of historic facts, and you can't see out of the back of your head. I do not think there is any record of a man being able to criticize the people that come after him. It is a sheer question of the amount of reading one man can do.

I don't know whether it is his own or whether it is a gem that he collected, but at any rate one of the things Frost said in London in 19—whenever it was—1912, was this: "Summary of prayer: 'Oh God, pay attention to *me*.'" And that is the approach of younger writers—not to divinity exactly!—and in general one has to limit one's reading to younger poets who are recommended by at least one other younger poet, as a sponsor. Of course a routine of that kind could lead to conspiracy, but at any rate . . .

As far as criticizing younger people, one has not the time to make a *comparative* estimate. People one is learning from, one does measure one against the other. I see a stirring now, but . . . For *general* conditions there is undoubtedly a *liveliness*. And Cal [Robert] Lowell is very good.

INTERVIEWER: You have given advice to the young all your life. Do you have anything special to say to them now?

POUND: To improve their curiosity and not to fake. But that is not enough. The mere registering of bellyache and the mere dumping of the ashcan is not enough. In fact the University of Pennsylvania student *Punchbowl* used to have as its motto, "Any damn fool can be spontaneous."

INTERVIEWER: You once wrote that you had four useful hints from living literary predecessors, who were Thomas Hardy, William Butler Yeats, Ford Madox Ford, and Robert Bridges. What were these hints?

POUND: Bridges' was the simplest. Bridges' was a warning against homophones. Hardy's was the degree to which he would concentrate on the subject matter, not on the manner. Ford's in general was the *freshness* of language. And Yeats you say was the fourth? Well, Yeats by 1908 had written simple lyrics in which there were no departures from the natural order of words.

INTERVIEWER: You were secretary to Yeats in 1913 and 1914. What sort of thing did you do for him?

POUND: Mostly reading aloud. Doughty's *Dawn in Britain*, and so on. And wrangling, you see. The Irish like contradiction. He tried to learn fencing at forty-five, which was amusing. He would thrash around with the foils like a whale. He sometimes gave the impression of being even a worse idiot than I am.

INTERVIEWER: There is an academic controversy about your influence on Yeats. Did you work over his poetry with him? Did you cut any of his poems in the way you cut *The Waste Land?*

POUND: I don't think I can remember anything like that. I am sure I objected to particular expressions. Once out at Rapallo I tried for God's sake to prevent him from printing a thing. I told him it was rubbish. All he did was print it with a preface saying that I *said* it was rubbish.

I remember when Tagore had taken to doodling on the edge of his proofs, and they told him it was art. There was a show of it in Paris. "Is this art?" Nobody was very keen on these doodlings, but of course so many people lied to him.

As far as the change in Yeats goes, I think that Ford Madox Ford might have some credit. Yeats never would have taken advice from Ford, but I think that Fordie helped him, via me, in trying to get towards a natural way of writing.

INTERVIEWER: Did anyone ever help you with your work as extensively as you have helped others? I mean by criticism or cutting.

POUND: Apart from Fordie, rolling on the floor undecorously and holding his head in his hands, and groaning on one occasion, I don't think anybody helped me through my manuscripts. Ford's stuff appeared too loose then, but he led the fight against tertiary archaisms.

INTERVIEWER: You have been closely associated with visual artists—Gaudier-Brzeska and Wyndham Lewis in the vorticist movement, and later Picabia, Picasso, and Brancusi. Has this had anything to do with you as a writer?

POUND: I don't believe so. One looked at paintings in galleries and one might have found out something. "The Game of Chess" poem shows the effect of modern abstract art, but vorticism from my angle was a renewal of the sense of construction. Color went dead and Manet and the impressionists revived it. Then what I would call the sense of form was blurred, and vorticism, as distinct from cubism, was an attempt to revive the sense of form—the form you had in Piero della Francesca's *De Prospettive Pingendi*, his treatise on the proportions and composition. I got started on the idea of comparative forms before I left America. A fellow named Poole did a book on composition. I did have *some* things in my head when I got to London, and I *had* heard of Catullus before I heard about modern French poetry. There's a bit of biography that might be rectified.

INTERVIEWER: I have wondered about your literary activities in America before you came to Europe. When did you first come over, by the way?

POUND: In 1898. At the age of twelve. With my great aunt.

INTERVIEWER: Were you reading French poetry then?

POUND: No, I suppose I was reading Grey's "Elegy in a Country Churchyard" or something. No, I wasn't reading French poetry. I was starting Latin next year.

INTERVIEWER: You entered college at fifteen, I believe?

POUND: I did it to get out of drill at Military Academy.

INTERVIEWER: How did you get started being a poet?

POUND: My grandfather on one side used to correspond with the local bank president in verse. My grandmother on the other side and her brothers used verse back and forth in their letters. It was taken for granted that anyone would write it.

INTERVIEWER: Did you learn anything in your university studies which helped you as a poet? I think you were a student for seven or eight years.

POUND: Only six. Well, six years and four months. I was writing all the time, especially as a graduate student. I started in freshman year studying Layamon's *Brut* and Latin. I got into college on my Latin; it was the only reason they *did* take me in. I did have the idea, at fifteen, of making a general survey. Of course whether I was or wasn't a poet was a matter for the gods to decide, but at least it was up to me to find out what had been done.

INTERVIEWER: You taught for four months only, as I remember. But you know that now the poets in America are mostly teachers. Do you have any ideas on the connection of teaching in the university with writing poetry?

POUND: It is the economic factor. A man's got to get in his rent somehow.

INTERVIEWER: How did you manage all the years in Europe?

POUND: Oh, God. A miracle of God. My income gained from October 1914 to October 1915 was £42.10.0. That figure is clearly engraved on my memory. . . .

I was never too good a hand at writing for the magazines. I once did a satirical article for *Vogue*, I think it was. On a painter whom I did not admire. They thought I had got just the right tone and then Verhaeren died and they asked me to do a note on Verhaeren. And I went down and said, "You want a nice bright snappy obituary notice of the gloomiest man in Europe."

"What, gloomy cuss, was he?"

"Yes," I said. "He wrote about peasants."

"Peasants or pheasants?"

"Peasants."

"Oh, I don't think we ought to touch it."

That is the way I crippled my earning capacity by not knowing enough to keep quiet.

INTERVIEWER: I read somewhere—I think you wrote it—that you once tried to write a novel. Did that get anywhere?

POUND: It got, fortunately, into the fireplace at Langham Place. I think there were two attempts, before I had any idea whatever of what a novel ought to be.

INTERVIEWER: Did they have anything to do with "Hugh Selwyn Mauberley?"

POUND: These were long before "Mauberley." "Mauberley" was later, but it *was* the definite attempt to get the novel cut down to the size of verse. It really is "Contacts and Life." Wadsworth seemed to think "Propertius" difficult because it was about Rome, so one applied the same thing to the contemporary outside.

INTERVIEWER: You said it was Ford who helped you toward a natural language, didn't you? Let's get back to London again.

POUND: One was hunting for a simple and natural language, and Ford was ten years older, and accelerated the process toward it. It was a continual discussion of that sort of thing. Ford knew the best of the people who were there before him, you see, and he had nobody to play with until Wyndham and I and my generation came along. He was definitely in opposition to the dialect, let us say, of Lionel Johnson and Oxford.

INTERVIEWER: You were for two or three decades at least in contact with all of the leading writers in English of the day and a lot of the painters, sculptors, and musicians. Of all these people, who were the most stimulating to you as an artist?

POUND: I saw most of Ford and Gaudier, I suppose. I should think that the people that I have written about were the most important to me. There isn't much revision to make there.

I may have limited my work, and limited the interest in it, by concentrating on the particular intelligence of particular people, instead of looking at the complete character and personality of my friends. Wyndham Lewis always claimed that I never *saw* people because I never noticed how wicked they were, what

S.O.B.'s they were. I wasn't the least interested in the vices of my friends, but in their intelligence.

INTERVIEWER: Was James a kind of a standard for you in London?

POUND: When he died one felt there was no one to ask about anything. Up to then one felt someone knew. After I was sixty-five I had great difficulty in realizing that I was older than James had been when I met him.

INTERVIEWER: Did you know Remy de Gourmont personally? You've mentioned him frequently.

POUND: Only by letter. There was one letter, which Jean de Gourmont also considered important, where he said, *"Franchement d'écrire ce qu'on pense, seul plaisir d'un écrivain."*

INTERVIEWER: It is amazing that you could come to Europe and quickly associate yourself with the best living writers. Had you been aware of any of the poets writing in America before you left? Was Robinson anything to you?

POUND: Aiken tried to sell me Robinson and I didn't fall. This was in London too. I then dragged it out of him that there was a guy at Harvard doing funny stuff. Mr. Eliot turned up a year or so later.

No, I should say that about 1900, you had Carman and Hovey, Carwine and Vance Cheney. The impression then was that the American stuff wasn't *quite* as good as the English at any point. And you had Mosher's pirated editions of the English stuff. No, I went to London because I thought Yeats knew more about poetry than anybody else. I made my life in London by going to see Ford in the afternoons and Yeats in the evenings. By mentioning one to the other one could always start a discussion. That was the exercise. I went to study with Yeats and found that Ford disagreed with him. So then I kept on disagreeing with *them* for twenty years.

INTERVIEWER: In 1942, you wrote that you and Eliot disagreed by calling each other protestants. I wonder when you and Eliot diverged.

POUND: Oh, Eliot and I started diverging from the beginning. The fun of an intellectual friendship is that you diverge on something or other and agree on a few points. Eliot, having had the Christian patience of tolerance all his life and so forth, and working very hard, must have found me very trying. We started disagreeing about a number of things from the time we met. We also agreed on a few things and I suppose both of us must have been right about something or other.

INTERVIEWER: Well, was there a point at which poetically and intellectually you felt further apart than you had been?

POUND: There's the whole problem of the relation of Christianity to Confucianism, and there's the whole problem of the different brands of Christianity. There is the struggle for orthodoxy— Eliot for the Church, me gunning round for particular theologians. In one sense Eliot's curiosity would appear to have been focused on a smaller number of problems. Even that is too much to say. The actual outlook of the experimental generation was all a question of the private ethos.

INTERVIEWER: Do you think that as poets you felt a divergence on technical grounds, unrelated to your subject matter?

POUND: I should think the divergence was first a difference in subject matter. He has undoubtedly got a natural language. In the language in the plays, he seems to me to have made a very great contribution. And in being able to make contact with an extant milieu, and an extant state of comprehension.

INTERVIEWER: That reminds me of the two operas—*Villon* and *Cavalcanti*—which you wrote. How did you come to compose music?

POUND: One wanted the word *and* the tune. One wanted great poetry *sung*, and the technique of the English opera libretto was not satisfactory. One wanted, with the quality of the texts of Villon and of Cavalcanti, to get something more extended than the single lyric. That's all.

INTERVIEWER: I suppose your interest in words to be sung was especially stimulated by your study of Provence. Do you feel that the discovery of Provençal poetry was your greatest breakthrough? Or perhaps the Fenollosa manuscripts?

POUND: The Provençal began with a very early interest, so that it wasn't really a discovery. And the Fenollosa was a windfall and one struggled against one's ignorance. One had the inside knowledge of Fenollosa's notes and the ignorance of a five-year-old child.

INTERVIEWER: How did Mrs. Fenollosa happen to hit upon you?

POUND: Well, I met her at Sarojini Naidu's and she said that Fenollosa had been in opposition to all the profs and academes, and she had seen some of my stuff and said I was the only person who could finish up these notes as Ernest would have wanted them done. Fenollosa saw what needed to be done but he didn't have time to finish it.

INTERVIEWER: Let me change the subject now, and ask you some questions which are more biographical than literary. I have read that you were born in Hailey, Idaho, in 1885. I suppose it must have been pretty rough out there then?

POUND: I left at the age of eighteen months and I don't remember the roughness.

INTERVIEWER: You did not grow up in Hailey?

POUND: I did not grow up in Hailey.

INTERVIEWER: What was your family doing there when you were born?

POUND: Dad opened the Government Land Office out there. I grew up near Philadelphia. The suburbs of Philadelphia.

INTERVIEWER: The wild Indian from the West then was not. . . ?

POUND: The wild Indian from the West is apocryphal, and the assistant assayer of the mint was not one of the most noted bandits of the frontier.

INTERVIEWER: I believe it's *true* that your grandfather built a railroad. What was the story of that?

POUND: Well, he got the railroad into Chippewa Falls, and they ganged up on him and would not let him buy any rails. That's in the *Cantos*. He went up to the north of New York State and found some rails on an abandoned road up there, bought them and had them shipped out, and then used his credit with the lumberjacks to get the road going to Chippewa Falls. What one learns in the home one learns in a way one doesn't learn in school.

INTERVIEWER: Does your particular interest in coinage start from your father's work at the mint?

POUND: You can go on for a long time on that. The government offices were more informal then, though I don't know that any other kids got in and visited. Now the visitors are taken through glass tunnels and see things from a distance, but you could then be taken around in the smelting room and see the gold piled up in the safe. You were offered a large bag of gold and told you could have it if you could take it away with you. You couldn't lift it.

When the Democrats finally came back in, they recounted all the silver dollars, four million dollars in silver. All the bags had rotted in these enormous vaults, and they were heaving it into the counting machines with shovels bigger than coal shovels. This spectacle of coin being shoveled around like it was litter—these fellows naked to the waist shoveling it around in the gas flares— things like that strike your imagination.

Then there's the whole technique of making metallic money. First, the testing of the silver is much more tricky than testing gold. Gold is simple. It is weighed, then refined and weighed again. You can tell the grade of the ore by the relative weights. But the test for silver is a cloudy solution; the accuracy of the eye in measuring the thickness of the cloud is an aesthetic perception, like the critical sense. I like the idea of the *fineness* of the metal, and it moves by analogy to the habit of testing verbal manifestations. At that time, you see, gold bricks, and specimens of iron pyrites mistaken for gold, were brought up to Dad's office. You heard the talk about the last guy who brought a gold brick and it turned out to be fool's gold.

INTERVIEWER: I know you consider monetary reform the key to good government. I wonder by what process you moved from aesthetic problems toward governmental ones. Did the great war, which slaughtered so many of your friends, do the moving?

POUND: The great war came as a surprise, and certainly to see the English—these people who had never done anything—get hold of themselves, fight it, was immensely impressive. But as soon as it was over they went dead, and then one spent the next twenty years trying to prevent the Second War. I can't say exactly where my study of government started. I think the *New Age* office helped me to see the war not as a separate event but as part of a system, one war after another.

INTERVIEWER: One point of connection between literature and politics which you make in your writing interests me particularly. In the *A.B.C. of Reading* you say that good writers are those who keep the language efficient, and that this is their function. You disassociate this function from party. Can a man of the wrong party use language efficiently?

POUND: Yes. That's the whole trouble! A gun is just as good, no matter who shoots it.

INTERVIEWER: Can an instrument which is orderly be used to create disorder? Suppose good language is used to forward bad government? Doesn't bad government make bad language?

POUND: Yes, but bad language is *bound* to make in addition bad government, whereas good language is *not* bound to make bad government. That again is clear Confucius: if the orders aren't clear they can't be carried out. Lloyd George's laws were such a mess, the lawyers never knew what they meant. And Talleyrand proclaimed that they changed the meaning of words between one conference and another. The means of communication breaks down, and that of course is what we are suffering now. We are enduring the drive to work on the subconscious without appealing to the reason. They repeat a trade name with the music a few times, and then repeat the music without it so that the music will give you the name. I think of the *assault*. We suffer from the use of language to conceal thought and to withhold all vital and

direct answers. There is the definite use of propaganda, forensic
language, merely to conceal and mislead.

INTERVIEWER: Where do ignorance and innocence end and the
chicanery begin?

POUND: There is natural ignorance and there is artificial ignorance. I should say at the present moment the artificial ignorance
is about eighty-five per cent.

INTERVIEWER: What kind of action can you hope to take?

POUND: The only chance for victory over the brainwash is the
right of every man to have his ideas judged one at a time. You
never get clarity as long as you have these package words, as long
as a word is used by twenty-five people in twenty-five different
ways. That seems to me to be the first fight, if there is going to
be any intellect left.

It is doubtful whether the individual soul is going to be allowed
to survive at all. Now you get a Buddhist movement with everything *except* Confucius taken into it. An Indian Circe of negation
and dissolution.

We are up against so many mysteries. There is the problem
of benevolence, the point at which benevolence has ceased to be
operative. Eliot says that they spend their time trying to imagine
systems so perfect that nobody will have to be good. A lot of
questions asked in that essay of Eliot's cannot be dodged, like the
question of whether there need be any change from the Dantesquan scale of values or the Chaucerian scale of values. If so,
how much? People who have lost reverence have lost a great deal.
That was where I split with Tiffany Thayer. All these large words
fall into clichés.

There is the mystery of the scattering, the fact that the people
who presumably understand each other are geographically scat-
tered. A man who fits in his milieu as Frost does, is to be considered a happy man.

Oh, the luck of a man like Mavrocordato, who is in touch with
other scholars, so that there is somewhere where he can verify a
point! Now for certain points where I want verification there is a

fellow named Dazzi in Venice that I write to and he comes up with an answer, as it might be about the forged Donation of Constantine. But the advantages which were supposed to inhere in the university—where there are other people to *contrôl* * opinion or to *contrôl* the data—were very great. It is crippling not to have had them. Of course I have been trying over a ten-year period to get any member of an American faculty to mention any other member of his same faculty, in his own department or outside it, whose intelligence he respects or with whom he will discuss serious matters. In one case the gentleman regretted that someone else had *left* the faculty.

I have been unable to get straight answers out of people on what appeared to me to be vital questions. That may have been due to my violence or obscurity with which I framed the questions. Often, I think, so-called obscurity is not obscurity in the language but in the other person's not being able to make out *why* you are saying a thing. For instance the attack on Endymion was complicated because Gifford and company couldn't see why the deuce Keats was doing it.

Another struggle has been the struggle to keep the value of a local and particular character, of a particular culture in this awful maelstrom, this awful avalanche toward uniformity. The whole fight is for the conservation of the individual soul. The enemy is the supression of history; against us is the bewildering propaganda and brainwash, luxury and violence. Sixty years ago, poetry was the poor man's art: a man off on the edge of the wilderness, or Frémont, going off with a Greek text in his pocket. A man who wanted the best could have it on a lonely farm. Then there was the cinema, and now television.

INTERVIEWER: The political action of yours that everybody remembers is your broadcasts from Italy during the war. When you gave these talks, were you conscious of breaking the American law?

POUND: No, I was completely surprised. You see I had that

---

* Pound indicates that he is using the French *contrôler:* "to verify, check information, a fact."

promise. I was given the freedom of the microphone twice a week. "He will not be asked to say anything contrary to his conscience or contrary to his duty as an American citizen." I thought that covered it.

INTERVIEWER: Doesn't the law of treason talk about "giving aid and comfort to the enemy," and isn't the enemy the country with whom we are at war?

POUND: I thought I was fighting for a constitutional point. I mean to say, I may have been completely nuts, but I certainly *felt* that it wasn't committing treason.

Wodehouse went on the air and the British asked him not to. Nobody asked me not to. There was no announcement until the collapse that the people who had spoken on the radio would be prosecuted.

Having worked for years to prevent war, and seeing the folly of Italy and America being at war—! I certainly wasn't telling the troops to revolt. I thought I was fighting an internal question of constitutional government. And if any man, any individual man, can say he has had a bad deal from me because of race, creed, or color, let him come out and state it with particulars. The *Guide to Kulchur* was dedicated to Basil Bunting and Louis Zukovsky, a Quaker and a Jew.

I don't know whether you think the Russians ought to be in Berlin or not. I don't know whether I was doing any good or not, whether I was doing any harm. Oh, I was probably offside. But the ruling in Boston was that there is no treason without treasonable intention.

What I was right about was the conservation of individual rights. If, when the executive or any other branch exceeds its legitimate powers, no one protests, you will lose all your liberties. My method of opposing tyranny was wrong over a thirty-year period; it had nothing to do with the Second World War in particular. If the individual, or heretic, gets hold of some essential truth, or sees some error in the system being practiced, he commits so many marginal errors himself that he is worn out before he can establish his point.

The world in twenty years has piled up hysteria—anxiety over a third war, bureaucratic tyranny, and hysteria from paper forms. The immense and undeniable loss of freedoms, as they were in 1900, is undeniable. We have seen the acceleration in efficiency of the tyrannizing factors. It's enough to keep a man worried. Wars are made to make debt. I suppose there's a possible out in space satellites and other ways of making debt.

INTERVIEWER: When you were arrested by the Americans, did you then expect to be convicted? To be hanged?

POUND: At first I puzzled over having missed a cog somewhere. I expected to turn myself in and to be asked about what I learned. I did and I wasn't. I know that I checked myself, on several occasions during the broadcasts, on reflecting that it was not up to me to do certain things, or to take service with a foreign country. Oh, it was paranoia to think one could argue against the usurpations, against the folks who got the war started to get America into it. Yet I hate the idea of obedience to something which is wrong.

Then later I was driven into the courtyard at Chiavari. They had been shooting them, and I thought I was finished then and there. Then finally a guy came in and said he was damned if he would hand me over to the Americans unless I wanted to be handed over to them.

INTERVIEWER: In 1942, when the war started for America, I understand you tried to leave Italy and come back to the United States. What were the circumstances of the refusal?

POUND: Those circumstances were by hearsay. I am a bit hazy in my head about a considerable period, and I think that . . . I know that I had a chance to get as far as Lisbon, and be cooped up there for the rest of the war.

INTERVIEWER: Why did you want to get back to the States at that time?

POUND: I wanted to get back during the election, before the election.

INTERVIEWER: The election was in 1940, wasn't it?

POUND: That would be 1940. I don't honestly remember what happened. My parents were too old to travel. They would have had to stay there in Rapallo. Dad retired there on his pension.

INTERVIEWER: During those years in the war in Italy did you write poetry? The *Pisan Cantos* were written when you were interned. What did you write during those years?

POUND: Arguments, arguments and arguments. Oh, I did some of the Confucius translation.

INTERVIEWER: How was it that you began to write poetry again only after you were interned? You didn't write any cantos at all during the war, did you?

POUND: Let's see—the Adams stuff came out just before the war shut off. No. There was *Oro e Lavoro*. I was writing economic stuff in Italian.

INTERVIEWER: Since your internment, you've published three collections of *Cantos*, *Thrones* just recently. You must be near the end. Can you say what you are going to do in the remaining *Cantos*?

POUND: It is difficult to write a paradiso when all the superficial indications are that you ought to write an apocalypse. It is obviously much easier to find inhabitants for an inferno or even a purgatorio. I am trying to collect the record of the top flights of the mind. I might have done better to put Agassiz on top instead of Confucius.

INTERVIEWER: Are you more or less stuck?

POUND: Okay, I am stuck. The question is, am I dead, as Messrs. A.B.C. might wish? In case I conk out, this is provisionally what I have to do: I must clarify obscurities; I must make clearer definite ideas or dissociations. I must find a verbal formula to combat the rise of brutality—the principle of order versus the split atom. There was a man in the bughouse, by the way, who insisted that the atom had never been split.

An epic is a poem containing history. The modern mind contains heteroclite elements. The past epos has succeeded when all or a great many of the answers were assumed, at least between author and audience, or a great mass of audience. The attempt in an experimental age is therefore rash. Do you know the story: "What are you drawing, Johnny?"

"God."

"But nobody knows what He looks like."

"They will when I get through!"

That confidence is no longer obtainable.

There *are* epic subjects. The struggle for individual rights is an epic subject, consecutive from jury trial in Athens to Anselm versus William Rufus, to the murder of Becket and to Coke and through John Adams.

Then the struggle appears to come up against a block. The nature of sovereignty is epic matter, though it may be a bit obscured by circumstance. Some of this *can* be traced, pointed; obviously it has to be condensed to get into the form. The nature of the individual, the heteroclite contents of contemporary consciousness. It's the fight for light versus subconsciousness; it demands obscurities and penumbras. A lot of contemporary writing avoids inconvenient areas of the subject.

I am writing to resist the view that Europe and civilization are going to Hell. If I am being "crucified for an idea"—that is, the coherent idea around which my muddles accumulated—it is probably the idea that European culture ought to survive, that the best qualities of it ought to survive along with whatever other cultures, in whatever universality. Against the propaganda of terror and the propaganda of luxury, have you a nice simple answer? One has worked on certain materials trying to establish bases and axes of reference. In writing so as to be understood, there is always the problem of rectification without giving up what is correct. There is the struggle not to sign on the dotted line for the opposition.

INTERVIEWER: Do the separate sections of the *Cantos*, now—the last three sections have appeared under separate names—mean that you are attacking particular problems in particular sections?

POUND: No. *Rock Drill* was intended to imply the necessary resistance in getting a certain main thesis across—hammering. I was not following the three divisions of the *Divine Comedy* exactly. One can't follow the Dantesquan cosmos in an age of experiment. But I have made the division between people dominated by emotion, people struggling upwards, and those who have some part of the divine vision. The thrones in Dante's *Paradiso* are for the spirits of the people who have been responsible for good government. The thrones in the *Cantos* are an attempt to move out from egoism and to establish some definition of an order possible or at any rate conceivable on earth. One is held up by the low percentage of reason which seems to operate in human affairs. *Thrones* concerns the states of mind of people responsible for something more than their personal conduct.

INTERVIEWER: Now that you come near the end, have you made any plans for revising the *Cantos*, after you've finished?

POUND: I don't know. There's need of elaboration, of clarification, but I don't know that a comprehensive revision is in order. There is no doubt that the writing is too obscure as it stands, but I hope that the order of ascension in the Paradiso will be toward a greater limpidity. Of course there ought to be a corrected edition because of errors that have crept in.

INTERVIEWER: Let me change the subject again, if I may. In all those years in St. Elizabeth's, did you get a sense of contemporary America from your visitors?

POUND: The trouble with visitors is that you don't get enough of the opposition. I suffer from the cumulative isolation of not having had enough contact—fifteen years living more with ideas than with persons.

INTERVIEWER: Do you have any plans for going back to the States? Do you want to?

POUND: I undoubtedly want to. But whether it is nostalgia for America that isn't there any more or not I don't know. This is a difference between an abstract Adams–Jefferson–Adams–Jackson America, and whatever is really going on. I undoubtedly have moments when I should like very much to live in America. There are these concrete difficulties against the general desire. Richmond is a beautiful city, but you can't live in it unless you drive an automobile. I'd like at least to spend a month or two a year in the U.S.

INTERVIEWER: You said the other day that as you grew older you felt more American all the time. How does this work?

POUND: It works. Exotics were necessary as an attempt at a foundation. One is transplanted and grows, and one is pulled up and taken back to what one has been transplanted from and it is no longer there. The contacts aren't there and I suppose one reverts to one's organic nature and finds it merciful. Have you ever read Andy White's memoirs? He's the fellow who founded Cornell University. That was the period of euphoria, when everybody thought that all the good things in America were going to function, before the decline, about 1900. White covers a period of history that goes back to Buchanan on one side. He alternated between being Ambassador to Russia and head of Cornell.

INTERVIEWER: Your return to Italy has been a disappointment, then?

POUND: Undoubtedly. Europe was a shock. The shock of no longer feeling oneself in the center of something is probably part of it. Then there is the incomprehension, Europe's incomprehension, of organic America. There are so many things which I, as an American, cannot say to a European with any hope of being understood. Somebody said that I am the last American living the tragedy of Europe.

DONALD HALL

Note: Mr. Pound's health made it impossible for him to finish proofreading this interview. The text is complete, but may contain details which Mr. Pound would have changed under happier circumstances.

3. Marianne Moore

Marianne Craig Moore was born in St. Louis, Missouri, on November 15, 1887. She attended Metzger Institute in Carlisle, Pennsylvania, then Bryn Mawr, from which she was graduated in 1909. The following year she was graduated from Carlisle Commercial College. From 1911 to 1915 she taught stenography and other commercial subjects at the United States Industrial Indian School, Carlisle, and from 1921 to 1925 was an assistant in the New York Public Library.

Miss Moore's first poems appeared in Bryn Mawr College publications; in 1917 some of her work was published in *The Egoist*, London, and later in Harriet Monroe's *Poetry*. In 1921 Winifred Ellerman (Bryher) and the poet Hilda Doolittle (H.D.), without the knowledge of Miss Moore, brought out *Poems* (The Egoist Press). Four years later *Observations* appeared in the United States and won the Dial Award as an outstanding contribution to American literature. In 1925, Miss Moore joined the editorial staff of *The Dial* and continued work with that magazine until its demise. She took up residence in Brooklyn, where she still lives.

Marianne Moore has won nearly all the prizes for poetry which are presented in this country, and in 1947 she was elected a member of the National Institute of Arts and Letters. Her published work includes *Observations* (1924), *Selected Poems* (1935), *The Pangolin and Other Verse* (1936), *What Are Years* (1941), *Nevertheless* (1944), *Collected Poems* (1951), *The Fables of La Fontaine* (translation, 1954), *Predilections* (essays, 1955), *Like a Bulwark* (1956), *O to Be a Dragon* (1959), *A Marianne Moore Reader* (1961).

T. S. Eliot wrote in 1935: "My conviction has remained unchanged for the last fourteen years—that Miss Moore's poems form part of the small body of durable poetry written in our time . . . in which an original sensibility and alert intelligence and deep feeling have been engaged in maintaining the life of the English language."

RESCUE WITH YUL BRYNNER

(appointed by ~~President Eisenhower~~ special consultant
to the United Nations Commission on Refugees,
(1959-1960)

with Dances Galanta by Zoltán Kodály
favorites of Budapest Symphony Orchestra -
now refugee Symphonia Hungarica in Marl-
CBS;December 10, 1960

Head, down ~~low~~ over the guitar,
he barely seemed to hum, ending "all come home";
did not smile;came by air;
did not have to come.

    The guitar's an event.
Guests of honor ~~is old doesn't~~ dance; ~~can't~~ smile.
"Have a home?" a boy asks. "Shall we live in a tent?"
        "In a house", Yul answers. His neat cloth hat
has nothing like the glitter ~~that~~ reflected on the face
of milkweed-~~seed~~ brown dominating a ~~palace~~ place
~~in those hells devoid of solace~~ that was nothing like the place
where he is now. His deliberate pace
is a kind's however. "You'll have plenty of space."

"Recital"? 'concert is the word.'-
in Marl Austria's Marl, by the Budapest Symphonia Symphony -
    displaced but not deterred,
listened to by me - I arose with detachment then
    ~~detachedly then~~ -
    Y like a ~~frog or~~ grasshopper that did not
    know it ~~had~~ missed the mower , a pigmy citizen;
        ~~in any~~ case, too slow a grower.
There were thirty million; there are thirteen still -
healthy to begin with, kept waiting till they're ill/
History judges. It ~~certainly will~~
~~remember~~ Winnipeg's incredible
conditions: "Ill;no a sponsor;and no kind of skill."
    Odd - a reporter with ~~small~~ guitar - a puzzle.
Mysterious Yul did not come to dazzle.

    Magic bird with multiple tongue -
five tongues - ~~embarked on~~ a crazy twelve-month tramp
or plod), he flew among
the damned, / found each camp
    where hope had slowly died -/(some had never even a flame).
    ~~& came to end that sort of death;~~
Instead/~~did not~~ feather himself, he exemplified/this rule that
    "Two small fishes and five loaves of bread"
    Nourished seeds of dignity. All were fed.
He said,"You may feel strange;~~not dressed the way they dress.~~
Nobody notices; you'll find some happiness.
No new "big fear"; no distress."
He can sing-~~twinned with~~an enchantress -
elephant-borne ~~fairy with blue~~ sequinned-spangled dress -
~~curled~~ aloft by trunk, with star-tipped wand,
~~tru-er~~ to the beat ~~than~~ Symphonia ~~Hungaria~~. Hungarica.
as true   as

Manuscript of a poem by Marianne Moore.

HILDEGARDE WATSON

Marianne Moore

American poetry is a great literature, and it has come to its maturity only in the last forty years; Walt Whitman and Emily Dickinson in the last century were rare examples of genius in a hostile environment. One decade gave America the major figures of our modern poetry: Wallace Stevens was born in 1879, and T. S. Eliot in 1888. To the ten years which these dates enclose belong H.D., Robinson Jeffers, John Crowe Ransom, William Carlos Williams, Ezra Pound, and Marianne Moore.

Marianne Moore, surely the leading woman in modern American literature, began to publish during the First World War. She was printed and praised in Europe by the expatriates T. S. Eliot and Ezra Pound. In Chicago Harriet Monroe's magazine Poetry, *which provided the enduring showcase for the new poetry, published her too. But she was mainly a poet of New York, of the Greenwich Village group which created magazines called* Others *and* Broom. *The poets with whom she was mostly associated were Alfred*

Kreymborg, William Carlos Williams, and Wallace Stevens—
Stateside representatives of the miraculous generation.

Marianne Moore has settled not in Bloomsbury or Rapallo but
in Brooklyn. She moved there from the Village in 1929, into the
apartment house where she still lives. To visit her you cross Brooklyn Bridge, turn left at Myrtle Avenue, follow the elevated for a
mile or two, and then turn right onto her street. It is pleasantly
lined with a few trees, and Miss Moore's apartment is conveniently
near a grocery store and the Presbyterian church which she attends.

The interview took place in November 1960, the day before the
election. The front door of Miss Moore's apartment opens onto a
long narrow corridor. Rooms lead off to the right, and at the end
of the corridor is a large sitting room which overlooks the street.
On top of a bookcase which ran the length of the corridor was a
Nixon button.

Miss Moore and the interviewer sat in her sitting room, a
microphone between them. Piles of books stood everywhere. On
the walls hung a variety of paintings. One came from Mexico, a
gift of Mabel Dodge; others were examples of the heavy, tea-
colored oils which Americans hung in the years before 1914. The
furniture was old-fashioned and dark.

Miss Moore spoke with an accustomed scrupulosity, and with
a humor which her readers will recognize. When she ended a
sentence with a phrase which was particularly telling, or even tart,
she glanced quickly at the interviewer to see if he was amused,
and then snickered gently. Later Miss Moore took the interviewer to an admirable lunch at a nearby restaurant. She decided
not to wear her Nixon button because it clashed with her coat
and hat.

INTERVIEWER: Miss Moore, I understand that you were born
in St. Louis only about ten months before T. S. Eliot. Did your
families know each other?

MOORE: No, we did not know the Eliots. We lived in Kirkwood,
Missouri, where my grandfather was pastor of the First Presby-

terian Church. T. S. Eliot's grandfather—Dr. William Eliot—was a Unitarian. We left when I was about seven, my grandfather having died in 1894, February 20th. My grandfather like Dr. Eliot had attended ministerial meetings in St. Louis. Also, at stated intervals, various ministers met for luncheon. After one of these luncheons my grandfather said, "When Dr. William Eliot asks the blessing and says, 'and this we ask in the name of our Lord Jesus Christ,' he is Trinitarian enough for me." The Mary Institute, for girls, was endowed by him as a memorial to his daughter Mary, who had died.

INTERVIEWER: How old were you when you started to write poems?

MOORE: Well, let me see, in Bryn Mawr. I think I was eighteen when I entered Bryn Mawr. I was born in 1887, I entered college in 1906. Now how old would I have been? Can you deduce my probable age?

INTERVIEWER: Eighteen or nineteen.

MOORE: I had no literary plans, but I was interested in the undergraduate monthly magazine, and to my surprise (I wrote one or two little things for it) the editors elected me to the board. It was my sophomore year—I am sure it was—and I stayed on, I believe. And then when I had left college I offered contributions (we weren't paid) to the *Lantern*, the alumnae magazine. But I didn't feel that my product was anything to shake the world.

INTERVIEWER: At what point did poetry become world-shaking for you?

MOORE: Never! I believe I was interested in painting then. At least I said so. I remember Mrs. Otis Skinner asking at commencement time, the year I was graduated, "What would you like to be?"

"A painter," I said.

"Well, I'm not surprised," Mrs. Skinner answered. I had something on that she liked, some kind of summer dress. She commended it—said, "I'm not at all surprised."

I like stories. I like fiction. And—this sounds rather pathetic, bizarre as well—I think verse perhaps was for me the next best thing to it. Didn't I write something one time, "Part of a Poem, Part of a Novel, Part of a Play"? I think I was all too truthful. I could visualize scenes, and deplored the fact that Henry James had to do it unchallenged. Now, if I couldn't write fiction, I'd like to write plays. To me the theater is the most pleasant, in fact my favorite, form of recreation.

INTERVIEWER: Do you go often?

MOORE: No. Never. Unless someone invites me. Lillian Hellman invited me to *Toys in the Attic*, and I am very happy that she did. I would have had no notion of the vitality of the thing, have lost sight of her skill as a writer if I hadn't seen the play; would like to go again. The accuracy of the vernacular! That's the kind of thing I am interested in, am always taking down little local expressions and accents. I think I should be in some philological operation or enterprise, am really much interested in dialect and intonations. I scarcely think of any that comes into my so-called poems at all.

INTERVIEWER: I wonder what Bryn Mawr meant for you as a poet. You write that most of your time there was spent in the biological laboratory. Did you like biology better than literature as a subject for study? Did the training possibly affect your poetry?

MOORE: I had hoped to make French and English my major studies, and took the required two-year English course—five hours a week—but was not able to elect a course until my junior year. I did not attain the requisite academic stand of eighty until that year. I then elected seventeenth-century imitative writing—Fuller, Hooker, Bacon, Bishop Andrewes, and others. Lectures in French were in French, and I had had no spoken French.

Did laboratory studies affect my poetry? I am sure they did. I found the biology courses—minor, major, and histology—exhilarating. I thought, in fact, of studying medicine. Precision, economy of statement, logic employed to ends that are disinterested, drawing and identifying, liberate—at least have some bearing on—the imagination, it seems to me.

INTERVIEWER: Whom did you know in the literary world, before you came to New York? Did you know Bryher and H.D.?

MOORE: It's very hard to get these things seriatim. I met Bryher in 1921 in New York. H.D. was my classmate at Bryn Mawr. She was there, I think, only two years. She was a non-resident and I did not realize that she was interested in writing.

INTERVIEWER: Did you know Ezra Pound and William Carlos Williams through her? Didn't she know them at the University of Pennsylvania?

MOORE: Yes. She did. I didn't meet them. I had met no writers until 1916 when I visited New York, when a friend in Carlisle wanted me to accompany her.

INTERVIEWER: So you were isolated really from modern poetry until 1916?

MOORE: Yes.

INTERVIEWER: Was that your first trip to New York, when you went there for six days and decided that you wanted to live there?

MOORE: Oh, no. Several times my mother had taken my brother and me sightseeing and to shop; on the way to Boston, or Maine, and to Washington and Florida. My senior year in college in 1909, I visited Dr. Charles Spraguesmith's daughter, Hilda, at Christmas time in New York. And Louis Anspacher lectured in a very ornamental way at Cooper Union. There was plenty of music at Carnegie Hall, and I got a sense of what was going on in New York.

INTERVIEWER: And what was going on made you want to come back?

MOORE: It probably did, when Miss Cowdrey in Carlisle invited me to come with her for a week. It was the visit in 1916 that made me want to live there. I don't know what put it into her head to do it, or why she wasn't likely to have a better time without me. She was most skeptical of my venturing forth to bohemian parties. But I was fearless about that. In the first place, I didn't think anyone would try to harm me, but if they did I felt impervious. It never occurred to me that chaperones were important.

INTERVIEWER: Do you suppose that moving to New York, and the stimulation of the writers whom you found there, led you to write more poems than you would otherwise have written?

MOORE: I'm sure it did—seeing what others wrote, liking this or that. With me it's always some fortuity that traps me. I certainly never intended to write poetry. That never came into my head. And now, too, I think each time I write that it may be the last time; then I'm charmed by something and seem to have to say something. Everything I have written is the result of reading or of interest in people, I'm sure of that. I had no ambition to be a writer.

INTERVIEWER: Let me see. You taught at the Carlisle Indian School, after Bryn Mawr. Then after you moved to New York in 1918 you taught at a private school and worked in a library. Did these occupations have anything to do with you as a writer?

MOORE: I think they hardened my muscles considerably, my mental approach to things. Working as a librarian was a big help, a tremendous help. Miss Leonard of the Hudson Park branch of the New York Public Library opposite our house came to see me one day. I wasn't in, and she asked my mother did she think I would care to be on the staff, work in the library, because I was so fond of books and liked to talk about them to people. My mother said no, she thought not; the shoemaker's children never have shoes, I probably would feel if I joined the staff that I'd have no time to read. When I came home she told me, and I said, "Why, certainly. Ideal. I'll tell her. Only I couldn't work more than half a day." If I had worked all day and maybe evenings or overtime, like the mechanics, why, it would *not* have been ideal.

As a free service we were assigned books to review and I did like that. We didn't get paid but we had the chance to diagnose. I reveled in it. Somewhere I believe I have carbon copies of those "P-slip" summaries. They were the kind of things that brought the worst-best out. I was always wondering why they didn't honor me with an art book or medical book or even a history, or criticism. But no, it was fiction, silent-movie fiction.

INTERVIEWER: Did you travel at this time? Did you go to Europe at all?

MOORE: In 1911. My mother and I went to England for about two months, July and August probably. We went to Paris and we stayed on the left bank, in a pension in the rue Valette, where Calvin wrote his *Institutes*, I believe. Not far from the Panthéon and the Luxembourg Gardens. I have been much interested in Sylvia Beach's book—reading about Ezra Pound and his Paris days. Where was I and what was I doing? I think, with the objective, an evening stroll—it was one of the hottest summers the world has ever known, 1911—we walked along to 12, rue de l'Odéon, to see Sylvia Beach's shop. It wouldn't occur to me to say, "Here am I, I'm a writer, would you talk to me a while?" I had no feeling at all like that. I wanted to observe things. And we went to every museum in Paris, I think, except two.

INTERVIEWER: Have you been back since?

MOORE: Not to Paris. Only to England in 1935 or 1936. I like England.

INTERVIEWER: You have mostly stayed put in Brooklyn, then, since you moved here in 1929?

MOORE: Except for four trips to the West: Los Angeles, San Francisco, Puget Sound, and British Columbia. My mother and I went through the canal previously, to San Francisco, and by rail to Seattle.

INTERVIEWER: Have you missed the Dodgers here, since *they* went West?

MOORE: Very much, and I am told that they miss us.

INTERVIEWER: I am still interested in those early years in New York. William Carlos Williams, in his *Autobiography*, says that you were "a rafter holding up the superstructure of our uncompleted building," when he talks about the Greenwich Village group of writers. I guess these were people who contributed to *Others*.

MOORE: I never was a rafter holding up anyone! I have his *Autobiography* and took him to task for his misinformed statements about Robert McAlmon and Bryher. In my indignation I missed some things I ought to have seen.

INTERVIEWER: To what extent did the *Others* contributors form a group?

MOORE: We did foregather a little. Alfred Kreymborg was editor, and was married to Gertrude Lord at the time, one of the loveliest persons you could ever meet. And they had a little apartment somewhere in the village. There was considerable unanimity about the group.

INTERVIEWER: Someone called Alfred Kreymborg your American discoverer. Do you suppose this is true?

MOORE: It could be said, perhaps; he did all he could to promote me. Miss Monroe and the Aldingtons had asked me simultaneously to contribute to *Poetry* and the *Egoist* in 1917 at the same time. Alfred Kreymborg was not inhibited. I was a little different from the others. He thought I might pass as a novelty, I guess.

INTERVIEWER: What was your reaction when H. D. and Bryher brought out your first collection, which they called *Poems*, in 1921 without your knowledge? Why had you delayed to do it yourself?

MOORE: To issue my slight product—conspicuously tentative—seemed to me premature. I disliked the term "poetry" for any but Chaucer's or Shakespeare's or Dante's. I do not now feel quite my original hostility to the word, since it is a convenient almost unavoidable term for the thing (although hardly for me—my observations, experiments in rhythm, or exercises in composition). What I write, as I have said before, could only be called poetry because there is no other category in which to put it. For the chivalry of the undertaking—issuing my verse for me in 1921, certainly in format choicer than the content—I am intensely grateful. Again, in 1925, it seemed to me not very self-interested of Faber and Faber, and simultaneously of the Macmillan Company, to propose a *Selected Poems* for me. Desultory occasional magazine publications seemed to me sufficient, conspicuous enough.

INTERVIEWER: Had you been sending poems to magazines be·
fore the *Egoist* printed your first poem?

MOORE: I must have. I have a little curio, a little wee book
about two by three inches, or two and a half by three inches, in
which I systematically entered everything sent out, when I got it
back, if they took it, and how much I got for it. That lasted
about a year, I think. I can't care as much as all that. I don't
know that I submitted anything that wasn't extorted from me.

I have at present three onerous tasks, and each interferes with
the others, and I don't know how I am going to write anything.
If I get a promising idea I set it down, and it stays there. I don't
make myself do anything with it. I've had several things in the
New Yorker. And I said to them, "I might never write again,"
and not to expect me to. I never knew anyone who had a passion
for words who had as much difficulty in saying things as I do
and I very seldom say them in a manner I like. If I do it's because
I don't know I'm trying. I've written several things for the *New
Yorker*—and I did want to write *them.*

INTERVIEWER: When did you last write a poem?

MOORE: It appeared in August. What was it about? Oh . . .
Carnegie Hall. You see, anything that really rouses me . . .

INTERVIEWER: How does a poem start for you?

MOORE: A felicitous phrase springs to mind—a word or two,
say—simultaneous usually with some thought or object of equal
attraction: "Its leaps should be *set/* to the flageo*let*"; "Katydid-
wing subdivided by *sun/*till the nettings are *legion.*" I like light
rhymes, inconspicuous rhymes and un-pompous conspicuous
rhymes: Gilbert and Sullivan:

> Yet, when the danger's near,
> We manage to appear
> As insensible to fear
> As anybody here.

I have a passion for rhythm and accent, so blundered into
versifying. Considering the stanza the unit, I came to hazard hy-

phens at the end of the line, but found that readers are distracted from the content by hyphens, so I try not to use them. My interest in La Fontaine originated entirely independent of content. I then fell a prey to that surgical kind of courtesy of his.

> I fear that appearances are worshiped throughout France
>   Whereas pre-eminence perchance
>   Merely means a pushing person.

I like the unaccented syllable and accented near-rhyme:

> By love and his blindness
> Possibly a service was done,
> Let lovers say. A lonely man has no criterion.

INTERVIEWER: What in your reading or your background led you to write the way you do write? Was imagism a help to you?

MOORE: No. I wondered why anyone would adopt the term.

INTERVIEWER: The descriptiveness of your poems has nothing to do with them, you think?

MOORE: No; I really don't. I was rather sorry to be a pariah, or at least that I had no connection with anything. But I *did* feel gratitude to *Others*.

INTERVIEWER: Where do you think your style of writing came from? Was it a gradual accumulation, out of your character? Or does it have literary antecedents?

MOORE: Not so far as I know. Ezra Pound said, "Someone has been reading Laforgue, and French authors." Well, sad to say, I had not read any of them until fairly recently. Retroactively I see that Francis Jammes' titles and treatment are a good deal like my own. I seem almost a plagiarist.

INTERVIEWER: And the extensive use of quotations?

MOORE: I was just trying to be honorable and not to steal things. I've always felt that if a thing had been said in the *best* way, how can you say it better? If I wanted to say something and somebody had said it ideally, then I'd take it but give the person credit for it. That's all there is to it. If you are charmed by an author, I think it's a very strange and invalid imagination that doesn't long to share it. Somebody else should read it, don't you think?

INTERVIEWER: Did any prose stylists help you in finding your poetic style? Elizabeth Bishop mentions Poe's prose in connection with your writing, and you have always made people think of Henry James.

MOORE: Prose stylists, very much. Doctor Johnson on Richard Savage: "He was in two months illegitimated by the Parliament, and disowned by his mother, doomed to poverty and obscurity, and launched upon the ocean of life only that he might be swallowed by its quicksands, or dashed upon its rocks. . . . It was his peculiar happiness that he scarcely ever found a stranger whom he did not leave a friend; but it must likewise be added, that he had not often a friend long without obliging him to become a stranger." Or Edmund Burke on the colonies: "You can shear a wolf; but will he comply?" Or Sir Thomas Browne: "States are not governed by Ergotisms." He calls a bee "that industrious flie," and his home his "hive." His manner is a kind of erudition-proof sweetness. Or Sir Francis Bacon: "Civil War is like the heat of fever; a foreign war is like the heat of exercise." Or Cellini: "I had by me a dog black as a mulberry. . . . I swelled up in my rage like an asp." Or Caesar's *Commentaries*, and Xenophon's *Cynegeticus*: the gusto and interest in every detail! In Henry James it is the essays and letters especially that affect me. In Ezra Pound, *The Spirit of Romance*: his definiteness, his indigenously unmistakable accent. Charles Norman says in his biography of Ezra Pound that he said to a poet, "Nothing, *nothing*, that you couldn't in some circumstance, under stress of some emotion, *actually say*." And Ezra said of Shakespeare and Dante, "Here we are with the masters; of neither can we say, 'He is the greater'; of each we must say, 'He is unexcelled.'"

INTERVIEWER: Do you have in your own work any favorites and unfavorites?

MOORE: Indeed, I do. I think the most difficult thing for me is to be satisfactorily lucid, yet have enough implication in it to suit myself. That's a problem. And I don't approve of my "enigmas," or as somebody said, "the not ungreen grass." I said to my mother one time, "How did you ever permit me to let this be printed?" And she said, "You didn't ask my advice."

INTERVIEWER: One time I heard you give a reading, and I think you said that you didn't like "In Distrust of Merits," which is one of your most popular poems.

MOORE: I do like it; it is sincere but I wouldn't call it a poem. It's truthful; it is testimony—to the fact that war is intolerable, and unjust.

INTERVIEWER: How can you call it not a poem, on what basis?

MOORE: Haphazard; as form, what has it? It is just a protest—disjointed, exclamatory. Emotion overpowered me. First this thought and then that.

INTERVIEWER: Your mother said that you hadn't asked her advice. Did you ever? Do you go for criticism to your family or friends?

MOORE: Well, not friends, but my brother if I get a chance. When my mother said "You didn't ask my advice" must have been years ago, because when I wrote "A Face," I had written something first about "the adder and the child with a bowl of porridge," and she said "It won't do." "All right," I said, "but I have to produce something." Cyril Connolly had asked me for something for *Horizon*. So I wrote "A Face." That is one of the few things I ever set down that didn't give me any trouble. She said, "I like it." I remember that.

Then, much before that, I wrote "The Buffalo." I thought it would probably outrage a number of persons because it had to me a kind of pleasing jerky progress. I thought, "Well, if it seems bad my brother will tell me, and if it has a point he'll detect it." And he said, with considerable gusto, "It takes my fancy." I was happy as could be.

INTERVIEWER: Did you ever suppress anything because of family objections?

MOORE: Yes, "the adder and the child with a bowl of porridge."
I never even wanted to improve it. You know, Mr. Saintsbury
said that Andrew Lang wanted him to contribute something on
Poe, and he did, and Lang returned it. Mr. Saintsbury said, "Once
a thing has been rejected, I would not offer it to the most different
of editors." That shocked me. I have offered a thing, submitted it
thirty-five times. Not simultaneously, of course.

INTERVIEWER: A poem?

MOORE: Yes. I am very tenacious.

INTERVIEWER: Do people ever ask you to write poems for them?

MOORE: Continually. Everything from on the death of a dog to
a little item for an album.

INTERVIEWER: Do you ever write them?

MOORE: Oh, perhaps; usually quote something. Once when I
was in the library we gave a party for Miss Leonard, and I wrote
a line or two of doggerel about a bouquet of violets we gave her.
It has no life or point. It was meant well but didn't amount to
anything. Then in college, I had a sonnet as an assignment. The
epitome of weakness.

INTERVIEWER: I'm interested in asking about the principles, and
the methods, of your way of writing. What is the rationale behind syllabic verse? How does it differ from free verse in which
the line length is controlled visually but not arithmetically?

MOORE: It never occurred to me that what I wrote was something to define. I am governed by the pull of the sentence as the
pull of a fabric is governed by gravity. I like the end-stopped line
and dislike the reversed order of words; like symmetry.

INTERVIEWER: How do you plan the shape of your stanzas? I
am thinking of the poems, usually syllabic, which employ a repeated stanza form. Do you ever experiment with shapes before
you write, by drawing lines on a page?

MOORE: Never, I never "plan" a stanza. Words cluster like
chromosomes, determining the procedure. I may influence an arrangement or thin it, then try to have successive stanzas identical
with the first. Spontaneous initial originality—say, impetus—seems

difficult to reproduce consciously later. As Stravinsky said about pitch, "If I transpose it for some reason, I am in danger of losing the freshness of first contact and will have difficulty in recapturing its attractiveness."

No, I never "draw lines." I make a rhyme conspicuous, to me at a glance, by underlining with red, blue, or other pencil—as many colors as I have rhymes to differentiate. However, if the phrases recur in too incoherent an architecture—as print—I notice that the words as a tune do not sound right. I may start a piece, find it obstructive, lack a way out, and not complete the thing for a year, or years, am thrifty. I salvage anything promising and set it down in a small notebook.

INTERVIEWER: I wonder if the act of translating La Fontaine's *Fables* helped you as a writer.

MOORE: Indeed it did. It was the best help I've ever had. I suffered frustration. I'm so naïve, so docile, I *tend* to take anybody's word for anything the person says, even in matters of art. The publisher who had commissioned the *Fables* died. I had no publisher. Well, I struggled on for a time and it didn't go very well. I thought, I'd better ask if they don't want to terminate the contract; then I could offer it elsewhere. I thought Macmillan, who took an interest in me, might like it. *Might*. The editor in charge of translations said, "Well, I studied French at Cornell, took a degree in French, I love French, and . . . well, I think you'd better put it away for a while." "How long?" I said. "About ten years; besides, it will hurt your own work. You won't write so well afterward."

"Oh," I said, "that's one reason I was undertaking it; I thought it would train me and give me momentum." Much dejected, I asked, "What is wrong? Have I not a good ear? Are the meanings not sound?"

"Well, there are conflicts," the editor reiterated, as it seemed to me, countless times. I don't know yet what they are or were. (A little "editorial.")

I said, "Don't write me an extenuating letter, please. Just send back the material in the envelope I put with it." I had submitted it in January and this was May. I had had a kind of uneasy hope that all would be well; meanwhile had volumes, hours, and years of work yet to do and might as well go on and do it, I had thought. The ultimatum was devastating.

At the same time Monroe Engel of the Viking Press wrote to me and said that he had supposed I had a commitment for my *Fables*, but if I hadn't would I let the Viking Press see them? I feel an everlasting gratitude to him.

However, I said, "I can't offer you something which somebody else thinks isn't fit to print. I would have to have someone to stabilize it and guarantee that the meanings are sound."

Mr. Engel said, "Who do you think could do that? Whom would you like?"

I said, "Harry Levin," because he had written a cogent, very shrewd review of Edna St. Vincent Millay's and George Dillon's translation of Baudelaire. I admired its finesse.

Mr. Engel said, "I'll ask him. But you won't hear for a long time. He's very busy. And how much do you think we ought to offer him?"

"Well," I said, "not less than ten dollars a Book; there would be no incentive in undertaking the bother of it, if it weren't twenty."

He said, "That would reduce your royalties too much on an advance."

I said, "I don't want an advance, wouldn't even consider one."

And then Harry Levin said, quite soon, that he would be glad to do it as a "refreshment against the chores of the term," but of course he would accept no remuneration. It was a very dubious refreshment, let me tell you. (He is precise, and not abusive, and did not "resign.")

INTERVIEWER: I've been asking you about your poems, which is of course what interests me most. But you were editor of *The*

Dial, too, and I want to ask you a few things about that. You were editor from 1925 until it ended in 1929, I think. How did you first come to be associated with it?

MOORE: Let me see. I think I took the initiative. I sent the editors a couple of things and they sent them back. And Lola Ridge had a party—she had a large apartment on a ground floor somewhere—and John Reed and Marsden Hartley, who was very confident with the brush, and Scofield Thayer, editor of *The Dial,* were there. And much to my disgust, we were induced each to read something we had written. And Scofield Thayer said of my piece, "Would you send that to us at *The Dial?*"

"I did send it," I said.

And he said, "Well, send it again." That is how it began, I think. Then he said, one time, "I'd like you to meet my partner, Sibley Watson," and invited me to tea at 152 W. 13th St. I was impressed. Doctor Watson is rare. He said nothing, but what he did say was striking and the significance would creep over you because unanticipated. And they asked me to join the staff, at *The Dial.*

INTERVIEWER: I have just been looking at that magazine, the years when you edited it. It's an incredible magazine.

MOORE: *The Dial?* There *were* good things in it, weren't there?

INTERVIEWER: Yes. It combined George Saintsbury and Ezra Pound in the same issue. How do you account for it? What made it so good?

MOORE: Lack of fear, for one thing. We didn't care what other people said. I never knew a magazine which was so self-propulsive. Everybody liked what he was doing, and when we made grievous mistakes we were sorry but we laughed over them.

INTERVIEWER: Louise Bogan said that *The Dial* made clear "the obvious division between American *avant-garde* and American conventional writing." Do you think this kind of division continues or has continued? Was this in any way a deliberate policy?

MOORE: I think that individuality was the great thing. We were not conforming to anything. We certainly didn't have a policy, except I remember hearing the word "intensity" very often. A thing must have "intensity." That seemed to be the criterion.

The thing applied to it, I think, that should apply to your own writing. As George Grosz said, at that last meeting he attended at the National Institute, "How did I come to be an artist? Endless curiosity, observation, research—and a great amount of joy in the thing." It was a matter of taking a liking to things. Things that were in accordance with your taste. I think that was it. And we didn't care how unhomogeneous they might seem. Didn't Aristotle say that it is the mark of a poet to see resemblances between apparently incongruous things? There was any amount of attraction about it.

INTERVIEWER: Do you think there is anything in the change of literary life in America that would make *The Dial* different if it existed today under the same editors? Were there any special conditions in the twenties that made the literary life of America different?

MOORE: I think it is always about the same.

INTERVIEWER: I wonder, if it had survived into the thirties, if it might have made that rather dry literary decade a little better.

MOORE: I think so. Because we weren't in captivity to anything.

INTERVIEWER: Was it just finances that made it stop?

MOORE: No, it wasn't the depression. Conditions changed. Scofield Thayer had a nervous breakdown, and he didn't come to meetings. Doctor Watson was interested in photography—was studying medicine; is a doctor of medicine, and lived in Rochester. I was alone. I didn't know that Rochester was about a night's journey away, and I would say to Doctor Watson, "Couldn't you come in for a make-up meeting, or send us these manuscripts and say what you think of them?" I may, as usual, have exaggerated my enslavement and my preoccupation with tasks—writing letters and reading manuscripts. Originally I had said I would come if I didn't have to write letters and didn't have to see contributors. And presently I was doing both. I think it was largely chivalry

—the decision to discontinue the magazine—because I didn't have time for work of my own.

INTERVIEWER: I wonder how you worked as an editor. Hart Crane complains, in one of his letters, that you rearranged "The Wine Menagerie" and changed the title. Do you feel that you were justified? Did you ask for revisions from many poets?

MOORE: No. We had an inflexible rule: do not ask changes of so much as a comma. Accept it or reject it. But in that instance I felt that in compassion I should disregard the rule. Hart Crane complains of me? Well, I complain of *him*. He liked *The Dial* and we liked him—friends, and with certain tastes in common. He was in dire need of money. It seemed careless not to so much as ask if he might like to make some changes ("like" in quotations). His gratitude was ardent and later his repudiation of it commensurate—he perhaps being in both instances under a disability with which I was not familiar. (Penalizing us for compassion?) I say "us," and should say "me." Really I am not used to having people in that bemused state. He was so *anxious* to have us take that thing, and so *delighted*. "Well, if you would modify it a little," I said, "we would like it better." I never attended "their" wild parties, as Lachaise once said. It was lawless of me to suggest changes; I disobeyed.

INTERVIEWER: Have you had editors suggest changes to you? Changes in your own poems, I mean?

MOORE: No, but my ardor to be helped being sincere, I sometimes *induce* assistance: the *Times*, the *Herald Tribune*, the *New Yorker*, have a number of times had to patch and piece me out. If you have a genius of an editor, you are blessed: e.g., T. S. Eliot and Ezra Pound, Harry Levin, and others; Irita Van Doren and Miss Belle Rosenbaum.

Have I found "help" helpful? I certainly have; and in three instances when I was at *The Dial*, I hazarded suggestions the results of which were to me drama. Excoriated by Herman George Scheffauer for offering to suggest a verbal change or two in his translation of Thomas Mann's *Disorder and Early Sorrow*, I must have posted the suggestions before I was able to withdraw them. In any case, his joyous subsequent retraction of abuse, and his pleasure in the narrative, were not unwelcome. Gilbert Seldes strongly commended me for excisions proposed by me in his "Jonathan Edwards" (for *The Dial*); and I have not ceased to marvel at the overrating by Mark Van Doren of editorial conscience on my reverting (after an interval) to keeping some final lines I had wished he would omit. (Verse! but not a sonnet.)

We should try to judge the work of others by the most that it is, and our own, if not by the least that it is, take the least into consideration. I feel that I would not be worth a button if not grateful to be preserved from myself, and informed if what I have written is not to the point. I think we should feel free, like La Fontaine's captious critic, to say, if asked, "Your phrases are too long, and the content is not good. Break up the type and put it in the font." As Kenneth Burke says in *Counter-Statement*: "[Great] artists feel as opportunity what others feel as a menace. This ability does not, I believe, derive from exceptional strength, it probably arises purely from professional interest the artist may take in his difficulties."

Lew Sarett says, in the *Poetry Society Bulletin*, we ask of a poet: Does this mean something? Does the poet say what he has to say and in his own manner? Does it stir the reader?

Shouldn't we replace vanity with honesty, as Robert Frost recommends? Annoyances abound. We should not find them lethal—a baffled printer's emendations for instance (my "elephant with frog-colored skin" instead of "fog-colored skin," and "the power of the invisible is the invisible," instead of "the power of the visible is the invisible") sounding like a parody on my meticulousness; a "glasshopper" instead of a "grasshopper."

INTERVIEWER: Editing *The Dial* must have acquainted you with the writers of the day whom you did not know already. Had you known Hart Crane earlier?

MOORE: Yes, I did. You remember *Broom*? Toward at the beginning of that magazine, in 1921, Lola Ridge was very hospitable, and she invited to a party—previous to my work on *The Dial*—Kay Boyle and her husband, a French soldier, and Hart Crane, Elinor Wylie, and some others. I took a great liking to Hart Crane. We talked about French bindings, and he was diffident and modest and seemed to have so much intuition, such a feel for things, for books—really a bibliophile—that I took special interest in him. And Doctor Watson and Scofield Thayer liked him—felt that he was one of our talents, that he couldn't fit himself into an IBM position to find a livelihood; that we ought to, whenever we could, take anything he sent us.

I know a cousin of his, Joe Nowak, who is rather proud of him. He lives here in Brooklyn, and is * at the Dry Dock Savings Bank and used to work in antiques. Joe was very convinced of Hart's sincerity and his innate love of all that I have specified. Anyhow, *The Bridge* is a grand theme. Here and there I think he could have firmed it up. A writer is unfair to himself when he is unable to be hard on himself.

INTERVIEWERS: Did Crane have anything to do with *Others*?

MOORE: *Others* antedated *Broom*. *Others* was Alfred Kreymborg and Skipwith Cannéll, Wallace Stevens, William Carlos Williams. Wallace Stevens—odd; I nearly met him a dozen times before I did meet him in 1941 at Mount Holyoke, at the college's *Entretiens de Pontigny* of which Professor Gustav Cohen was chairman. Wallace Stevens was Henry Church's favorite American poet. Mr. Church had published him and some others, and me, in *Mésure*, in Paris. Raymond Queneau translated us.

During the French program at Mount Holyoke one afternoon Wallace Stevens had a discourse, the one about Goethe dancing, on a packet-boat in black wool stockings. My mother and I were there; and I gave a reading with commentary. Henry Church had an astoundingly beautiful Panama hat—a sort of pork-pie with a

---

* *Was*; killed; his car run into by a reckless driver in April 1961.—M.M.

wide brim, a little like Bernard Berenson's hats. I have never seen as fine a weave, and he had a pepper-and-salt shawl which he draped about himself. This lecture was on the lawn.

Wallace Stevens was extremely friendly. We should have had a tape recorder on that occasion, for at lunch they seated us all at a kind of refectory table and a girl kept asking him questions such as, "Mr. Stevens have you read the—*Four—Quartets?*"

"Of course, but I can't read much of Eliot or I wouldn't have any individuality of my own."

INTERVIEWER: Do you read new poetry now? Do you try to keep up?

MOORE: I am always seeing it—am sent some every day. Some, good. But it does interfere with my work. I can't get much done. Yet I would be a monster if I tossed everything away without looking at it; I write more notes, letters, cards in an hour than is sane.

Although everyone is penalized by being quoted inexactly, I wonder if there is anybody alive whose remarks are so often paraphrased as mine—printed as verbatim. It is really martyrdom. In his book *Ezra Pound*, Charles Norman was very scrupulous. He got several things exactly right. The first time I met Ezra Pound, when he came here to see my mother and me, I said that Henry Eliot seemed to me more nearly the artist than anyone I had ever met. "Now, now," said Ezra. "Be careful." Maybe that isn't exact, but he quotes it just the way I said it.

INTERVIEWER: Do you mean Henry Ware Eliot, T. S. Eliot's brother?

MOORE: Yes. After the Henry Eliots moved from Chicago to New York to—is it 68th Street? It's the street on which Hunter College is—to an apartment there, they invited me to dinner, I should think at T. S. Eliot's suggestion, and I took to them immediately. I felt as if I'd known them a great while. It was some time before I felt that way about T. S. Eliot.

About inaccuracies—when I went to see Ezra Pound at St. Elizabeth's, about the third time I went, the official who escorted me to the grounds said, "Good of you to come to see him," and I said, "Good? You have no idea how much he has done for me, and others." This pertains to an early rather than final visit.

I was not in the habit of asking experts or anybody else to help me with things that I was doing, unless it was a librarian or someone whose business it was to help applicants; or a teacher. But I was desperate when Macmillan declined my *Fables*. I had worked about four years on them and sent Ezra Pound several—although I hesitated. I didn't like to bother him. He had enough trouble without that; but finally I said, "Would you have time to tell me if the rhythms grate on you? Is my ear not good?"

INTERVIEWER: He replied?

MOORE: Yes, said, "The least touch of merit upsets these blighters."

INTERVIEWER: When you first read Pound in 1916, did you recognize him as one of the great ones?

MOORE: Surely did. *The Spirit of Romance*. I don't think anybody could read that book and feel that a flounderer was writing.

INTERVIEWER: What about the early poems?

MOORE: Yes. They seemed a little didactic, but I liked them.

INTERVIEWER: I wanted to ask you a few questions about poetry in general. Somewhere you have said that originality is a by-product of sincerity. You often use moral terms in your criticism. Is the necessary morality specifically literary, a moral use of words, or is it larger? In what way must a man be good if he is to write good poems?

MOORE: If emotion is strong enough, the words are unambiguous. Someone asked Robert Frost (is this right?) if he was selective. He said, "Call it passionate preference." Must a man be good to write good poems? The villains in Shakespeare are not illiterate, are they? But rectitude *has* a ring that is implicative, I would say. And with *no* integrity, a man is not likely to write the kind of book I read.

INTERVIEWER: Eliot, in his introduction to your *Selected Poems*, talks about your function as poet relative to the living language, as he calls it. Do you agree that this is a function of a poet? How does the poetry have the effect on the living language? What's the mechanics of it?

MOORE: You accept certain modes of saying a thing. Or strongly repudiate things. You do something of your own, you modify, invent a variant or revive a root meaning. Any doubt about that?

INTERVIEWER: I want to ask you a question about your correspondence with the Ford Motor Company, those letters which were printed in the *New Yorker*. They were looking for a name for the car they eventually called the Edsel, and they asked you to think of a name that would make people admire the car—

MOORE: Elegance and grace, they said it would have—

INTERVIEWER: ". . . some visceral feeling of elegance, fleetness, advanced features and design. A name, in short, which flashes a dramatically desirable picture in people's minds."

MOORE: Really?

INTERVIEWER: That's what they said, in their first letter to you. I was thinking about this in connection with my question about language. Do you remember Pound's talk about expression and meaning? He says that when expression and meaning are far apart, the culture is in a bad way. I was wondering if this request doesn't ask you to remove expression a bit further from meaning.

MOORE: No, I don't think so. At least, to exposit the irresistible-ness of the car. I got deep in motors and turbines and recessed wheels. No. That seemed to me a very worthy pursuit. I was more interested in the mechanics. I am interested in mechanisms, mechanics in general. And I enjoyed the assignment, for all that it was abortive. Dr. Pick at Marquette University procured a young demonstrator of the Edsel to call for me in a black one, to convey me to the auditorium. Nothing was wrong with that Edsel! I thought it was a very handsome car. It came out the wrong year.

INTERVIEWER: Another thing: in your criticism you make frequent analogies between the poet and the scientist. Do you think this analogy is helpful to the modern poet? Most people would consider the comparison a paradox, and assume that the poet and the scientist are opposed.

MOORE: Do the poet and scientist not work analogously? Both are willing to waste effort. To be hard on himself is one of the main strengths of each. Each is attentive to clues, each must narrow the choice, must strive for precision. As George Grosz says, "In art there is no place for gossip and but a small place for the satirist." The objective is fertile procedure. Is it not? Jacob Bronowski says in the *Saturday Evening Post* that science is not a mere collection of discoveries, but that science is the process of discovering. In any case it's not established once and for all; it's evolving.

INTERVIEWER: One last question. I was intrigued when you wrote that "America has in Wallace Stevens at least one artist whom professionalism will not demolish." What sort of literary professionalism did you have in mind? And do you find this a feature of America still?

MOORE: Yes. I think that writers sometimes lose verve and pugnacity, and he never would say "frame of reference" or "I wouldn't know." A question I am often asked is: "What work can I find that will enable me to spend my whole time writing?" Charles Ives, the composer, says, "You cannot set art off in a corner and hope for it to have vitality, reality, and substance. The fabric weaves itself whole. My work in music helped my business and my work in business helped my music." I am like Charles Ives. I guess Lawrence Durrell and Henry Miller would not agree with me.

INTERVIEWER: But how does professionalism make a writer lose his verve and pugnacity?

MOORE: Money may have something to do with it, and being regarded as a pundit; Wallace Stevens was really very much annoyed at being catalogued, categorized, and compelled to be scientific about what he was doing—to give satisfaction, to answer the teachers. He wouldn't do that. I think the same of William Carlos Williams. I think he wouldn't make so much of the great American language if he were plausible; and tractable. That's the beauty of it; he is willing to be reckless; if you can't be that, what's the point of the whole thing?

DONALD HALL

4. T. S. Eliot

Thomas Stearns Eliot was born September 26, 1888, in St. Louis, of a distinguished Boston family, deeply rooted in the New England tradition and in the Unitarian Church. He lived in St. Louis until he was eighteen, and in 1906, after one year at Milton, entered Harvard, where he had a brilliant career, and received his M.A. in four years. After a year at the Sorbonne, he returned to Harvard and worked for his Ph.D. His dissertation on F. H. Bradley and Meinong's *Gegenstandstheorie* was accepted, he says, "because it was unreadable," and he never took his degree. In 1914 Eliot visited Germany in the summer, and that winter, after the outbreak of the war, read philosophy at Oxford. He settled in England at that time and has lived there since. From 1917 to 1919 he was assistant editor of the *Egoist* and published his first book of poems, *Prufrock and Other Observations*, and many essays including *Ezra Pound, His Metric and Poetry*. It was in 1922, however, with the appearance of *The Waste Land*, that his name came to the forefront of contemporary literature.

Among other titles for which he is famous are the poems *Ash Wednesday* (1930) and *Four Quartets* (1943); the plays *Murder in the Cathedral* (1935), *Family Reunion* (1939), and *The Cocktail Party* (1950); and essays, *The Sacred Wood* (1920), *Andrew Marvell* (1922), *Thoughts after Lambeth* (1931), *The Uses of Poetry and the Uses of Criticism* (1933), and *Essays Ancient and Modern* (1936).

The Criterion, Eliot's magazine, in which *The Waste Land* first appeared, existed for seventeen years and was highly regarded in literary and philosophical circles. During his directorship Eliot worked as an editor at the publishing firm of Faber and Faber.

Eliot became a British subject in 1927. By 1933 he was able to call himself "an Anglo-Catholic in religion, a classicist in literature, and a royalist in politics." In 1948 he received the Order of Merit from King George VI and was awarded the Nobel Prize in literature.

he was exploring his own mind also. The compositions in verse and
in prose fiction to which I have just referred may I think be ignored, except for the information they can yield about their author; and his other writings, those concerned directly with theological, social or political matter, should be considered consider
as by-products of a mind of which the primary activity was literar
criticism.

I first met Middleton Murry by appointment at some meeting
place whence he was to conduct me to his home for dinner and a
discussion of his projects for The Athenaeum, a defunct weekly
which was to be revived under his editorship. I had heard of
him earlier, in the circle of Lady Ottoline Morrell where I had
already met Katharine Mansfield on one occasion, but we had held
no communication before he wrote to propose this meeting. I do
not know what he had been told about me; what is important is that
he had read (having had it brought to his attention no doubt) at
Garsington) my first book of Verse, Prufrock, and that it was
entirely because of this verse that he wished to ask me to
become his Assistant Editor. Of my cri-
tical writings he knew nothing: I gave him some copies of The
Egoist to enable him to judge of my abilities. It speaks of the
man, however, that he had made up his mind that he wanted my help
with this venture without having seen any criticism of mine,
wholly on the strength of Prufrock. After a good deal of hesitation I declined; and I think that I was wise to do so, and to
remain for some years at my desk in the City. I did however
become one of Murry's regular contributors, reviewing some book

Part of a manuscript by T. S. Eliot.

D. CAMMELL

T. S. Eliot

The interview took place in New York, at the apartment of Mrs. Louis Henry Cohn, of House of Books, Ltd., who is a friend of Mr. and Mrs. Eliot. The bookcases of the attractive living room contain a remarkable collection of modern authors. On a wall near the entrance hangs a drawing of Mr. Eliot, done by his sister-in-law, Mrs. Henry Ware Eliot. An inscribed wedding photograph of the Eliots stands in a silver frame on a table. Mrs. Cohn and Mrs. Eliot sat on a sofa at one end of the room, while Mr. Eliot and the interviewer faced each other in the center. The microphone of a tape recorder lay on the floor between them.

Mr. Eliot looked particularly well. He was visiting the United States briefly on his way back to London from a holiday in Nassau. He was tanned, and he seemed to have put on weight in the three years since the interviewer had seen him. Altogether, he looked younger and seemed jollier. He frequently glanced at Mrs. Eliot *during the interview, as if he were sharing with her an answer which he was not making.*

The interviewer had talked with Mr. Eliot previously in London. The small office at Faber and Faber, a few flights above Russell Square, displays a gallery of photographs on its walls: here is a large picture of Virginia Woolf, with an inset portrait of Pius XII; here are I. A. Richards, Paul Valéry, W. B. Yeats, Goethe, Marianne Moore, Charles Whibley, Djuna Barnes, and others. Many young poets have stared at the faces there, during a talk with Mr. Eliot. One of them has told a story which illustrates some of the unsuspected in Mr. Eliot's conversation. After an hour of serious literary discussion, Mr. Eliot paused to think if he had a final word of advice; the young poet, an American, was about to go up to Oxford as Mr. Eliot had done forty years before. Then, as gravely as if he were recommending salvation, Mr. Eliot advised the purchase of long woolen underwear because of Oxford's damp stone. Mr. Eliot is able to be avuncular while he is quite aware of comic disproportion between manner and message.

Similar combinations modified many of the comments which are reported here, and the ironies of gesture are invisible on the page. At times, actually, the interview moved from the ironic and the mildly comic to the hilarious. The tape is punctuated by the head-back Boom Boom of Mr. Eliot's laughter, particularly in response to mention of his early derogation of Ezra Pound, and to a question about the unpublished, and one gathers improper, King Bolo poems of his Harvard days.

INTERVIEWER: Perhaps I can begin at the beginning. Do you remember the circumstances under which you began to write poetry in St. Louis when you were a boy?

ELIOT: I began I think about the age of fourteen, under the inspiration of Fitzgerald's *Omar Khayyam*, to write a number of very gloomy and atheistical and despairing quatrains in the same style, which fortunately I suppressed completely—so completely that they don't exist. I never showed them to anybody. The first poem that shows is one which appeared first in the *Smith Academy Record,* and later in *The Harvard Advocate,* which was written as an exercise for my English teacher and was an imitation of Ben Jonson. He thought it very good for a boy of fifteen or sixteen. Then I wrote a few at Harvard, just enough to qualify for election to an editorship on *The Harvard Advocate,* which I enjoyed. Then I had an outburst during my junior and senior years. I became much more prolific, under the influence first of Baudelaire and then of Jules Laforgue, whom I discovered I think in my junior year at Harvard.

INTERVIEWER: Did anyone in particular introduce you to the French poets? Not Irving Babbitt, I suppose.

ELIOT: No, Babbitt would be the last person! The one poem that Babbitt always held up for admiration was Gray's *Elegy.* And that's a fine poem but I think this shows certain limitations on Babbitt's part, God bless him. I have advertised my source, I think; it's Arthur Symons's book on French poetry,* which I came across in the Harvard Union. In those days the Harvard Union was a meeting place for any undergraduate who chose to belong to it. They had a very nice little library, like the libraries in many Harvard houses now. I liked his quotations and I went to a foreign bookshop somewhere in Boston (I've forgotten the name and I don't know whether it still exists) which specialized in French and German and other foreign books and found Laforgue, and other poets. I can't imagine why that bookshop should have had a few poets like Laforgue in stock. Goodness knows how long they'd had them or whether there were any other demands for them.

INTERVIEWER: When you were an undergraduate, were you aware of the dominating presence of any older poets? Today the poet in his youth is writing in the age of Eliot and Pound and Stevens. Can you remember your own sense of the literary times?

---

* *The Symbolist Movement in Literature.*

I wonder if your situation may not have been extremely different.

ELIOT: I think it was rather an advantage not having any living poets in England or America in whom one took any particular interest. I don't know what it would be like but I think it would be a rather troublesome distraction to have such a lot of dominating presences, as you call them, about. Fortunately we weren't bothered by each other.

INTERVIEWER: Were you aware of people like Hardy or Robinson at all?

ELIOT: I was slightly aware of Robinson because I read an article about him in *The Atlantic Monthly* which quoted some of his poems, and that wasn't my cup of tea at all. Hardy was hardly known to be a poet at that time. One read his novels, but his poetry only really became conspicuous to a later generation. Then there was Yeats, but it was the early Yeats. It was too much Celtic twilight for me. There was really nothing except the people of the 90s who had all died of drink or suicide or one thing or another.

INTERVIEWER: Did you and Conrad Aiken help each other with your poems, when you were co-editors on the *Advocate*?

ELIOT: We were friends but I don't think we influenced each other at all. When it came to foreign writers, he was more interested in Italian and Spanish, and I was all for the French.

INTERVIEWER: Were there any other friends who read your poems and helped you?

ELIOT: Well, yes. There was a man who was a friend of my brother's, a man named Thomas H. Thomas who lived in Cambridge and who saw some of my poems in *The Harvard Advocate*. He wrote me a most enthusiastic letter and cheered me up. And I wish I had his letters still. I was very grateful to him for giving me that encouragement.

INTERVIEWER: I understand that it was Conrad Aiken who introduced you and your work to Pound.

ELIOT: Yes it was. Aiken was a very generous friend. He tried to place some of my poems in London, one summer when he was over, with Harold Monro and others. Nobody would think of publishing them. He brought them back to me. Then in 1914, I think, we were both in London in the summer. He said, "You go to Pound. Show him your poems." He thought Pound might like them. Aiken liked them, though they were very different from his.

INTERVIEWER: Do you remember the circumstances of your first meeting with Pound?

ELIOT: I think I went to call on him first. I think I made a good impression, in his little triangular sitting room in Kensington. He said, "Send me your poems." And he wrote back, "This is as good as anything I've seen. Come around and have a talk about them." Then he pushed them on Harriet Monroe, which took a little time.

INTERVIEWER: In an article about your *Advocate* days, for the book in honor of your sixtieth birthday, Aiken quotes an early letter from England in which you refer to Pound's verse as "touchingly incompetent." I wonder when you changed your mind.

ELIOT: Hah! *That* was a bit brash, wasn't it? Pound's verse was first shown me by an editor of *The Harvard Advocate*, W. G. Tinckom-Fernandez, who was a crony of mine and Conrad Aiken's and the other Signet * poets of the period. He showed me those little things of Elkin Mathews, *Exultations* and *Personae*.† He said, "This is up your street; you ought to like this." Well, I didn't, really. It seemed to me rather fancy old-fashioned romantic stuff, cloak-and-dagger kind of stuff. I wasn't very much impressed by it. When I went to see Pound, I was not particularly an admirer of his work, and though I now regard the work I saw then as very accomplished, I am certain that in his later work is to be found the grand stuff.

---

* Harvard's literary club.
† Early books of Pound, published by Elkin Mathews in 1909.

INTERVIEWER: You have mentioned in print that Pound cut *The Waste Land* from a much larger poem into its present form. Were you benefited by his criticism of your poems in general? Did he cut other poems?

ELIOT: Yes. At that period, yes. He was a marvelous critic because he didn't try to turn you into an imitation of himself. He tried to see what you were trying to do.

INTERVIEWER: Have you helped to rewrite any of your friends' poems? Ezra Pound's, for instance?

ELIOT: I can't think of any instances. Of course I have made innumerable suggestions on manuscripts of young poets in the last twenty-five years or so.

INTERVIEWER: Does the manuscript of the original, uncut *Waste Land* exist?

ELIOT: Don't ask me. That's one of the things I don't know. It's an unsolved mystery. I sold it to John Quinn. I also gave him a notebook of unpublished poems, because he had been kind to me in various affairs. That's the last I heard of them. Then he died and they didn't turn up at the sale.

INTERVIEWER: What sort of thing did Pound cut from *The Waste Land*? Did he cut whole sections?

ELIOT: Whole sections, yes. There was a long section about a shipwreck. I don't know what that had to do with anything else, but it was rather inspired by the Ulysses Canto in *The Inferno*, I think. Then there was another section which was an imitation *Rape of the Lock*. Pound said, "It's no use trying to do something that somebody else has done as well as it can be done. Do something different."

INTERVIEWER: Did the excisions change the intellectual structure of the poem?

ELIOT: No. I think it was just as structureless, only in a more futile way, in the longer version.

INTERVIEWER: I have a question about the poem which is related to its composition. In *Thoughts after Lambeth* you denied the allegation of critics who said that you expressed "the disillusionment of a generation" in *The Waste Land*, or you denied that it was your intention. Now F. R. Leavis, I believe, has said that the poem exhibits no progression; yet on the other hand, more recent critics, writing after your later poetry, found *The Waste Land* Christian. I wonder if this was part of your intention.

ELIOT: No, it wasn't part of my conscious intention. I think that in *Thoughts after Lambeth*, I was speaking of intentions more in a negative than in a positive sense, to say what was not my intention. I wonder what an "intention" means! One wants to get something off one's chest. One doesn't know quite what it is that one wants to get off the chest until one's got it off. But I couldn't apply the word "intention" positively to any of my poems. Or to any poem.

INTERVIEWER: I have another question about you and Pound and your earlier career. I have read somewhere that you and Pound decided to write quatrains, in the late teens, because *vers libre* had gone far enough.

ELIOT: I think that's something Pound said. And the suggestion of writing quatrains was his. He put me onto *Emaux et Camées.**

INTERVIEWER: I wonder about your ideas about the relation of form to subject. Would you then have chosen the form before you knew quite what you were going to write in it?

ELIOT: Yes, in a way. One studied originals. We studied Gautier's poems and then we thought, "Have I anything to say in which this form will be useful?" And we experimented. The form gave the impetus to the content.

INTERVIEWER: Why was *vers libre* the form you chose to use in your early poems?

ELIOT: My early *vers libre*, of course, was started under the endeavor to practice the same form as Laforgue. This meant merely rhyming lines of irregular length, with the rhymes coming in irregular places. It wasn't quite so *libre* as much *vers*, especially the sort which Ezra called "Amygism." † Then, of course, there

---

* Poems by Théophile Gautier.
† A reference to Amy Lowell, who captured and transformed imagism.

were things in the next phase which were freer, like "Rhapsody on a Windy Night." I don't know whether I had any sort of model or practice in mind when I did that. It just came that way.

INTERVIEWER: Did you feel, possibly, that you were writing against something, more than from any model? Against the poet laureate perhaps?

ELIOT: No, no, no. I don't think one was constantly trying to reject things, but just trying to find out what was right for oneself. One really ignored poet laureates as such, the Robert Bridges. I don't think good poetry can be produced in a kind of political attempt to overthrow some existing form. I think it just supersedes. People find a way in which they can say something. "I can't say it that way, what way can I find that will do?" One didn't really *bother* about the existing modes.

INTERVIEWER: I think it was after "Prufrock" and before "Gerontion" that you wrote the poems in French which appear in your *Collected Poems*. I wonder how you happened to write them. Have you written any since?

ELIOT: No, and I never shall. That was a very curious thing which I can't altogether explain. At that period I thought I'd dried up completely. I hadn't written anything for some time and was rather desperate. I started writing a few things in French and found I *could*, at that period. I think it was that when I was writing in French I didn't take the poems so seriously, and that, not taking them seriously, I wasn't so worried about not being able to write. I did these things as a sort of *tour de force* to see what I could do. That went on for some months. The best of them have been printed. I must say that Ezra Pound went through them, and Edmond Dulac, a Frenchman we knew in London, helped with them a bit. We left out some, and I suppose they disappeared completely. Then I suddenly began writing in English again and lost all desire to go on with French. I think it was just something that helped me get started again.

INTERVIEWER: Did you think at all about becoming a French symbolist poet like the two Americans of the last century?

ELIOT: Stuart Merrill and Viélé-Griffin. I only did that during the romantic year I spent in Paris after Harvard. I had at that time the idea of giving up English and trying to settle down and scrape along in Paris and gradually write French. But it would have been a foolish idea even if I'd been much more bilingual than I ever was, because, for one thing, I don't think that one can be a bilingual poet. I don't know of any case in which a man wrote great or even fine poems equally well in two languages. I think one language must be the one you express yourself in in poetry, and you've got to give up the other for that purpose. And I think that the English language really has more resources in some respects than the French. I think, in other words, I've probably done better in English than I ever would have in French even if I'd become as proficient in French as the poets you mentioned.

INTERVIEWER: Can I ask you if you have any plans for poems now?

ELIOT: No, I haven't any plans for anything at the moment, except that I think I would like, having just got rid of *The Elder Statesman* (I only passed the final proofs just before we left London), to do a little prose writing of a critical sort. I never think more than one step ahead. Do I want to do another play or do I want to do more poems? I don't know until I find I want to do it.

INTERVIEWER: Do you have any unfinished poems that you look at occasionally?

ELIOT: I haven't much in that way, no. As a rule, with me an unfinished thing is a thing that might as well be rubbed out. It's better, if there's something good in it that I might make use of elsewhere, to leave it at the back of my mind than on paper in a drawer. If I leave it in a drawer it remains the same thing but if it's in the memory it becomes transformed into something else. As I have said before, *Burnt Norton* began with bits that had to be cut out of *Murder in the Cathedral*. I learned in *Murder in the Cathedral* that it's no use putting in nice lines that you think are good poetry if they don't get the action on at all. That was when Martin Browne was useful. He would say, "There are very nice lines here, but they've nothing to do with what's going on on stage."

INTERVIEWER: Are any of your minor poems actually sections cut out of longer works? There are two that sound like "The Hollow Men."

ELIOT: Oh, those were the preliminary sketches. Those things were earlier. Others I published in periodicals but not in my collected poems. You don't want to say the same thing twice in one book.

INTERVIEWER: You seem often to have written poems in sections. Did they begin as separate poems? I am thinking of "Ash Wednesday," in particular.

ELIOT: Yes, like "The Hollow Men," it originated out of separate poems. As I recall, one or two early drafts of parts of "Ash Wednesday" appeared in *Commerce* and elsewhere. Then gradually I came to see it as a sequence. That's one way in which my mind does seem to have worked throughout the years poetically —doing things separately and then seeing the possibility of fusing them together, altering them, and making a kind of whole of them.

INTERVIEWER: Do you write anything now in the vein of *Old Possum's Book of Practical Cats* or *King Bolo*?

ELIOT: Those things do come from time to time! I keep a few notes of such verse, and there are one or two incomplete cats that probably will never be written. There's one about a glamour cat. It turned out too sad. This would never do. I can't make my children weep over a cat who's gone wrong. She had a very questionable career, did this cat. It wouldn't do for the audience of my previous volume of cats. I've never done any dogs. Of course dogs don't seem to lend themselves to verse quite so well, collectively, as cats. I may eventually do an enlarged edition of my cats. That's more likely than another volume. I did add one poem, which was originally done as an advertisement for Faber and Faber. It seemed to be fairly successful. Oh, yes, one wants to keep one's hand in, you know, in every type of poem, serious and frivolous and proper and improper. One doesn't want to lose one's skill.

INTERVIEWER: There's a good deal of interest now in the process of writing. I wonder if you could talk more about your actual habits in writing verse. I've heard you composed on the typewriter.

ELIOT: Partly on the typewriter. A great deal of my new play, *The Elder Statesman*, was produced in pencil and paper, very roughly. Then I typed it myself first before my wife got to work on it. In typing myself I make alterations, very considerable ones. But whether I write or type, composition of any length, a play for example, means for me regular hours, say ten to one. I found that three hours a day is about all I can do of actual composing. I could do polishing perhaps later. I sometimes found at first that I wanted to go on longer, but when I looked at the stuff the next day, what I'd done after the three hours were up was never satisfactory. It's much better to stop and think about something else quite different.

INTERVIEWER: Did you ever write any of your non-dramatic poems on schedule? Perhaps the *Four Quartets*?

ELIOT: Only "occasional" verse. The *Quartets* were not on schedule. Of course the first one was written in '35, but the three which were written during the war were more in fits and starts. In 1939 if there hadn't been a war I would probably have tried to write another play. And I think it's a very good thing I didn't have the opportunity. From my personal point of view, the one good thing the war did was to prevent me from writing another play too soon. I saw some of the things that were wrong with *Family Reunion*, but I think it was much better that any possible play was blocked for five years or so to get up a head of steam. The form of the *Quartets* fitted in very nicely to the conditions under which I was writing, or could write at all. I could write them in sections and I didn't have to have quite the same continuity; it didn't matter if a day or two elapsed when I did not write, as they frequently did, while I did war jobs.

INTERVIEWER: We have been mentioning your plays without talking about them. In *Poetry and Drama* you talked about your first plays. I wonder if you could tell us something about your intentions in *The Elder Statesman*.

ELIOT: I said something, I think, in *Poetry and Drama* about my ideal aims, which I never expect fully to realize. I started, really, from *The Family Reunion*, because *Murder in the Cathedral* is a period piece and something out of the ordinary. It is written in rather a special language, as you do when you're dealing with another period. It didn't solve any of the problems I was interested in. Later I thought that in *The Family Reunion* I was giving so much attention to the versification that I neglected the structure of the play. I think *The Family Reunion* is still the best of my plays in the way of poetry, although it's not very well constructed.

In *The Cocktail Party* and again in *The Confidential Clerk*, I went further in the way of structure. *The Cocktail Party* wasn't altogether satisfactory in that respect. It sometimes happens, disconcertingly, at any rate with a practitioner like myself, that it isn't always the things constructed most according to plan that are the most successful. People criticized the third act of *The Cocktail Party* as being rather an epilogue, so in *The Confidential Clerk* I wanted things to turn up in the third act which were fresh events. Of course, *The Confidential Clerk* was so well constructed in some ways that people thought it was just meant to be farce.

I wanted to get to learn the technique of the theater so well that I could then forget about it. I always feel it's not wise to violate rules until you know how to observe them.

I hope that *The Elder Statesman* goes further in getting more poetry in, at any rate, than *The Confidential Clerk* did. I don't feel that I've got to the point I aim at and I don't think I ever will, but I would like to feel I was getting a little nearer to it each time.

INTERVIEWER: Do you have a Greek model behind *The Elder Statesman?*

ELIOT: The play in the background is the *Oedipus at Colonus.* But I wouldn't like to refer to my Greek originals as models. I have always regarded them more as points of departure. That was one of the weaknesses of *The Family Reunion;* it was rather too close to the *Eumenides.* I tried to follow my original too literally and in that way led to confusion by mixing pre-Christian and post-Christian attitudes about matters of conscience and sin and guilt.

So in the subsequent three I have tried to take the Greek myth as a sort of springboard, you see. After all, what one gets essential and permanent, I think, in the old plays, is a situation. You can take the situation, rethink it in modern terms, develop your own characters from it, and let another plot develop out of that. Actually you get further and further away from the original. *The Cocktail Party* had to do with Alcestis simply because the question arose in my mind, what would the life of Admetus and Alcestis be, after she'd come back from the dead; I mean if there'd been a break like that, it couldn't go on just as before. Those two people were the center of the thing when I started and the other characters only developed out of it. The character of Celia, who came to be really the most important character in the play, was originally an appendage to a domestic situation.

INTERVIEWER: Do you still hold to the theory of levels in poetic drama (plot, character, diction, rhythm, meaning) which you put forward in 1932?

ELIOT: I am no longer very much interested in my own theories about poetic drama, especially those put forward before 1934. I have thought less about theories since I have given more time to writing for the theater.

INTERVIEWER: How does the writing of a play differ from the writing of poems?

ELIOT: I feel that they take quite different approaches. There is all the difference in the world between writing a play for an audience and writing a poem, in which you're writing primarily for yourself—although obviously you wouldn't be satisfied if the poem didn't mean something to other people afterward. With a poem you can say, "I got my feeling into words for myself. I now have the equivalent in words for that much of what I have felt." Also in a poem you're writing for your own voice, which is very important. You're thinking in terms of your own voice, whereas in a play from the beginning you have to realize that you're preparing something which is going into the hands of other people, unknown at the time you're writing it. Of course I won't say there aren't moments in a play when the two approaches may not converge, when I think ideally they *should*. Very often in Shakespeare they do, when he is writing a poem and thinking in terms of the theater and the actors and the audience all at once. And the two things are one. That's wonderful when you can get that. With me it only happens at odd moments.

INTERVIEWER: Have you tried at all to control the speaking of your verse by the actors? To make it seem more like verse?

ELIOT: I leave that primarily to the producer. The important thing is to have a producer who has the feeling of verse and who can guide them in just how emphatic to make the verse, just how far to depart from prose or how far to approach it. I only guide the actors if they ask me questions directly. Otherwise I think that they should get their advice through the producer. The important thing is to arrive at an agreement with him first, and then leave it to him.

INTERVIEWER: Do you feel that there's been a general tendency in your work, even in your poems, to move from a narrower to a larger audience?

ELIOT: I think that there are two elements in this. One is that I think that writing plays (that is *Murder in the Cathedral* and *The Family Reunion*) made a difference to the writing of the *Four Quartets*. I think that it led to a greater simplification of language and to speaking in a way which is more like conversing with your reader. I see the later *Quartets* as being much simpler and easier to understand than *The Waste Land* and "Ash Wednesday." Sometimes the thing I'm trying to say, the subject matter, may be difficult, but it seems to me that I'm saying it in a simpler way.

The other element that enters into it, I think, is just experience and maturity. I think that in the early poems it was a question of not being able to—of having more to say than one knew how to say, and having something one wanted to put into words and rhythm which one didn't have the command of words and rhythm to put in a way immediately apprehensible.

That type of obscurity comes when the poet is still at the stage of learning how to use language. You have to say the thing the difficult way. The only alternative is not saying it at all, at that stage. By the time of the *Four Quartets*, I couldn't have written in the style of *The Waste Land*. In *The Waste Land*, I wasn't even bothering whether I understood what I was saying. These things, however, become easier to people with time. You get used to having *The Waste Land*, or *Ulysses*, about.

INTERVIEWER: Do you feel that the *Four Quartets* are your best work?

ELIOT: Yes, and I'd like to feel that they get better as they go on. The second is better than the first, the third is better than the second, and the fourth is the best of all. At any rate, that's the way I flatter myself.

INTERVIEWER: This is a very general question, but I wonder if you could give advice to a young poet about what disciplines or attitudes he might cultivate to improve his art.

ELIOT: I think it's awfully dangerous to give general advice. I think the best one can do for a young poet is to criticize in detail a particular poem of his. Argue it with him if necessary; give him your opinion, and if there are any generalizations to be made, let him do them himself. I've found that different people have different ways of working and things come to them in different ways. You're never sure when you're uttering a statement that's generally valid for all poets or when it's something that only applies to yourself. I think nothing is worse than to try to form people in your own image.

INTERVIEWER: Do you think there's any possible generalization to be made about the fact that all the better poets now, younger than you, seem to be teachers?

ELIOT: I don't know. I think the only generalization that can be made of any value will be one which will be made a generation later. All you can say at this point is that at different times there are different possibilities of making a living, or different limitations on making a living. Obviously a poet has got to find a way of making a living apart from his poetry. After all, artists do a great deal of teaching, and musicians too.

INTERVIEWER: Do you think that the optimal career for a poet would involve no work at all but writing and reading?

ELIOT: No, I think that would be—but there again one can only talk about oneself. It is very dangerous to give an optimal career for everybody, but I feel quite sure that if I'd started by having independent means, if I hadn't had to bother about earning a living and could have given all my time to poetry, it would have had a deadening influence on me.

INTERVIEWER: Why?

ELIOT: I think that for me it's been very useful to exercise other activities, such as working in a bank, or publishing even. And I think also that the difficulty of not having as much time as I would like has given me a greater pressure of concentration. I mean it has prevented me from writing too much. The danger, as a rule, of having nothing else to do is that one might write too much rather than concentrating and perfecting smaller amounts. That would be *my* danger.

INTERVIEWER: Do you consciously attempt, now, to keep up with the poetry that is being written by young men in England and America?

ELIOT: I don't now, not with any conscientiousness. I did at one time when I was reading little reviews and looking out for new talent as a publisher. But as one gets older, one is not quite confident in one's own ability to distinguish new genius among younger men. You're always afraid that you are going as you have seen your elders go. At Faber and Faber now I have a younger colleague who reads poetry manuscripts. But even before that, when I came across new stuff that I thought had real merit, I would show it to younger friends whose critical judgment I trusted and get their opinion. But of course there is always the danger that there is merit where you don't see it. So I'd rather have younger people to look at things first. If they like it, they will show it to me, and see whether I like it too. When you get something that knocks over younger people of taste and judgment and older people as well, then that's likely to be something important. Sometimes there's a lot of resistance. I shouldn't like to feel that I was resisting, as my work was resisted when it was new, by people who thought that it was imposture of some kind or other.

INTERVIEWER: Do you feel that younger poets in general have repudiated the experimentalism of the early poetry of this century? Few poets now seem to be resisted the way you were resisted, but some older critics like Herbert Read believe that poetry after you has been a regression to out-dated modes. When you talked about Milton the second time, you spoke of the function of poetry as a retarder of change, as well as a maker of change, in language.

ELIOT: Yes, I don't think you want a revolution every ten years.

INTERVIEWER: But is it possible to think that there has been a counterrevolution rather than an exploration of new possibilities?

ELIOT: No, I don't see anything that looks to me like a counter-revolution. After a period of getting away from the traditional forms, comes a period of curiosity in making new experiments with traditional forms. This can produce very good work if what has happened in between has made a difference: when it's not merely going back, but taking up an old form, which has been out of use for a time, and making something new with it. That is not counterrevolution. Nor does mere regression deserve the name. There is a tendency in some quarters to revert to Georgian scenery and sentiments: and among the public there are always people who prefer mediocrity, and when they get it, say, "What a relief! Here's some real poetry again." And there are also people who like poetry to be modern but for whom the really creative stuff is too strong—they need something diluted.

What seems to me the best of what I've seen in young poets is not reaction at all. I'm not going to mention any names, for I don't like to make public judgments about younger poets. The best stuff is a further development of a less revolutionary character than what appeared in earlier years of the century.

INTERVIEWER: I have some unrelated questions that I'd like to end with. In 1945 you wrote, "A poet must take as his material his own language as it is actually spoken around him." And later you wrote, "The music of poetry, then, will be a music latent in the common speech of his time." After the second remark, you disparaged "standardized BBC English." Now isn't one of the changes of the last fifty years, and perhaps even more of the last five years, the growing dominance of commercial speech through the means of communication? What you referred to as "BBC English" has become immensely more powerful through the ITA and BBC television, not to speak of CBS, NBC, and ABC. Does this development make the problem of the poet and his relationship to common speech more difficult?

ELIOT: You've raised a very good point there. I think you're right, it does make it more difficult.

INTERVIEWER: I wanted *you* to make the point.

ELIOT: Yes, but you wanted the point to be *made*. So I'll take the responsibility of making it: I do think that where you have these modern means of communication and means of imposing the speech and idioms of a small number on the mass of people at large, it does complicate the problem very much. I don't know to what extent that goes for film speech, but obviously radio speech has done much more.

INTERVIEWER: I wonder if there's a possibility that what you mean by common speech will disappear.

ELIOT: That is a very gloomy prospect. But very likely indeed.

INTERVIEWER: Are there other problems for a writer in our time which are unique? Does the prospect of human annihilation have any particular effect on the poet?

ELIOT: I don't see why the prospect of human annihilation should affect the poet differently from men of other vocations. It will affect him as a human being, no doubt in proportion to his sensitiveness.

INTERVIEWER: Another unrelated question: I can see why a man's criticism is better for his being a practicing poet, better although subject to his own prejudices. But do you feel that writing criticism has helped you as a poet?

ELIOT: In an indirect way it has helped me somehow as a poet —to put down in writing my critical valuation of the poets who have influenced me and whom I admire. It is merely making an influence more conscious and more articulate. It's been a rather natural impulse. I think probably my best critical essays are essays on the poets who had influenced me, so to speak, long before I thought of writing essays about them. They're of more value, probably, than any of my more generalized remarks.

INTERVIEWER: G. S. Fraser wonders, in an essay about the two of you, whether you ever met Yeats. From remarks in your talk about him, it would seem that you did. Could you tell us the circumstances?

ELIOT: Of course I had met Yeats many times. Yeats was always very gracious when one met him and had the art of treating younger writers as if they were his equals and contemporaries. I can't remember any one particular occasion.

INTERVIEWER: I have heard that you consider that your poetry belongs in the tradition of American literature. Could you tell us why?

ELIOT: I'd say that my poetry has obviously more in common with my distinguished contemporaries in America than with anything written in my generation in England. That I'm sure of.

INTERVIEWER: Do you think there's a connection with the American past?

ELIOT: Yes, but I couldn't put it any more definitely than that, you see. It wouldn't be what it is, and I imagine it wouldn't be so good; putting it as modestly as I can, it wouldn't be what it is if I'd been born in England, and it wouldn't be what it is if I'd stayed in America. It's a combination of things. But in its sources, in its emotional springs, it comes from America.

INTERVIEWER: One last thing. Seventeen years ago you said, "No honest poet can ever feel quite sure of the permanent value of what he has written. He may have wasted his time and messed up his life for nothing." Do you feel the same now, at seventy?

ELIOT: There may be honest poets who do feel sure. I don't.

DONALD HALL

5. Boris Pasternak

Boris Pasternak was born in Moscow on February 10, 1890, the eldest son of Leonid Pasternak, the painter, and Rosa Kaufman-Pasternak, the musician. He was educated at a Moscow *gymnasium* and later at Moscow University, where he went to study law. Early in his life he became interested in both musical and poetic composition, and was greatly influenced by Scriabin, who was one of his close friends. He gave up his formal study of music, however, as well as that of law, to go to Marburg, Germany, and read philosophy.

Shortly before the outbreak of the First World War, Pasternak returned to Russia and worked in a factory in the Urals. After the revolution he was employed in the library of the Commissariat for Education; during this period he joined groups interested in the arts, and continued his experiments in new techniques of poetic composition. His main collection of poems, which appeared between 1917 and 1932, gave him an eminent position in Russian literature of the day. In 1932, however, an autobiographical poem, *Spectorsky,* led to violent accusations of "anti-sociability." The hero of the poem was described by its critics as being "socially insignificant." From 1933 on, Pasternak lived in seclusion, in the suburbs of Moscow, devoting his time almost exclusively to translations from English and German—principally the plays and poetry of Shakespeare and Goethe. *Dr. Zhivago* was his first creative work after a silence of twenty-five years.

Pasternak was awarded the Nobel Prize for literature in 1958, and he died in May 1960.

His published work also includes: *Twin in the Clouds* (1917), *Above the Barrier* (1917), *My Sister, Life* (1922), *Dissertations on Art* (1922), *Themes and Variations* (1923), *Aerial Ways* (1925), *The Year 1905* (1925), *Lieutenant Schmidt* (1926), *Second Birth* (1930), *Safe Conduct* (1931), *Early Trains* (1942), *The Collected Poems of Boris Pasternak* (1959).

Мне очень близка мелодическая неподдельность большей части сказанного Вами, Ваша подверженность этому началу, Ваша подверженность этому возрождению в его последнем, блоковском выражении. И тоже, как Вы особенно убедитесь по последним моим работам, находясь под властью этого влеченья, надо только стараться, чтоб эта нота, как у родоначальника влеченья, что и ввела работу, совершила открытие, доводила воплощенье и выраженье мысли до конца и ясности, а не оставалась напоминаньем о дорогом когда-то звуке, отголоском, расплывающимся в воздухе не без последствий. Отчасти Вы доводите округлость Вашу описали до железной обстоятельнос

Fragment of a letter from Boris Pasternak to a fellow poet: "The melodic authenticity of most of your work is very dear to me, as is your faithfulness to the principle of melody and to 'ascent' in the supreme sense that Alexander Block gave that word. You will understand from a reading of my most recent works that I, too, am under the power of the same influence, but we must try to make sure that, as in Alexander Block, this note works, reveals, incarnates, and expresses thoughts to their ultimate clarity, instead of being only a reminder of sounds which originally charmed us, an inconsequential echo dying in the air."

ANNENKOV

Boris Pasternak

I decided to visit Boris Pasternak about ten days after my arrival in Moscow one January. I had heard much about him from my parents, who had known him for many years, and I had heard and loved his poems since my earliest years.

I had messages and small presents to take to him from my parents and from other admirers. But Pasternak had no phone, I discovered in Moscow. I dismissed the thought of writing a note as too impersonal. I feared that in view of the volume of his correspondence he might have some sort of standard rejection form for requests to visit him. It took a great effort to call unannounced on a man so famous. I was afraid that Pasternak in later years would not live up to my image of him suggested by his poems—lyric, impulsive, above all youthful.

My parents had mentioned that when they saw Pasternak in 1957, just before he received the Nobel Prize, he had held open house on Sundays—a tradition among Russian writers which extends to Russians abroad. As an adolescent in Paris, I remember being taken to call on the writer Remizov and the famous philosopher Berdyaev on Sunday afternoons.

On my second Sunday in Moscow I suddenly decided to go to Peredelkino. It was a radiant day, and in the center of the city, where I stayed, the fresh snow sparkled against the Kremlin's gold cupolas. The streets were full of sightseers—out-of-town families bundled in peasant-like fashion walking toward the Kremlin. Many carried bunches of fresh mimosa—sometimes one twig at a time. On winter Sundays large shipments of mimosa are brought to Moscow. Russians buy them to give to one another or simply to carry, as if to mark the solemnity of the day.

I decided to take a taxi to Peredelkino, although I knew of an electric train which went from the Kiev railroad station near the outskirts of Moscow. I was suddenly in a great hurry to get there, although I had been warned time and again by knowledgeable Muscovites of Pasternak's unwillingness to receive foreigners. I was prepared to deliver my messages and perhaps shake his hand and turn back.

The cab driver, a youngish man with the anonymous air of taxi-drivers everywhere, assured me that he knew Peredelkino very well —it was about thirty kilometers out on the Kiev highway. The fare would be about thirty roubles (about three dollars). He seemed to find it completely natural that I should want to drive out there on that lovely sunny day.

But the driver's claim to know the road turned out to be a boast, and soon we were lost. We had driven at fair speed along the four-lane highway free of snow and of billboards or gas stations. There were a few discreet road signs but they failed to direct us to Peredelkino, and so we began stopping whenever we encountered anyone to ask directions. Everyone was friendly and willing to help, but nobody seemed to know of Peredelkino. We drove for a long time on an unpaved, frozen road through endless white fields. Finally we entered a village from another era, in complete contrast with the immense new apartment houses in the outskirts of Moscow—low, ancient-looking log cottages bordering a straight main street. A horse-drawn sled went by; kerchiefed women were grouped near a small wooden church. We found we were in a settlement very close to Peredelkino. After a ten-minute drive on a small winding road through dense evergreens I was in front of Pasternak's house. I had seen photographs of it in magazines and suddenly there it was on my right: brown, with bay windows, standing on a slope against a background of fir trees and overlooking the road by which we had accidentally entered the town.

Peredelkino is a loosely settled little town, hospitable-looking and cheerful at sunny midday. Many writers and artists live in it year round in houses provided, as far as I know, for their lifetimes, and there is a large rest home for writers and journalists run by the Soviet Writers' Union. But part of the town still belongs to small artisans and peasants and there is nothing "arty" in the atmosphere.

Tchoukovsky, the famous literary critic and writer of children's books, lives there in a comfortable and hospitable house lined with books—he runs a lovely small library for the town's children. Constantin Fedine, one of the best known of living Russian novelists, lives next door to Pasternak. He is now the first secretary of the Writers' Union—a post long held by Alexander Fadeyev, who also lived here until his death in 1956. Later, Pasternak showed me Isaac Babel's house where he was arrested in the late 1930s and to which he never returned.

Pasternak's house was on a gently curving country road which leads down the hill to a brook. On that sunny afternoon the hill was crowded with children on skis and sleds, bundled like teddy bears. Across the road from the house was a large fenced field—a communal field cultivated in summer; now it was a vast white expanse dominated by a little cemetery on a hill, like a bit of background out of a Chagall painting. The tombs were surrounded by wooden fences painted a bright blue, the crosses were planted at odd angles, and there were bright pink and red paper flowers half buried in the snow. It was a cheerful cemetery.

The house's veranda made it look much like an American frame house of forty years ago, but the firs against which it stood marked it as Russian. They grew very close together and gave the feeling of deep forest, although there were only small groves of them around the town.

I paid the driver and with great trepidation pushed open the gate separating the garden from the road and walked up to the dark house. At the small veranda to one side there was a door with a withered, half-torn note in English pinned on it saying, "I am working now. I cannot receive anybody, please go away." After a moment's hesitation I chose to disregard it, mostly because it was so old-looking and also because of the little packages in my hands. I knocked, and almost immediately the door was opened—by Pasternak himself.

He was wearing an astrakhan hat. He was strikingly handsome; with his high cheek-bones and dark eyes and fur hat he looked like someone out of a Russian tale. After the mounting anxiety of the trip I suddenly felt relaxed—it seemed to me that I had never really doubted that I would meet Pasternak.

I introduced myself as Olga Andreyev, Vadim Leonidovitch's daughter, using my father's semi-formal name. It is made up of his own first name and his father's, the short-story writer and play-wright, Leonid, author of the play *He Who Gets Slapped* and *The Seven Who Were Hanged*, etc. Andreyev is a fairly common Russian name.

It took Pasternak a minute to realize that I had come from abroad to visit him. He greeted me with great warmth, taking my hand in both of his, and asking about my mother's health and my father's writing, and when I was last in Paris, and looking closely into my face in search of family resemblances. He was going out to pay some calls. Had I been a moment later I would have missed him. He asked me to walk part of the way with him —as far as his first stop, at the Writers' Club.

While Pasternak was getting ready to go I had a chance to look around the simply furnished dining room into which I had been shown. From the moment I had stepped inside I had been struck by the similarity of the house to Leo Tolstoi's house in Moscow, which I had visited the day before. The atmosphere in both combined austerity and hospitality in a way which I think must have been characteristic of a Russian intellectual's home in the nineteenth century. The furniture was comfortable, but old and unpretentious. The rooms looked ideal for informal entertaining, for children's gatherings, for the studious life. Although it was extremely simple for its period, Tolstoi's house was bigger and more elaborate than Pasternak's, but the unconcern about elegance or display was the same.

Usually, one walked into Pasternak's house through the kitchen, where one was greeted by a tiny, smiling, middle-aged cook who helped to brush the snow off one's clothes. Then came the dining room with a bay window where geraniums grew. On the walls hung charcoal studies by Leonid Pasternak, the writer's painter father. There were life-studies and portraits. One recognized Tolstoi, Gorki, Scriabin, Rachmaninoff. There were sketches of Boris Pasternak and his brother and sisters as children, of ladies in big hats with veils. . . . It was very much the world of Pasternak's early reminiscences, that of his poems about adolescent love.

Pasternak was soon ready to go. We stepped out into the brilliant sunlight and walked through the evergreen grove behind the house in rather deep snow which sifted into my low-cut boots.

Soon we were on a packed road, much more comfortable for walking although it had treacherous, icy patches. Pasternak took long, lanky steps. On particularly perilous spots he would take my arm; otherwise he gave all his attention to the conversation. Walks are an established part of life in Russia—like drinking tea or lengthy philosophical discussions—a part he apparently loved. We took what was obviously a very roundabout path to the Writers'

Club. The stroll lasted for about forty minutes. He first plunged into an elaborate discussion of the art of translating. He would stop from time to time to ask about the political and literary situations in France and in the United States. He said that he rarely read papers—"Unless I sharpen my pencil and glance over the sheet of newspaper into which I collect the shavings. This is how I learned last fall that there was a near revolution against De Gaulle in Algeria, and that Soustelle was ousted—*Sous*telle was *oust*ed," he repeated—a rough translation of his words, emphasizing both approval of De Gaulle's decision and the similarity in the words as he spoke them. But actually he seemed remarkably well informed about literary life abroad; it seemed to interest him greatly.

From the first moment I was charmed and impressed by the similarity of Pasternak's speech to his poetry—full of alliterations and unusual images. He related words to each other musically, without however at any time sounding affected or sacrificing the exact meaning. For somebody acquainted with his verse in Russian, to have conversed with Pasternak is a memorable experience. His word sense was so personal that one felt the conversation was somehow the continuation, the elaboration of a poem, a rushed speech, with waves of words and images following one another in a crescendo.

Later, I remarked to him on the musical quality of his speech. "In writing as in speaking," he said, "the music of the word is never just a matter of sound. It does not result from the harmony of vowels and consonants. It results from the relation between the speech and its meaning. And meaning—content—must always lead."

Often I found it difficult to believe that I was speaking to a man of seventy; Pasternak appeared remarkably young and in good health. There was something a little strange and forbidding in this youthfulness as if something—was it art?—had mixed itself with the very substance of the man to preserve him. His movements were completely youthful—the gestures of the hands, the manner in which he threw his head back. His friend, the poetess Marina Tsvetayeva, once wrote, "Pasternak looks at the same time like an Arab and like his horse." And indeed, with his dark complexion and somehow archaic features Pasternak did have something of an Arabic face. At certain moments he seemed suddenly to become aware of the impact of his own extraordinary face, of his whole personality. He seemed to withdraw for an instant, half closing his slanted brown eyes, turning his head away, vaguely reminiscent of a horse balking.

I had been told by some writers in Moscow—most of them didn't know him personally—that Pasternak was a man in love with his own image. But then I was told many contradictory things about him in the few days I spent in Moscow. Pasternak seemed a living legend—a hero for some, a man who had sold out to the enemies of Russia for others. Intense admiration for his poetry among writers and artists was universal. It was the title character of Dr. Zhivago that seemed most controversial. "Nothing but a worn-out intellectual of no interest whatsoever," said a well-known young poet, otherwise very liberal-minded and a great admirer of Pasternak's poetry.

In any event, I found that there was no truth to the charge that Pasternak was an egocentric. On the contrary, he seemed intensely aware of the world around him and reacted to every change of mood in people near him. It is hard to imagine a more perceptive conversationalist. He grasped the most elusive thought at once. The conversation lost all heaviness. Pasternak asked questions about my parents. Although he had seen them but a few times in his life, he remembered everything about them and their tastes. He recalled with surprising exactness some of my father's poems which he had liked. He wanted to know about writers I knew—Russians in Paris, and French, and Americans. American literature seemed particularly to interest him, although he knew only the important names. I soon discovered that it was difficult to make him talk about himself, which I had hoped he would do.

As we walked in the sunshine, I told Pasternak what interest and admiration *Dr. Zhivago* had aroused in the West and particularly in the United States, despite the fact that in my and many others' opinion the translation into English did not do justice to his book.

"Yes," he said, "I am aware of this interest and I am immensely happy and, proud of it. I get an enormous amount of mail from abroad about my work. In fact, it is quite a burden at times, all those inquiries that I have to answer, but then it is indispensable to keep up relations across boundaries. As for the translators of *Dr. Zhivago*, do not blame them too much. It's not their fault. They are used, like translators everywhere, to reproduce the literal sense rather than the tone of what is said—and of course it is the tone that matters. Actually, the only interesting sort of translation is that of classics. There is challenging work. As far as modern writing is concerned, it is rarely rewarding to translate it, although it might be easy. You said you were a painter. Well, translation is very much like copying paintings. Imagine yourself copying a Malevitch; wouldn't it be boring? And that is precisely what I have to do with the well-known Czech surrealist Nezval. He is not really bad, but all this writing of the twenties has terribly aged. This translation which I have promised to finish and my own correspondence take much too much of my time."

Do you have difficulty receiving your mail?

"At present I receive all of it, everything sent me, I assume. There's a lot of it—which I'm delighted to receive, though I'm troubled by the volume of it and the compulsion to answer it all.

"As you can imagine, some of the letters I get about *Dr. Zhivago* are quite absurd. Recently somebody writing about *Dr. Zhivago* in France was inquiring about the plan of the novel. I guess it baffles the French sense of order. . . . But how silly, for the plan of the novel is outlined by the poems accompanying it. This is partly why I chose to publish them alongside the novel. They are there also to give the novel more body, more richness. For the same reason I used religious symbolism—to give warmth to the book. Now some critics have gotten so wrapped up in those symbols— which are put in the book the way stoves go into a house, to warm it up—they would like me to commit myself and climb into the stove."

Have you read Edmund Wilson's critical essays on Dr. Zhivago?

"Yes, I have read them and appreciated their perception and intelligence, but you must realize that the novel must not be judged on theological lines. Nothing is further removed from my understanding of the world. One must live and write restlessly, with the help of the new reserves that life offers. I am weary of this notion of faithfulness to a point of view at all cost. Life around us is ever changing, and I believe that one should try to change one's slant accordingly—at least once every ten years. The great heroic devotion to one point of view is very alien to me—it's a lack of humility. Mayakovsky killed himself because his pride would not be reconciled with something new happening within himself—or around him."

We had reached a gate beside a long, low wooden fence. Pasternak stopped. He was due there, our conversation had already made him slightly late. I said good-by with regret. There were so many things that I wanted to ask him right then. Pasternak showed me the way to the railroad station, very close by, downhill behind the little cemetery. A little electric train took me into Moscow in less than an hour. It is the one described so accurately by Pasternak in *Early Trains*:

> . . . And, worshipful, I humbly watch
> Old peasant women, Muscovites,
> Plain artisans, plain laborers
> Young students and suburbanites.
>
> I see no traces of subjection
> Born of unhappiness, dismay,
> Or want. They bear their daily trials
> Like masters who have come to stay

Disposed in every sort of posture
In little knots, in quiet nooks
The children and the young sit still
Engrossed, like experts, reading books

Then Moscow greets us in a mist
Of darkness turning silver gray . . .

My subsequent two visits with Pasternak merge in my memory into one long literary conversation. Although he declined to give me a formal interview ("For this, you must come back when I am less busy, next fall perhaps") he seemed interested in the questions which I wanted to ask him. Except for meals, we were alone, and there were no interruptions. Both times as I was about to leave, Pasternak kissed my hand in the old-fashioned Russian manner, and asked me to come back the following Sunday.

I remember coming to Pasternak's house from the railroad station at dusk, taking a short cut I had learned near the cemetery. Suddenly the wind grew very strong; a snowstorm was beginning. I could see snow flying in great round waves past the station's distant lights. It grew dark very quickly; I had difficulty walking against the wind. I knew this to be customary Russian winter weather, but it was the first real *metol*—snowstorm—I had seen. It recalled poems by Pushkin and Block, and it brought to mind Pasternak's early poems, and the snowstorms of *Dr. Zhivago*. To be in his house a few minutes later, and to hear his elliptical sentences so much like his verse, seemed strange.

I had arrived too late to attend the midday dinner; Pasternak's family had retired, the house seemed deserted. Pasternak insisted that I have something to eat and the cook brought some venison and vodka into the dining room. It was about four o'clock and the room was dark and warm, shut off from the world with only the sound of snow and wind outside. I was hungry and the food delicious. Pasternak sat across the table from me discussing my grandfather, Leonid Andreyev. He had recently reread some of his stories and liked them. "They bear the stamp of those fabulous

Russian nineteen-hundreds. Those years are now receding in our memory, and yet they loom in the mind like great mountains seen in the distance, enormous. Andreyev was under a Nietzschean spell, he took from Nietzsche his taste for excesses. So did Scriabin. Nietzsche satisfied the Russian longing for the extreme, the absolute. In music and writing, men had to have this enormous scope before they acquired specificity, became themselves."

Pasternak told me about a piece he had recently written for a magazine, on the subject of "What is man?" "How old-fashioned Nietzsche seems, he who was the most important thinker in the days of my youth! What enormous influence—on Wagner, on Gorki . . . Gorki was impregnated with his ideas. Actually, Nietzsche's principal function was to be the transmitter of the bad taste of his period. It is Kierkegaard, barely known in those years, who was destined to influence deeply our own years. I would like to know the works of Berdyaev better; he is in the same line of thought, I believe—truly a writer of our time."

It grew quite dark in the dining room and we moved to a little sitting room on the same floor where a light was on. Pasternak brought me tangerines for dessert. I ate them with a strange feeling of something already experienced; tangerines appear in Pasternak's work very often—in the beginning of *Dr. Zhivago*, in early poems. They seem to stand for a sort of ritual thirst-quenching. And then there was another vivid evocation of a Pasternak poem, like the snowstorm which blew outside—an open grand piano, black and enormous, filling up most of the room:

> . . . *and yet we are nearest*
> *In twilight here, the music tossed upon*
> *the fire, year after year, like pages of a diary.* *

On these walls, as in the dining room, there were sketches by Leonid Pasternak. The atmosphere was both serious and relaxed.

---

* "The Trembling Piano," *Themes and Variations*.

It seemed a good time to ask Pasternak a question which interested me especially. I had heard from people who had seen him while he was working on *Dr. Zhivago* that he rejected most of his early verse as too tentative and dated. I had difficulty believing it. There is a classical perfection to *Themes and Variations* and *My Sister, Life,* experimental as they were in the 1920s. I found that writers and poets in Russia knew them by heart and would recite them with fervor. Often one would detect the influence of Pasternak in the verse of young poets. Mayakovsky and Pasternak, each in his own manner, are the very symbol of the years of the Revolution and the 1920s. Then art and the revolutionary ideas seemed inseparable. It was enough to let oneself be carried by the wave of overwhelming events and ideas. There were fewer heartbreaking choices to make (and I detected a longing for those years on the part of young Russian intellectuals). Was it true that Pasternak rejected those early works?

In Pasternak's reply I sensed a note of slight irritation. It might have been because he didn't like to be solely admired for those poems—did he realize perhaps that they are unsurpassable? Or was it the more general weariness of the artist dissatisfied with past achievements, concerned with immediate artistic problems only?

"These poems were like rapid sketches—just compare them with the works of our elders. Dostoevski and Tolstoi were not just novelists, Block not just a poet. In the midst of literature—the world of commonplaces, conventions, established names—they were three voices which spoke because they had something to say . . . and it sounded like thunder. As for the facility of the twenties, take my father for example. How much search, what efforts to finish one of his paintings! Our success in the twenties was partly due to chance. My generation found itself in the focal point of history. Our works were dictated by the times. They lacked universality; now they have aged. Moreover, I believe that it is no longer possible for lyric poetry to express the immensity of our experience. Life has grown too cumbersome, too complicated. We have acquired values which are best expressed in prose. I have tried to express them through my novel, I have them in mind as I write my play."

What about Zhivago? Do you still feel, as you told my parents in 1957, that he is the most significant figure of your work?

"When I wrote *Dr. Zhivago* I had the feeling of an immense debt toward my contemporaries. It was an attempt to repay it. This feeling of debt was overpowering as I slowly progressed with the novel. After so many years of just writing lyric poetry or translating, it seemed to me that it was my duty to make a statement about our epoch—about those years, remote and yet looming so closely over us. Time was pressing. I wanted to record the past and to honor in *Dr. Zhivago* the beautiful and sensitive aspects of the Russia of those years. There will be no return of those days, or of those of our fathers and forefathers, but in the great blossoming of the future I forsee their values will revive. I have tried to describe them. I don't know whether *Dr. Zhivago* is fully successful as a novel, but then with all its faults I feel it has more value than those early poems. It is richer, more humane than the works of my youth."

Among your contemporaries in the twenties which ones do you think have best endured?

"You know how I feel about Mayakovsky. I have told it at great length in my autobiography, *Safe Conduct*. I am indifferent to most of his later works, with the exception of his last unfinished poem 'At the Top of My Voice.' The falling apart of form, the poverty of thought, the unevenness which is characteristic of poetry in that period are alien to me. But there are exceptions. I love all of Essenin, who captures so well the smell of Russian earth. I place Tsvetayeva highest—she was a formed poet from her very beginning. In an age of affectations she had her own voice—human, classical. She was a woman with a man's soul. Her struggle with everyday life gave her strength. She strived and reached perfect clarity. She is a greater poet than Ahmatova, whose simplicity and lyricism I have always admired. Tsvetayeva's death was one of the great sadnesses of my life."

What about Andrei Beily, so influential in those years?

"Beily was too hermetic, too limited. His scope is comparable to that of chamber music—never greater. If he had really suffered, he might have written the major work of which he was capable. But he never came into contact with real life. Is it perhaps the fate of writers who die young like Beily, this fascination with new forms? I have never understood those dreams of a new language, of a completely original form of expression. Because of this dream, much of the work of the twenties which was but stylistic experimentation has ceased to exist. The most extraordinary discoveries are made when the artist is overwhelmed by what he has to say. Then he uses the old language in his urgency and the old language is transformed from within. Even in those years one felt a little sorry for Beily because he was so cut off from the real life which could have helped his genius to blossom."

What about today's young poets?

"I am impressed by the extent that poetry seems a part of everyday life for Russians. Printings of twenty thousand volumes of poetry by young poets are amazing to a Westerner, but actually poetry in Russia is not as alive as you might think. It is fairly limited to a group of intellectuals. And today's poetry is often rather ordinary. It is like the pattern of a wallpaper, pleasant enough but without real *raison d'être.* Of course some young people show talent—for example Evtuchenko."

Wouldn't you say, however, that the first half of the Russian twentieth century is a time of high achievement in poetry rather than in prose?

"I don't think that's so any longer. I believe that prose is today's medium—elaborate, rich prose like Faulkner's. Today's work must re-create whole segments of life. This is what I am trying to do in my new play. I say trying because everyday life has grown very complicated for me. It must be so anywhere for a well-known writer, but I am unprepared for such a role. I don't like a life deprived of secrecy and quiet. It seems to me that in my youth there was work, an integral part of life which illuminated everything else in it. Now it is something I have to fight for. All those demands by scholars, editors, readers cannot be ignored, but together with the translations they devour my time. . . . You must tell people abroad who are interested in me that this is my only serious problem—this terrible lack of time."

My last visit with Pasternak was a very long one. He had asked me to come early, in order to have a talk before the dinner which was to be a family feast. It was again a sunny Sunday. I arrived shortly before Pasternak returned from his morning stroll. As I was shown into his study, the house echoed with cheerful voices. Somewhere in the back of it, members of his family were assembled.

Pasternak's study was a large, rather bare room on the second floor. Like the rest of the house it had little furniture—a large desk near the bay window, a couple of chairs, a sofa. The light coming from the window looking over the large snowy field was brilliant. Pinned on the light gray wooden walls there was a multitude of art postcards. When he came in, Pasternak explained to me that those were all sent to him by readers, mostly from abroad. Many were reproductions of religious scenes—medieval Nativities, St. George killing the dragon, St. Magdalene . . . They were related to *Dr. Zhivago*'s themes.

After his walk, Pasternak looked especially well. He was wearing a collegiate-looking navy-blue blazer and was obviously in a good mood. He sat at the desk by the window and placed me across from him. As on other occasions, the atmosphere was relaxed and yet of great concentration. I remember vividly feeling happy—Pasternak looked so gay and the sun through the window was warm. As we sat there for two or more hours, I felt a longing to prolong those moments—I was leaving Moscow the next day—but the bright sunlight flooding the room inexorably faded as the day advanced.

Pasternak decided to tell me about his new play. He seemed to do so on the spur of the moment. Quite fascinated, I listened to him—there were few interruptions on my part. Once or twice, unsure of some historical or literary allusion, I asked him for explanation.

"I think that on account of your background—so close to the events of the Russian nineteenth century—you will be interested in the outlines of my new work. I am working on a trilogy. I have about a third of it written.

"I want to re-create a whole historical era, the nineteenth century in Russia with its main event, the liberation of the serfs. We have, of course, many works about that time, but there is no modern treatment of it. I want to write something panoramic, like Gogol's *Dead Souls*. I hope that my plays will be as real, as involved with everyday life as *Dead Souls*. Although they will be long, I hope that they can be played in one evening. I think that most plays should be cut for staging. I admire the English for knowing how to cut Shakespeare, not just to keep what is essential, but rather to emphasize what is significant. The Comédie Française came to Moscow recently. They don't cut Racine and I feel it is a serious mistake. Only what is expressive today, what works dramatically should be staged.

"My trilogy deals with three meaningful moments in the long process of liberating the serfs. The first play takes place in 1840— that is when unrest caused by serfdom is first felt throughout the country. The old feudal system is outlived, but no tangible hope is yet to be seen for Russia. The second one deals with the 1860s. Liberal landowners have appeared and the best among Russian aristocrats begin to be deeply stirred by Western ideas. Unlike the two first plays, which are set in a great country estate, the third part will take place in St. Petersburg in the 1880s. But this part is but a project yet, while the first and second plays are partially written. I can tell you in more detail about those if you like.

"The first play describes life at its rawest, most trivial, in the manner of the first part of *Dead Souls*. It is existence before it has been touched by any form of spirituality.

"Imagine a large estate lost in the heart of rural Russia around 1840. It is in a state of great neglect, nearly bankrupt. The masters of the estate, the Count and his wife, are away. They have gone on a trip to spare themselves the painful spectacle of the designation—by means of a lottery—of those among their peasants who must go into the Army. As you know, military service lasted for twenty-five years in Russia in those times. The masters are about to return and the household is getting ready to receive them. In the opening scene we see the servants cleaning house—sweeping, dusting, hanging fresh curtains. There is a lot of confusion, of running around—laughter and jokes among the young servant girls.

"Actually, the times are troubled in this part of the Russian countryside. Soon the mood among the servants becomes more somber. From their conversations we learn that there are hidden bandits in the neighboring woods; they are probably runaway soldiers. We also hear of legends surrounding the estate, like that of the 'house killer' from the times of Catherine the Great. She was a sadistic woman, an actual historical figure who took delight in terrifying and torturing her serfs—her crimes so extreme at a time when almost anything was permitted to serf-owners that she was finally arrested.

"The servants also talk about a plaster bust standing high on a cupboard. It is a beautiful young man's head in eighteenth-century hair dress. This bust is said to have a magical meaning. Its destinies are linked to those of the estate. It must therefore be dusted with extreme care, lest it be broken.

"The main character in the play is Prokor, the keeper of the estate. He is about to leave for town to sell wood and wheat—the estate lives off such sales—but he joins in the general mood instead of going. He remembers some old masquerade costumes stored away in a closet and decides to play a trick on his superstitious fellow servants. He dresses himself as a devil—big bulging eyes like a fish. Just as he emerges in his grotesque costume, the

masters' arrival is announced. In haste the servants group themselves at the entrance to welcome the Count and his wife. Prokor
has no other alternative but to hide himself in a closet.

"As the Count and Countess come in, we begin at once to
sense that there is a great deal of tension between them, and
we find out that during their trip home the Count has been
trying to get his wife to give him her jewels—all that's left besides
the mortgaged estate. She has refused, and when he threatened
her with violence a young valet traveling with them defended
her—an unbelievable defiance. He hasn't been punished yet, but
it's only a question of time before the Count's wrath is unleashed
against him.

"As the Count renews his threats against the Countess, the
young valet, who has nothing to lose anyway, suddenly reaches
for one of the Count's pistols which have just been brought in
from the carriage. He shoots at the Count. There is a great panic
—servants rushing around and screaming. The plaster statue
tumbles down from the cupboard and breaks into a thousand
pieces. It wounds one of the young servant girls, blinding her.
She is 'The Blind Beauty' for whom the trilogy is named. The
title is, of course, symbolic of Russia, oblivious for so long of its
own beauty and its own destinies. Although she is a serf, the
blind beauty is also an artist; she is a marvelous singer, an important member of the estate's chorus of serfs.

"As the wounded Count is carried out of the room, the Countess, unseen in the confusion, hands her jewels to the young valet,
who manages to make his escape. It is poor Prokor, still costumed
as a devil and hidden in the closet, who is eventually accused of
having stolen them. As the Countess does not reveal the truth,
he is convicted of the theft and sent to Siberia. . . .

"As you see, all this is very melodramatic, but I think that the
theater *should* try to be emotional, colorful. I think everybody's
tired of stages where nothing happens. The theater is the art of
emotions—it is also that of the concrete. The trend should be
toward appreciating melodrama again: Victor Hugo, Schiller. . . .

"I am working now on the second play. As it stands, it's broken into separate scenes. The setting is the same estate, but times have changed. We are in 1860, on the eve of the liberation of the serfs. The estate now belongs to a nephew of the Count. He would have already freed his serfs but for his fears of hurting the common cause. He is impregnated with liberal ideas and loves the arts. And his passion is theater. He has an outstanding theatrical company. Of course, the actors are his serfs, but their reputation extends to all of Russia.

"The son of the young woman blinded in the first play is the principal actor of the group. He is also the hero of this part of the trilogy. His name is Agafon, a marvelously talented actor. The Count has provided him with an outstanding education.

"The play opens with a snowstorm." Pasternak described it with large movements of his hands. "An illustrious guest is expected at the estate—none other than Alexandre Dumas, then traveling in Russia. He is invited to attend the premiere of a new play. The play is called *The Suicide*. I might write it—a play within a play as in *Hamlet*. I would love to write a melodrama in the taste of the middle of the nineteenth century. . . .

"Alexandre Dumas and his entourage are snowed in at a relay station not too far from the estate. A scene takes place there, and who should the relay-master be but Prokor, the former estate keeper? He has been back from Siberia for some years—released when the Countess disclosed his innocence on her deathbed. He has become increasingly prosperous running the relay station. And yet despite the advent of new times, the scene at the inn echoes the almost medieval elements of the first play: we see the local executioner and his aides stop at the inn. They are traveling from the town to their residence deep in the woods—by custom they are not allowed to live near other people.

"A very important scene takes place at the estate when the guests finally arrive there. There is a long discussion about art between Alexandre Dumas and Agafon. This part will illustrate my own ideas about art—not those of the 1860s, needless to say. Agafon dreams of going abroad, of becoming a Shakespearean actor, to play Hamlet.

"This play has a denouement somehow similar to that of the first one. An obnoxious character whom we first meet at the relay station is the local police chief. He is a sort of Sobakevitch, the character in *Dead Souls* who personifies humanity at its crudest. Backstage, after the performance of *The Suicide*, he tries to rape one of the young actresses. Defending her, Agafon hits the police chief with a champagne bottle, and he has to flee for fear of persecution. The Count, however, helps him, and eventually gets him to Paris.

"In the third play, Agafon comes back to Russia to live in St. Petersburg. No longer a serf (we are now in 1880) he's an extremely successful actor. Eventually he has his mother cured of her blindness by a famous European doctor.

"As for Prokor, in the last play he has become an affluent merchant. I want him to represent the middle class which did so much for Russia at the end of the nineteenth century. Imagine someone like Schukine, who collected all those beautiful paintings in Moscow at the turn of the century. Essentially, what I want to show at the end of the trilogy is just that: the birth of an enlightened and affluent middle class, open to occidental influences, progressive, intelligent, artistic. . . ."

It was typical of Pasternak to tell me about his plays in concrete terms, like a libretto. He didn't emphasize the ideas behind the trilogy, though it became apparent, after a while, that he was absorbed in ideas about art—not in its historical context, but as an element ever present in life. As he went on, I realized that what he was describing was simply the frame of his new work. Parts of it were completed, others were still to be filled in.

"At first, I consulted all sorts of documents on the nineteenth century. Now I'm finished with research. After all, what is important is not the historical accuracy of the work, but the successful re-creation of an era. It is not the object described that matters, but the light that falls on it, like that from a lamp in a distant room."

Toward the end of his description of his trilogy, Pasternak was obviously hurried. Dinner time was long past. He would glance at his watch from time to time. But, despite the fact that he didn't have the opportunity to clarify philosophical implications which would have given body to the strange framework of the dramas, I felt I had been witness to a remarkable evocation of the Russian past.

The story of our fathers sounds like the days of the Stuarts
Further away than Pushkin and can be seen only in dream. *

As we came down to the dining room, the family already was seated around the large table. "Don't they look like an impressionist painting?" said Pasternak. "With the geraniums in the background and this mid-afternoon light? There is a painting by Simon just like this. . . ."

Everyone stood as we entered and remained standing while Pasternak introduced me around the table. Besides Mme. Pasternak, two of Pasternak's sons were there—his oldest son by his first marriage, and his youngest son, who was eighteen or twenty years old—a handsome boy, dark, with quite a strong resemblance to his mother. He was a student in physics at the Moscow University. Professor Nihaus was also a guest. He is a famous Chopin teacher at the Moscow Conservatory to whom Mme. Pasternak had once been married. He was quite elderly, with an old-fashioned mustache, very charming and refined. He asked about Paris and musicians we knew there in common. There were also two ladies at the table whose exact relationship to the Pasternak family I didn't learn.

I was seated to the right of Pasternak. Mme. Pasternak was at his left. The table was simply set, covered with a white linen Russian tablecloth embroidered with red cross-stitches. The sil-

* From *The Year 1905*.

verware and china were very simple. There was a vase with
mimosa in the middle, and bowls of oranges and tangerines.
The hors d'oeuvres were already set on the table. Guests passed
them to each other while Pasternak poured the vodka. There
were caviar, marinated herring, pickles, macedoine of vegetables.
. . . The meal progressed slowly. Soon kvass was poured out—a
home-made fermented drink usually drunk in the country. Because
of fermentation the kvass corks would sometimes pop during the
night and wake everybody up—just like a pistol shot, said Mme.
Pasternak. After the hors d'oeuvres the cook served a succulent
stew made of game.

The conversation was general. Hemingway's works were discussed. Last winter he was one of the most widely read authors
in Moscow. A new collection of his writings had just been published. Mme. Pasternak and the ladies at the table remarked that
they found Hemingway monotonous—all those endless drinks
with little else happening to the heroes.

Pasternak, who had fallen silent for a while, took exception.

"The greatness of a writer has nothing to do with subject
matter itself, only with how much the subject matter touches
the author. It is the density of style which counts. Through
Hemingway's style you feel matter, iron, wood." He was punctuat-
ing his words with his hands, pressing them against the wood
of the table. "I admire Hemingway but I prefer what I know of
Faulkner. *Light in August* is a marvelous book. The character
of the little pregnant woman is unforgettable. As she walks from
Alabama to Tennessee something of the immensity of the South
of the United States, of its essence, is captured for us who have
never been there."

Later the conversation turned to music. Professor Nihaus and
Pasternak discussed fine points of interpretation of Chopin. Pasternak said how much he loved Chopin—"a good example of
what I was saying the other day—Chopin used the old Mozartian
language to say something completely new—the form was reborn
from within. Nonetheless, I am afraid that Chopin is considered

a little old-fashioned in the United States. I gave a piece on Chopin to Stephen Spender which was not published."

I told him how much Gide loved to play Chopin—Pasternak didn't know this and was delighted to hear it. The conversation moved on to Proust, whom Pasternak was slowly reading at that time.

"Now that I am coming to the end of A *la Recherche du Temps Perdu*, I am struck by how it echoes some of the ideas which absorbed us in 1910. I put them into a lecture about 'Symbolism and Immortality' which I gave on the day before Leo Tolstoi died and I went to Astapovo with my father. Its text has long been lost, but among many other things on the nature of symbolism it said that, although the artist will die, the happiness of living which he has experienced is immortal. If it is captured in a personal and yet universal form it can actually be relived by others through his work.

"I have always liked French literature," he continued. "Since the war I feel that French writing has acquired a new accent, less rhetoric. Camus' death is a great loss for all of us." (Earlier, I had told Pasternak of Camus' tragic end, which took place just before I came to Moscow. It was not written up in the Russian press. Camus is not translated into Russian.) "In spite of differences of themes, French literature is now much closer to us. But French writers when they commit themselves to political causes are particularly unattractive. Either they are cliquish and insincere or with their French sense of logic they feel they have to carry out their beliefs to their conclusion. They fancy they must be absolutists like Robespierre or Saint-Just."

Tea and cognac were served at the end of the meal. Pasternak looked tired suddenly and became silent. As always during my stay in Russia I was asked many questions about the West—about its cultural life and our daily existence.

Lights were turned on. I looked at my watch to discover that it was long past six o'clock. I had to go. I felt very tired, too.

Pasternak walked me to the door, through the kitchen. We said good-by outside on the little porch in the blue snowy evening. I was terribly sad at the thought of not returning to Peredelkino. Pasternak took my hand in his and held it for an instant, urging me to come back very soon. He asked me once again to tell his friends abroad that he was well, that he remembered them even though he hadn't time to answer their letters. I had already walked down the porch and into the path when he called me back. I was happy to have an excuse to stop, to turn back, to have a last glimpse of Pasternak standing bare-headed, in his blue blazer under the door light.

"Please," he called, "don't take what I have said about letters personally. Do write to me, in any language you prefer. I will answer you."

OLGA CARLISLE

6.

Katherine Anne Porter

Katherine Anne Porter was born May 15, 1890, at Indian Creek, Texas. She spent her early youth in Texas and Louisiana, and received her education from small convent schools in that area. She began writing, she has said, almost as soon as she could put words on paper. "I did not choose this vocation, and if I had any say in the matter, I would not have chosen it . . . yet for this vocation I was and am willing to live and die, and I consider very few other things of the slightest importance."

Supporting herself by book reviewing, political articles, hack writing, and editing, she worked continually at her own stories, although she did not publish until she was in her thirties. Her first collection of short stories, *Flowering Judas*, appeared in 1930 and earned her an immediate reputation. In 1931 she was awarded a Guggenheim Fellowship and went abroad to study and write—in Berlin, Basel, and Madrid.

When she returned to America she received a Book-of-the-Month Club Fellowship, and in 1938 another Guggenheim grant. In 1949 Miss Porter was given an honorary Litt. D. degree from the Woman's College of the University of North Carolina. She has been a vice-president of the National Institute of Arts and Letters, a fellow in the Library of Congress, and in 1952 was the only woman writer in the United States delegation to the Cultural Exposition in Paris sponsored by the Congress for Cultural Freedom.

Her published work includes: *Hacienda* (1934), *Noon Wine* (1937), *Pale Horse, Pale Rider* (1939), *The Leaning Tower and Other Stories* (1944), *The Days Before* (essays, 1952), and *Ship of Fools* (1962).

er ~~~~~ greeting for any one.   She sat there alone reading stale magazines until
the luncheon bugle sounded.   The exact vision of the Baumgartner's faces ~~~~~~~~~~
would not leave her. It was plain they too had ~~~~ some sort of shabby little incident
during the night— no matter what. Mrs. Treadwell did not even wish to guess what it
might have been, but that sad dull display of high manners after they had behaved
no doubt disgracefully to each other and their child— ~~~~~ to prove ~~~~~~~~ that
they were not so base as they had caused each other to seem. That dreadful little
door-holding, bowing scene had meant to say You can see, can't you, that in another
time or place, or another society, I might have been very different, much better than
you have ever seen me? Mrs. Treadwell leaned back and closed her eyes. What they
were saying to each other was only Love me, love me in spite of all! Whether or not
I love you, whether I am fit to love, whether you are able to love, even if there
is no such thing as love. Love me!

A small deep wandering sensation of disgust, self-distaste came with these
straying thoughts. She remembered as in a dream again her despairs, her long
weeping, her incurable grief over the failure of love or what she had been told was
love, and the ruin of her hopes— what hopes? she could not remember- and what had
it been but the childish refusal to admit and accept on some terms or other the
difference between what one had hoped was true and what one discovers to be the
mere ~~~~~ ~~~~~~~~~~~~— She had been hurt, she had recovered, and what had it all
been but a foolish piece of romantic carelessness?   She stood up to take a deep
breath and walk around the stuffy room. All morning long she had been trying in
the back of her mind to piece together exactly what had happened last night to her,
and what she had done. The scene with that young officer was clear enough. She remembered Herr Baumgartner hanging over the rail looking sick. Lizzi delivered to
her hands later, when she had been amusing herself painting her face; and then—

No good putting it off any longer. She could not find her gilded sandals when
she was putting her things in order. There were small random bloodspots on the
lower front of her night gown. And as she walked, she remembered, and stopped clutching
a chairback feeling faint; walked again, then left the room and set out to look
for Jenny Brown. She should know everything about it, being the "girl" of that
rather self-absorbed young man, Denny cabin mate... Mrs. Treadwell remembered very
well what had happened, what she had done; she wanted a few particulars of the damage
she had done, and above all to learn whether her enemy had recognized her.

Jenny Brown was reading the bulletin board. A ragged-edged imitation of an ancient
proclamation announced:" The victims of last night's violence and bloodshed are resting quietly. The suspected criminals are under surveillance, not yet apprehended,
~~~ ~~~~~~~~ ~~~~~~ but an early disclosure of several interesting identities is expected.
Signed Los Camelots de la Cucaracha.

Manuscript page from Katherine Anne Porter's novel Ship of Fools.

WILLIAM WALTON

Katherine Anne Porter

The Victorian house in which Katherine Anne Porter lives is narrow and white, reached by an iron-railed stairway curving up from the shady brick-walked Georgetown street. The parlor to which a maid admits the caller is an elegant mélange of several aspects of the past, both American and European. High-ceilinged, dim and cool after the midsummer glare, the room is dominated by a bottle-green settee from the period of Napoleon III. Outside the alcove of windows there is a rustle of wind through ginkgo trees, then a hush.

Finally, a voice in the upper hallway: its tone that of someone talking to a bird, or coquetting with an old beau—light and feathery, with a slight flutter. A few moments later, moving as lightly as her voice, Miss Porter hurries through the wide door-

way, unexpectedly modern in a soft green suit of woven Italian silk. Small and elegant, she explains her tardiness, relates an anecdote of the morning's mail, offers a minted ice tea, and speculates aloud on where we might best conduct our conversation.

She decides on the dining room, a quiet, austere place overlooking the small enclosed garden. Here the aspect is a different one. "I want to live in a world capital or the howling wilderness," she said once, and did. The drawing room was filled with pieces that had once been part of the house on rue Notre-Dame des Champs; this one is bright with Mexican folk art—whistles and toy animals collected during a recent tour for the Department of State—against simpler, heavier pieces of furniture. The round table at which we sit is of Vermont marble, mottled and colored like milk glass, on a wrought-iron base of her own design. There is a sixteenth-century cupboard from Avila, and a refectory table of the early Renaissance from a convent in Fiesole. Here we settle the tape recorder, under an image of the great god Horus.

We try to make a beginning. She is an experienced lecturer, familiar with microphone and tape recorder, but now she is to talk about herself as well as her work, the link between, and the inexorable winding of the tape from one spool to the other acts almost as a hypnotic. Finally we turn it off and talk for a while of other things, more frivolous and more autobiographical, hoping to surprise an easier revelation. . . .

INTERVIEWER: You were saying that you had never intended to make a career of writing.

PORTER: I've never made a career of anything, you know, not even of writing. I started out with nothing in the world but a kind of passion, a driving desire. I don't know where it came from, and I don't know why—or why I have been so stubborn about it that nothing could deflect me. But this thing between me and my writing is the strongest bond I have ever had—stronger than any bond or any engagement with any human being or with any other work I've ever done. I really started writing when I was six or seven years old. But I had such a multiplicity of half-talents, too: I wanted to dance, I wanted to play the piano, I sang, I drew. It wasn't really dabbling—I was investigating everything, experimenting in everything. And then, for one thing, there weren't very many amusements in those days. If you wanted music, you had to play the piano and sing yourself. Oh, we saw all the great things that came during the season, but after all, there would only be a dozen or so of those occasions a year. The rest of the time we depended upon our own resources: our own music and books. All the old houses that I knew when I was a child were full of books, bought generation after generation by members of the family. Everyone was literate as a matter of course. Nobody told you to read this or not to read that. It was there to read, and we read.

INTERVIEWER: Which books influenced you most?

PORTER: That's hard to say, because I grew up in a sort of mélange. I was reading Shakespeare's sonnets when I was thirteen years old, and I'm perfectly certain that they made the most profound impression upon me of anything I ever read. For a time I knew the whole sequence by heart; now I can only remember two or three of them. That was the turning point of my life, when I read the Shakespeare sonnets, and then all at one blow, all of Dante—in that great big book illustrated by Gustave Doré. The plays I saw on the stage, but I don't remember reading them with any interest at all. Oh, and I read all kinds of poetry—Homer, Ronsard, all the old French poets in translation. We also had a very good library of—well, you might say secular philosophers. I was incredibly influenced by Montaigne when I was very young. And one day when I was about fourteen, my father led me up to a great big line of books and said, "Why don't you read this? It'll knock some of the nonsense out of you!" It happened to be the entire set of Voltaire's philosophical dictionary with notes by Smollett. And I plowed through it; it took me about five years.

And of course we read all the eighteenth-century novelists, though Jane Austen, like Turgenev, didn't really engage me until

I was quite mature. I read them both when I was very young, but I was grown up before I really took them in. And I discovered for myself *Wuthering Heights*; I think I read that book every year of my life for fifteen years. I simply adored it. Henry James and Thomas Hardy were really my introduction to modern literature; Grandmother didn't much approve of it. She thought Dickens might do, but she was a little against Mr. Thackeray; she thought he was too trivial. So that was as far as I got into the modern world until I left home!

INTERVIEWER: Don't you think this background—the comparative isolation of Southern rural life, and the atmosphere of literary interest—helped to shape you as a writer?

PORTER: I think it's something in the blood. We've always had great letter writers, readers, great storytellers in our family. I've listened all my life to articulate people. They were all great storytellers, and every story had shape and meaning and point.

INTERVIEWER: Were any of them known as writers?

PORTER: Well, there was my sixth or seventh cousin once removed, poor William Sidney. O. Henry, you know. He was my father's second cousin—I don't know what that makes him to me. And he was more known in the family for being a bank robber. He worked in a bank, you know, and he just didn't seem to find a talent for making money; no Porter ever did. But he had a wife who was dying of TB and he couldn't keep up with the doctor's bills. So he took a pitiful little sum—oh, about three hundred and fifty dollars—and ran away when he was accused. But he came back, because his wife was dying, and went to prison. And there was Horace Porter, who spent his whole eight years as ambassador to France looking for the bones of John Paul Jones. And when he found them, and brought them back, he wrote a book about them.

INTERVIEWER: It seems to me that your work is pervaded by a sense of history. Is that part of the family legacy?

PORTER: We were brought up with a sense of our own history, you know. My mother's family came to this country in 1648 and went to the John Randolph territory of Virginia. And one of my great great grandfathers was Jonathan Boone, the brother of Daniel. On my father's side I'm descended from Colonel Andrew Porter, whose father came to Montgomery County, Pennsylvania, in 1720. He was one of the circle of George Washington during the Revolution, a friend of Lafayette, and one of the founders of the Society of the Cincinnati—oh, he really took it seriously!— and when he died in 1809—well, just a few years before that he was offered the post of Secretary of War, but he declined. We were never very ambitious people. We never had a President, though we had two governors and some in the Army and the Navy. I suppose we did have a desire to excel but not to push our way to higher places. We thought we'd *already* arrived!

INTERVIEWER: The "we" of family is very strong, isn't it? I remember that you once wrote of the ties of blood as the "absolute point of all departure and return." And the central character in many of your stories is defined, is defining herself often, in relation to a family organization. Even the measure of time is human —expressed in terms of the very old and the very young, and how much of human experience they have absorbed.

PORTER: Yes, but it wasn't a conscious made-up affair, you know. In those days you belonged together, you lived together, because you were a family. The head of our house was a grandmother, an old matriarch, you know, and a really lovely and beautiful woman, a good soul, and so she didn't do us any harm. But the point is that we did live like that, with Grandmother's friends, all reverend old gentlemen with frock coats, and old ladies with jet breastplates. Then there were the younger people, the beautiful girls and the handsome young boys, who were all ahead of me; when I was a little girl, eight or nine years old, they were eighteen to twenty-two, and they represented all glamour, all beauty, all joy and freedom to me. Then there was my own age, and then there were the babies. And the servants, the Negroes. We simply lived that way; to have four generations in one house, under one roof, there was nothing unusual about that. That was just my experience, and this is just the way I've reacted to it. Many other people didn't react, who were brought up in very much the same way.

I remember when I was very young, my older sister wanted to buy some old furniture. It was in Louisiana, and she had just been married. And I went with her to a wonderful old house in the country where we'd been told there was a very old gentleman who probably had some things to sell. His wife had died, and he was living there alone. So we went to this lovely old house, and, sure enough, there was this lonely beautiful old man, eighty-seven or -eight, surrounded by devoted Negro servants. But his wife was dead and his children were married and gone. He said, yes, he had a few things he wanted to sell. So he showed us through the house. And finally he opened a door, and showed us a bedroom with a beautiful four-poster bed, with a wonderful satin coverlet: the most wonderful, classical-looking bed you ever saw. And my sister said, "Oh, that's what I want." And he said, "Oh, madame, that is my marriage bed. That is the bed that my wife brought with her as a bride. We slept together in that bed for nearly sixty years. All our children were born there. Oh," he said, "I shall die in that bed, and then they can dispose of it as they like."

I remember that I felt a little suffocated and frightened. I felt a little trapped. But why? Only because I understood that. I was brought up in that. And I was at the age of rebellion then, and it really scared me. But I look back on it now and think how perfectly wonderful, what a tremendously beautiful life it was. Everything in it had meaning.

INTERVIEWER: But it seems to me that your work suggests someone who was searching for new—perhaps broader—meanings . . . that while you've retained the South of your childhood as a point of reference, you've ranged far from that environment itself. You seem to have felt little of the peculiarly Southern preoccupation with racial guilt and the death of the old agrarian life.

PORTER: I'm a Southerner by tradition and inheritance, and I have a very profound feeling for the South. And, of course, I belong to the guilt-ridden white-pillar crowd myself, but it just didn't rub off on me. Maybe I'm just not Jewish enough, or Puritan enough, to feel that the sins of the father are visited on the third and fourth generations. Or maybe it's because of my European influences—in Texas and Louisiana. The Europeans didn't have slaves themselves as late as my family did, but they *still* thought slavery was quite natural. . . . But, you know, I was always restless, always a roving spirit. When I was a little child I was always running away. I never got very far, but they were always having to come and fetch me. Once when I was about six, my father came to get me somewhere I'd gone, and he told me later he'd asked me, "Why are you so restless? Why can't you stay here with us?" and I said to him, "I want to go and see the world. I want to know the world like the palm of my hand."

INTERVIEWER: And at sixteen you made it final.

PORTER: At sixteen I ran away from New Orleans and got married. And at twenty-one I bolted again, went to Chicago, got a newspaper job, and went into the movies.

INTERVIEWER: The movies?

PORTER: The newspaper sent me over to the old S. and A. movie studio to do a story. But I got into the wrong line, and then was too timid to get out. "Right over this way, Little Boy Blue," the man said, and I found myself in a courtroom scene with Francis X. Bushman. I was horrified by what had happened to me, but they paid me five dollars for that first day's work, so I stayed on. It was about a week before I remembered what I had been sent to do; and when I went back to the newspaper they gave me eighteen dollars for my week's non-work and fired me!

I stayed on for six months—I finally got to nearly ten dollars a day—until one day they came in and said, "We're moving to the coast." "Well, I'm not," I said. "Don't you want to be a movie actress?" "Oh, no!" I said. "Well, be a fool!" they said, and they left. That was 1914 and World War had broken out, so in September I went home.

INTERVIEWER: And then?

PORTER: Oh, I sang old Scottish ballads in costume—I made it myself—all around Texas and Louisiana. And then I was supposed to have TB, and spent about six weeks in a sanitarium. It was just bronchitis, but I was in Denver, so I got a newspaper job.

INTERVIEWER: I remember that you once warned me to avoid that at all costs—to get a job "hashing" in a restaurant in preference.

PORTER: Anything, anything at all. I did it for a year and that is what confirmed me that it wasn't doing me any good. After that I always took little dull jobs that didn't take my mind and wouldn't take all of my time, and that, on the other hand, paid me just enough to subsist. I think I've only spent about ten per cent of my energies on writing. The other ninety per cent went to keeping my head above water.

And I think that's all wrong. Even Saint Teresa said, "I can pray better when I'm comfortable," and she refused to wear her haircloth shirt or starve herself. I don't think living in cellars and starving is any better for an artist than it is for anybody else; the only thing is that sometimes the artist has to take it, because it is the only possible way of salvation, if you'll forgive that old-fashioned word. So I took it rather instinctively. I was inexperienced in the world, and likewise I hadn't been trained to do anything, you know, so I took all kinds of laborious jobs. But, you know, I think I could probably have written better if I'd been a little more comfortable.

INTERVIEWER: Then you were writing all this time?

PORTER: All this time I was writing, writing no matter what else I was doing; no matter what I *thought* I was doing, in fact. I was living almost as instinctively as a little animal, but I realize now that all that time a part of me was getting ready to be an artist. That my mind was working even when I didn't know it, and didn't care if it was working or not. It is my firm belief that all our lives we are preparing to be somebody or something, even if we don't do it consciously. And the time comes one morning when you wake up and find that you have become irrevocably what you were preparing all this time to be. Lord, that could be a sticky moment, if you had been doing the wrong things, something against your grain. And, mind you, I know that can happen. I have no patience with this dreadful idea that whatever you have in you has to come out, that you can't suppress true talent. People *can* be destroyed; they can be bent, distorted, and completely crippled. To say that you can't destroy yourself is just as foolish as to say of a young man killed in war at twenty-one or twenty-two that that was his fate, that he wasn't going to have anything anyhow.

I have a very firm belief that the life of no man can be explained in terms of his experiences, of what has happened to him, because in spite of all the poetry, all the philosophy to the contrary, we are not really masters of our fate. We don't really direct our lives unaided and unobstructed. Our being is subject to all the chances of life. There are so many things we are capable of, that we could be or do. The potentialities are so great that we never, any of us, are more than one-fourth fulfilled. Except that there may be one powerful motivating force that simply carries you along, and I think that was true of me. . . . When I was a very little girl I wrote a letter to my sister saying I wanted glory. I don't know quite what I meant by that now, but it was something different from fame or success or wealth. I know that I wanted to be a good writer, a good artist.

INTERVIEWER: But weren't there certain specific events that crystallized that desire for you—something comparable to the experience of Miranda in *Pale Horse, Pale Rider?*

PORTER: Yes, that was the plague of influenza, at the end of the First World War, in which I almost died. It just simply divided my life, cut across it like that. So that everything before that was just getting ready, and after that I was in some strange way altered, ready. It took me a long time to go out and live in the world again. I was really "alienated," in the pure sense. It was, I think, the fact that I really had participated in death, that I knew what death was, and had almost experienced it. I had what the

Christians call the "beatific vision," and the Greeks called the "happy day," the happy vision just before death. Now if you have had that, and survived it, come back from it, you are no longer like other people, and there's no use deceiving yourself that you are. But you see, I did: I made the mistake of thinking I was quite like anybody else, of trying to live like other people. It took me a long time to realize that that simply wasn't true, that I had my own needs and that I had to live like me.

INTERVIEWER: And that freed you?

PORTER: I just got up and bolted. I went running off on that wild escapade to Mexico, where I attended, you might say, and assisted at, in my own modest way, a revolution.

INTERVIEWER: That was the Obregón Revolution of 1921?

PORTER: Yes—though actually I went to Mexico to study the Aztec and Mayan art designs. I had been in New York, and was getting ready to go to Europe. Now, New York was full of Mexican artists at that time, all talking about the renaissance, as they called it, in Mexico. And they said, "Don't go to Europe, go to Mexico. That's where the exciting things are going to happen." And they were right! I ran smack into the Obregón Revolution, and had, in the midst of it, the most marvelous, natural, spontaneous experience of my life. It was a terribly exciting time. It was alive, but death was in it. But nobody seemed to think of that: life was in it, too.

INTERVIEWER: What do you think are the best conditions for a writer, then? Something like your Mexican experience, or—

PORTER: Oh, I can't say what they are. It would be such an individual matter. Everyone needs something different. . . . But what I find most dreadful among the young artists is this tendency toward middle-classness—this idea that they have to get married and have lots of children and live just like everybody else, you know? Now, I am all for human life, and I am all for marriage and children and all that sort of thing, but quite often you can't have that and do what you were supposed to do, too. Art is a vocation, as much as anything in this world. For the real artist, it is the most natural thing in the world, not as necessary as air and water, perhaps, but as food and water. But we really do lead almost a monastic life, you know; to follow it you very often have to give up something.

INTERVIEWER: But for the unproven artist that is a very great act of faith.

PORTER: It *is* an act of faith. But one of the marks of a gift is to have the courage of it. If they haven't got the courage, it's just too bad. They'll fail, just as people with lack of courage in other vocations and walks of life fail. Courage is the first essential.

INTERVIEWER: In choosing a pattern of life compatible with the vocation?

PORTER: The thing is not to follow a pattern. Follow your own pattern of feeling and thought. The thing is, to accept your own life and not try to live someone else's life. Look, the thumbprint is not like any other, and the thumbprint is what you must go by.

INTERVIEWER: In the current vernacular then, you think it's necessary for an artist to be a "loner"—not to belong to any literary movement?

PORTER: I've never belonged to any group or huddle of any kind. You cannot be an artist and work collectively. Even the fact that I went to Mexico when everybody else was going to Europe—I went to Mexico because I felt I had business there. And there I found friends and ideas that were sympathetic to me. That was my entire milieu. I don't think anyone even knew I was a writer. I didn't show my work to anybody or talk about it, because—well, no one was particularly interested in that. It was a time of revolution, and I was running with almost pure revolutionaries!

INTERVIEWER: And you think that was a more wholesome environment for a writer than, say, the milieu of the expatriated artist in Europe at the same time?

PORTER: Well, I know it was good for me. I would have been completely smothered—completely disgusted and revolted—by the goings-on in Europe. Even now when I think of the twenties and the legend that has grown up about them, I think it was a horrible time: shallow and trivial and silly. The remarkable thing is that anybody survived in such an atmosphere—in a place where they could call F. Scott Fitzgerald a great writer!

INTERVIEWER: You don't agree?

PORTER: Of course I don't agree. I couldn't read him then and I can't read him now. There was just one passage in a book called *Tender Is the Night*—I read that and thought, "Now I will read this again," because I couldn't be sure. Not only didn't I like his writing, but I didn't like the people he wrote about. I thought they weren't worth thinking about, and I still think so. It seems to me that your human beings have to have some kind of meaning. I just can't be interested in those perfectly stupid meaningless lives. And I don't like the same thing going on now—the way the artist simply will not face up to the final reckoning of things.

INTERVIEWER: In a philosophical sense?

PORTER: I'm thinking of it now in just the artistic sense—in the sense of an artist facing up to his own end meanings. I suppose I shouldn't be mentioning names, but I read a story some time ago, I think it was in the *Paris Review*, called "The McCabes." * Now I think William Styron is an extremely gifted man: he's very ripe and lush and with a kind of Niagara Falls of energy, and a kind of power. But he depends so on violence and a kind of exaggerated heat—at least it looks like heat, but just turns out to be summer lightning. Because there is nothing in the world more meaningless than that whole escapade of this man going off and winding up in the gutter. You sit back and think, "Well, let's see, where are we now?" All right, it's possible that that's just what Styron meant—the whole wicked pointlessness of things. But I tell you, nothing is pointless, and nothing is meaningless if the artist will face it. And it's his business to face it. He hasn't got the right to sidestep it like that. Human life itself may be almost pure chaos, but the work of the artist—the only thing he's good

---

* "The McCabes" was mistakenly not identified as a section from Styron's novel *Set This House on Fire.*

for—is to take these handfuls of confusion and disparate things, things that seem to be irreconcilable, and put them together in a frame to give them some kind of shape and meaning. Even if it's only his view of a meaning. That's what he's for—to give his view of life. Surely, we understand very little of what is happening to us at any given moment. But by remembering, comparing, waiting to know the consequences, we can sometimes see what an event really meant, what it was trying to teach us.

INTERVIEWER: You once said that every story begins with an ending, that until the end is known there is no story.

PORTER: That is where the artist begins to work: With the consequences of acts, not the acts themselves. Or the events. The event is important only as it affects your life and the lives of those around you. The reverberations, you might say, the overtones: that is where the artist works. In that sense it has sometimes taken me ten years to understand even a little of some important event that had happened to me. Oh, I could have given a perfectly factual account of what had happened, but I didn't know what it meant until I knew the consequences. If I didn't know the ending of a story, I wouldn't begin. I always write my last lines, my last paragraph, my last page first, and then I go back and work towards it. I know where I'm going. I know what my goal is. And how I get there is God's grace.

INTERVIEWER: That's a very classical view of the work of art— that it must end in resolution.

PORTER: Any true work of art has got to give you the feeling of reconciliation—what the Greeks would call catharsis, the purification of your mind and imagination—through an ending that is endurable because it is right and true. Oh, not in any pawky individual idea of morality or some parochial idea of right and wrong. Sometimes the end is very tragic, because it needs to be. One of the most perfect and marvelous endings in literature—it raises my hair now—is the little boy at the end of *Wuthering Heights*, crying that he's afraid to go across the moor because there's a man and woman walking there.

And there are three novels that I reread with pleasure and delight—three almost perfect novels, if we're talking about form, you know. One is *A High Wind in Jamaica* by Richard Hughes, one is *A Passage to India* by E. M. Forster, and the other is *To the Lighthouse* by Virginia Woolf. Every one of them begins with an apparently insoluble problem, and every one of them works out of confusion into order. The material is all used so that you are going toward a goal. And that goal is the clearing up of disorder and confusion and wrong, to a logical and human end. I don't mean a happy ending, because after all at the end of *A High Wind in Jamaica* the pirates are all hanged and the children are all marked for life by their experience, but it comes out to an orderly end. The threads are all drawn up. I have had people object to Mr. Thompson's suicide at the end of *Noon Wine*, and I'd say, "All right, where was he going? Given what he was, his own situation, what else could he do?" Every once in a while when I see a character of mine just going towards perdition, I think, "Stop, stop, you can always stop and choose, you know." But no, being what he was, he already *has* chosen, and he can't go back on it now. I suppose the first idea that man had was the idea of fate, of the servile will, of a deity who destroyed as he would, without regard for the creature. But I think the idea of free will was the second idea.

INTERVIEWER: Has a story never surprised you in the writing? A character suddenly taken a different turn?

PORTER: Well, in the vision of death at the end of "Flowering Judas" I knew the real ending—that she was not going to be able to face her life, what she'd done. And I knew that the vengeful spirit was going to come in a dream to tow her away into death, but I didn't know until I'd written it that she was going to wake up saying, "No!" and be afraid to go to sleep again.

INTERVIEWER: That was, in a fairly literal sense, a "true" story, wasn't it?

PORTER: The truth is, I have never written a story in my life that didn't have a very firm foundation in actual human experience—somebody else's experience quite often, but an experience that became my own by hearing the story, by witnessing the thing, by hearing just a word perhaps. It doesn't matter, it just takes a little—a tiny seed. Then it takes root, and it grows. It's an organic thing. That story had been on my mind for years, growing out of this one little thing that happened in Mexico. It was forming and forming in my mind, until one night I was quite desperate. People are always so sociable, and I'm sociable too, and if I live around friends. . . . Well, they were insisting that I come and play bridge. But I was very firm, because I knew the time had come to write that story, and I had to write it.

INTERVIEWER: What was that "little thing" from which the story grew?

PORTER: Something I saw as I passed a window one evening. A girl I knew had asked me to come and sit with her, because a man was coming to see her, and she was a little afraid of him. And as I went through the courtyard, past the flowering judas tree, I glanced in the window and there she was sitting with an open book on her lap, and there was this great big fat man sitting beside her. Now Mary and I were friends, both American girls living in this revolutionary situation. She was teaching at an Indian school, and I was teaching dancing at a girls' technical school in Mexico City. And we were having a very strange time of it. I was more skeptical, and so I had already begun to look with a skeptical eye on a great many of the revolutionary leaders. Oh, the idea was all right, but a lot of men were misapplying it.

And when I looked through that window that evening, I saw something in Mary's face, something in her pose, something in the whole situation, that set up a commotion in my mind. Because until that moment I hadn't really understood that she was not able to take care of herself, because she was not able to face her own nature and was afraid of everything. I don't know why I saw it. I don't believe in intuition. When you get sudden flashes of perception, it is just the brain working faster than usual. But you've been getting ready to know it for a long time, and when it comes, you feel you've known it always.

INTERVIEWER: You speak of a story "forming" in your mind. Does it begin as a visual impression, growing to a narrative? Or how?

PORTER: All my senses were very keen; things came to me through my eyes, through all my pores. Everything hit me at once, you know. That makes it very difficult to describe just exactly what is happening. And then, I think the mind works in such a variety of ways. Sometimes an idea starts completely inarticulately. You're not thinking in images or words or—well, it's exactly like a dark cloud moving in your head. You keep wondering what will come out of this, and then it will dissolve itself into a set of—well, not images exactly, but really thoughts. You begin to think directly in words. Abstractly. Then the words transform themselves into images. By the time I write the story my people are up and alive and walking around and taking things into their own hands. They exist as independently inside my head as you do before me now. I have been criticized for not enough detail in describing my characters, and not enough furniture in the house. And the odd thing is that I see it all so clearly.

INTERVIEWER: What about the technical problems a story presents—its formal structure? How deliberate are you in matters of technique? For example, the use of the historical present in "Flowering Judas"?

PORTER: The first time someone said to me, "Why did you write 'Flowering Judas' in the historical present?" I thought for a moment and said, "Did I?" I'd never noticed it. Because I didn't *plan* to write it any way. A story forms in my mind and forms and forms, and when it's ready to go, I strike it down—it takes just the time I sit at the typewriter. I never think about form at all. In fact, I would say that I've never been interested in anything about writing after having learned, I hope, to write. That is, I mastered my craft as well as I could. There is a technique, there is a craft, and you have to learn it. Well, I did as well as I could with that, but now all in the world I am interested in is telling a story. I have something to tell you that I, for some reason, think is worth telling, and so I want to tell it as clearly and purely and simply as I can. But I had spent fifteen years at least learning to write. I practiced writing in every possible way that I could. I wrote a pastiche of other people, imitating Dr. Johnson and Laurence Sterne, and Petrarch and Shakespeare's sonnets, and then I tried writing my own way. I spent fifteen years learning to trust myself: that's what it comes to. Just as a pianist runs his scales for ten years before he gives his concert: because when he gives that concert, he can't be thinking of his fingering or of his hands; he has to be thinking of his interpretation, of the music he's playing. He's thinking of what he's trying to communicate. And if he hasn't got his technique perfected by then, he needn't give the concert at all.

INTERVIEWER: From whom would you say you learned most during this period of apprenticeship?

PORTER: The person who influenced me most, the real revelation in my life as a writer—though I don't write in the least like him—was Laurence Sterne, in *Tristram Shandy*. Why? Because, you know, I loved the grand style, and he made it look easy. The others, the great ones, really frightened me; they were so grand and magnificent they overawed me completely. But Laurence Sterne—well, it was just exactly as if he said, "Oh, come on, do it this way. It's so easy." So I tried to do it that way, and that taught me something, that taught me more than anybody else had. Because Laurence Sterne is a most complex and subtle man.

INTERVIEWER: What about your contemporaries? Did any of them contribute significantly to your development as a writer?

PORTER: I don't think I learned very much from my contemporaries. To begin with, we were all such individuals, and we were all so argumentative and so bent on our own courses that although I got a kind of support and personal friendship from my contemporaries, I didn't get very much help. I didn't show my work to anybody. I didn't hand it around among my friends for criticism, because, well, it just didn't occur to me to do it. Just as I didn't even try to publish anything until quite late because I didn't think I was ready. I published my first story in 1923. That was "María Concepción," the first story I ever finished. I rewrote "María Concepción" fifteen or sixteen times. That was a real battle, and I was thirty-three years old. I think it is the most curious lack of judgment to publish before you are ready. If there are echoes of other people in your work, you're not ready. If anybody has to help you rewrite your story, you're not ready. A story should be a finished work before it is shown. And after that, I will not allow anyone to change anything, and I will not change anything on anyone's advice. "Here is my story. It's a finished story. Take it or leave it!"

INTERVIEWER: You are frequently spoken of as a stylist. Do you think a style can be cultivated, or at least refined?

PORTER: I've been called a stylist until I really could tear my hair out. And I simply don't believe in style. The style is you. Oh, you can cultivate a style, I suppose, if you like. But I should say it remains a cultivated style. It remains artificial and imposed, and I don't think it deceives anyone. A cultivated style would be like a mask. Everybody knows it's a mask, and sooner or later you must show yourself—or at least, you show yourself as someone who could not afford to show himself, and so created something to hide behind. Style is the man. Aristotle said it first, as far as I know, and everybody has said it since, because it is one of those unarguable truths. You do not create a style. You work, and develop yourself; your style is an emanation from your own being. Symbolism is the same way. I never consciously took or adopted a symbol in my life. I certainly did not say, "This blooming tree upon which Judas is supposed to have hanged himself is going to be the center of my story." I named "Flowering Judas" after it was written, because when reading back over it I suddenly saw the whole symbolic plan and pattern of which I was totally unconscious while I was writing. There's a pox of symbolist theory going the rounds these days in American colleges in the writing courses. Miss Mary McCarthy, who is one of the wittiest and most acute and in some ways the worst-tempered woman in American letters, tells about a little girl who came to her with a story. Now Miss McCarthy is an extremely good critic, and she found this to be a good story, and she told the girl that it was—that she considered it a finished work, and that she could with a clear conscience go on to something else. And the little girl said, "But Miss McCarthy, my writing teacher said, 'Yes, it's a good piece of work, but now we must go back and put in the symbols!'" I think that's an amusing story, and it makes my blood run cold.

INTERVIEWER: But certainly one's command of the language can be developed and refined?

PORTER: I love the purity of language. I keep cautioning my students and anyone who will listen to me not to use the jargon of trades, not to use scientific language, because they're going to be out of date the day after tomorrow. The scientists change their vocabulary, their jargon, every day. So do the doctors, and the politicians, and the theologians—every body, every profession, every trade changes its vocabulary all of the time. But there is a basic pure human speech that exists in every language. And that is the language of the poet and the writer. So many words that had good meanings once upon a time have come to have meanings almost evil—certainly shabby, certainly inaccurate. And "psychology" is one of them. It has been so abused. This awful way a whole segment, not a generation but too many of the young writers, have got so soaked in the Freudian and post-Freudian vocabulary that they can't speak—not only can't speak English, but they can't speak *any* human language anymore. You can't write about people out of textbooks, and you can't use a jargon. You have to speak clearly and simply and purely in a language that a six-year-old child can understand; and yet have the meanings and the overtones of language, and the implications, that appeal to the highest intelligence—that is, the highest intelligence that one is able to reach. I'm not sure that I'm able to appeal to the highest intelligence, but I'm willing to try.

INTERVIEWER: You speak of the necessity of writing out of your own understanding rather than out of textbooks, and I'm sure any writer would agree. But what about the creation of masculine characters then? Most women writers, even the best of them like George Eliot, have run aground there. What about you? Was Mr. Thompson, say, a more difficult imaginative problem than Miranda?

PORTER: I never did make a profession of understanding people, man or woman or child, and the only thing I know about people is exactly what I have learned from the people right next to me. I have always lived in my immediate circumstances, from day to day. And when men ask me how I know so much about men, I've got a simple answer: everything I know about men, I've learned from men. If there is such a thing as a man's mind and a woman's mind—and I'm sure there is—it isn't what most critics mean when they talk about the two. If I show wisdom, they say I have a masculine mind. If I am silly and irrelevant—and Edmund Wilsons says I often am—why then they say I have a typically feminine mind! (That's one thing about reaching my age: you can always quote the authorities about what you are.) But I haven't ever found it unnatural to be a woman.

INTERVIEWER: But haven't you found that being a woman presented to you, as an artist, certain special problems? It seems to me that a great deal of the upbringing of women encourages the dispersion of the self in many small bits, and that the practice of any kind of art demands a corralling and concentrating of that self and its always insufficient energies.

PORTER: I think that's very true and very right. You're brought up with the notion of feminine chastity and inaccessibility, yet with the curious idea of feminine availability in all spiritual ways, and in giving service to anyone who demands it. And I suppose that's why it has taken me twenty years to write this novel; it's been interrupted by just anyone who could jimmy his way into my life.

INTERVIEWER: Hemingway said once that a writer writes best when he's in love.

PORTER: I don't know whether you write better, but you feel so good you *think* you're writing better! And certainly love does create a rising of the spirit that makes everything you do seem easier and happier. But there must come a time when you no longer depend upon it, when the mind—not the will, really, either —takes over.

INTERVIEWER: In judging that the story is ready? You said a moment ago that the actual writing of a story is always done in a single spurt of energy—

PORTER: I always write a story in one sitting. I started "Flowering Judas" at seven p.m. and at one-thirty I was standing on a snowy windy corner putting it in the mailbox. And when I wrote my short novels, two of them, I just simply took the manuscript, packed a suitcase and departed to an inn in Georgetown, Pennsylvania, without leaving any forwarding address! Fourteen days later I had finished *Old Mortality* and *Noon Wine*.

INTERVIEWER: But the new novel *Ship of Fools* has been in the writing since 1942. The regime for writing this must have been a good deal different.

PORTER: Oh, it was. I went up and sat nearly three years in the country, and while I was writing it I worked every day, anywhere from three to five hours. Oh, it's true I used to do an awful lot of just sitting there thinking what comes next, because this is a great big unwieldy book with an enormous cast of characters— it's four hundred of my manuscript pages, and I can get four hundred and fifty words on a page. But all that time in Connecticut, I kept myself free for work; no telephone, no visitors—oh, I really lived like a hermit, everything but being fed through a grate! But it is, as Yeats said, a "solitary sedentary trade." And I did a lot of gardening, and cooked my own food, and listened to music, and of course I would read. I was really very happy. I can live a solitary life for months at a time, and it does me good, because I'm working. I just get up bright and early—sometimes at five o'clock—have my black coffee, and go to work.

INTERVIEWER: You work best in the morning, then?

PORTER: I work whenever I'm let. In the days when I was taken up with everything else, I used to do a day's work, or housework, or whatever I was doing, and then work at night. I worked when I could. But I prefer to get up very early in the morning and work. I don't want to speak to anybody or see anybody. Perfect silence. I work until the vein is out. There's something about the way you feel, you know when the well is dry, that you'll have to wait till tomorrow and it'll be full up again.

INTERVIEWER: The important thing, then, is to avoid any breaks or distractions while you're writing?

PORTER: To keep at a boiling point. So that I can get up in the morning with my mind still working where it was yesterday. Then I can stop in the middle of a paragraph and finish it the next day. I began writing *Ship of Fools* twenty years ago, and I've been away from it for several years at a time and stopped in the middle of a paragraph—but, you know, I can't tell where the crack is mended, and I hope nobody else can.

INTERVIEWER: You find no change in style, or in attitudes, over the years?

PORTER: It's astonishing how little I've changed: nothing in my point of view or my way of feeling. I'm going back now to finish some of the great many short stories that I have begun and not been able to finish for one reason or another. I've found one that I think I can finish. I have three versions of it: I started it in 1923, and it's based on an episode in my life that took place when I was twenty. Now here I am, seventy, and it's astonishing how much it's like me now. Oh, there are certain things, certain turns of sentence, certain phrases that I think I can sharpen and make more clear, more simple and direct, but my point of view, my being, is strangely unchanged. We change, of course, every day; we are not the same people who sat down at this table, yet there is a basic and innate being that is unchanged.

INTERVIEWER: *Ship of Fools* too is based upon an event that took place ten years or more before the first writing, isn't it? A sea voyage just before the beginning of the European war.

PORTER: It is the story of my first voyage to Europe in 1931. We embarked on an old German ship at Vera Cruz and we landed in Bremerhaven twenty-eight days later. It was a crowded ship, a great mixture of nationalities, religions, political beliefs—all that sort of thing. I don't think I spoke a half-dozen words to anybody. I just sat there and watched—not deliberately, though. I kept a diary in the form of a letter to a friend, and after I got home the friend sent it back. And, you know, it is astonishing what happened on that boat, and what happened in my mind afterwards. Because it is fiction now.

INTERVIEWER: The title—isn't it from a medieval emblem?— suggests that it might also be an allegory.

PORTER: It's just exactly what it seems to be. It's an allegory if you like, though I don't think much of the allegorical as a standard. It's a parable, if you like, of the ship of this world on its voyage to eternity.

INTERVIEWER: I remember your writing once—I think in the preface to *Flowering Judas*—of an effort to understand what you called the "majestic and terrible failure" of Western man. You were speaking then of the World War and what it signified of human folly. It seems to me that *Ship of Fools* properly belongs to that investigation of betrayal and self-delusion—

PORTER: Betrayal and treachery, but also self-betrayal and self-deception—the way that all human beings deceive themselves about the way they operate. . . . There seems to be a kind of order in the universe, in the movement of the stars and the turning of the earth and the changing of the seasons, and even in the cycle of human life. But human life itself is almost pure chaos. Everyone takes his stance, asserts his own rights and feelings, mistaking the motives of others, and his own. . . . Now, nobody knows the end of the life he's living, and neither do I. Don't forget I am a passenger on that ship; it's not the other people altogether who are the fools! We don't really know what is going to happen to us, and we don't know why. Quite often the best we can do is to keep our heads, and try to keep at least one line unbroken and unobstructed. Misunderstanding and separation are the natural conditions of man. We come together only at these pre-arranged meeting grounds; we were all passengers on that ship, yet at his destination, each one was alone.

INTERVIEWER: Did you find that the writing of *Ship of Fools* differed from the writing of shorter fiction?

PORTER: It's just a longer voyage, that's all. It was the question of keeping everything moving at once. There are about forty-five main characters, all taking part in each others' lives, and then there was a steerage of sugar workers, deportees. It was all a matter of deciding which should come first, in order to keep the harmonious moving forward. A novel is really like a symphony, you know, where instrument after instrument has to come in at its own time, and no other. I tried to write it as a short novel, you know, but it just wouldn't confine itself. I wrote notes and sketches. And finally I gave in. "Oh, no, this is simply going to have to be a novel," I thought. That was a real horror. But it needed a book to contain its full movement: of the sea, and the ship on the sea, and the people going around the deck, and into the ship, and up from it. That whole movement, felt as one forward motion: I can feel it while I'm reading it. I didn't "intend" it, but it took hold of me.

INTERVIEWER: As writing itself, perhaps, "took hold" of you—we began by your saying that you had never intended to be a professional anything, even a professional writer.

PORTER: I look upon literature as an art, and I practice it as an art. Of course, it is also a vocation, and a trade, and a profession, and all kinds of things; but first it's an art, and you should practice it as that, I think. I know a great many people disagree, and they are welcome to it. I think probably the important thing is to get your work done, in the way you can—and we all have our different and separate ways. But I look upon literature as an art, and I believe that if you misuse it or abuse it, it will leave you. It is not a thing that you can nail down and use as you want. You have to let it use you, too.

BARBARA THOMPSON

7. Henry Miller

Henry Miller was born in the Yorkville section of New York City on December 26, 1891. He attended City College for two months before taking a job with a cement company and entering a period of "rigorous athleticism" which lasted for seven years. Mr. Miller states that he took up with his first mistress, "a woman old enough to be my mother," when he was seventeen. In 1913 he began to travel, touring the western United States, and working at odd jobs. In 1914 he returned to New York and worked in the tailor shop owned by his father, leaving after an attempt to turn the shop over to the employees.

Mr. Miller wrote his first book, never published, in 1922, during a three-week vacation from Western Union. He dates 1925, however, as being the year in which he began writing in earnest, selling prose poems ("Mezzotints") from door to door. Beginning at this time, and for many years thereafter, he endured great poverty, depending for sustenance mainly on the patronage of others. Now his work, according to Lawrence Clark Powell, the University of California librarian, is the most widely read of any living American other than Upton Sinclair, or any dead American other than Mark Twain and Jack London.

His work includes *Tropic of Cancer* (1934), *Black Spring* (1936), *Tropic of Capricorn* (1939), *The Colossus of Maroussi* (1941), *The Wisdom of the Heart* (1941), *The Air-Conditioned Nightmare* (1945), *Remember to Remember* (1947), *The Books in My Life* (1952), *Big Sur and the Oranges of Hieronymus Bosch* (1957), *Stand Still Like the Hummingbird* (1962), and *Watercolors, Drawings and His Essay "The Angel Is My Watermark!"* (1962). For many years he has been working on *The Rosy Crucifixion*, an autobiographical trilogy, of which *Sexus* (1949), *Plexus* (1953), and Book I of *Nexus* (1960) have appeared. American editions of *Tropic of Cancer* and *Tropic of Capricorn* were published in 1961 and 1962, respectively.

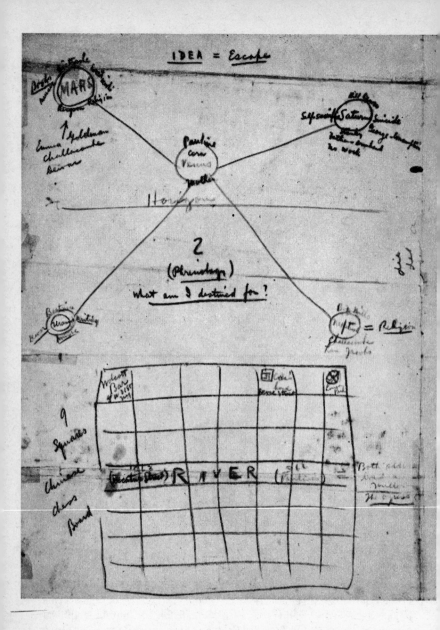

Manuscript plan of Henry Miller's Tropic of Capricorn, *"embracing planetary conjunction; topographical map of region and monuments and streets and cemeteries; fatal, or otherwise, influence of fields—according to type; Major Events; Dominant Idea; Psychological Pattern."*

SELF-PORTRAIT

Henry Miller

In 1934, Henry Miller, then aged forty-two and living in Paris, published his first book. In 1961 the book was finally published in his native land, where it promptly became a best-seller and a cause célèbre. By now the waters have been so muddied by controversy about censorship, pornography, and obscenity that one is likely to talk about anything but the book itself.

But this is nothing new. Like D. H. Lawrence, Henry Miller has long been a byword and a legend. Championed by critics and artists, venerated by pilgrims, emulated by beatniks, he is above everything else a culture hero—or villain, to those who see him as a menace to law and order. He might even be described as a folk hero: hobo, prophet, and exile, the Brooklyn boy who went to Paris when everyone else was going home, the starving bohemian enduring the plight of the creative artist in America, and in latter years the sage of Big Sur.

His life is all written out in a series of picaresque narratives in the first person historical present: his early Brooklyn years in Black Spring, *his struggles to find himself during the twenties in* Tropic of Capricorn *and the three volumes of the* Rosy Crucifixion, *his adventures in Paris during the thirties in* Tropic of Cancer.

In 1939 he went to Greece to visit Lawrence Durrell; his sojourn there provides the narrative basis of The Colossus of Maroussi. *Cut off by the war and forced to return to America, he made the year-long odyssey recorded in* The Air-Conditioned Nightmare. *Then in 1944 he settled on a magnificent empty stretch of California coast, leading the life described in* Big Sur and the Oranges of Hieronymus Bosch. *Now that his name has made Big Sur a center for pilgrimage, he has been driven out and is once again on the move.*

At seventy Henry Miller looks rather like a Buddhist monk who has swallowed a canary. He immediately impresses one as a warm and humorous human being. Despite his bald head with its halo of white hair, there is nothing old about him. His figure, surprisingly slight, is that of a young man; all his gestures and movements are young.

His voice is quite magically captivating, a mellow, resonant but quiet bass with great range and variety of modulation; he cannot be as unconscious as he seems of its musical spell. He speaks a modified Brooklynese frequently punctuated by such rhetorical pauses as "Don't you see?" and "You know?" and trailing off with a series of diminishing reflective noises, "Yas, yas . . . hmm . . . hmm . . . yas . . . hm . . . hm." To get the full flavor and honesty of the man, one must hear the recordings of that voice.

The interview was conducted in September 1961, in London.

INTERVIEWER: First of all, would you explain how you go about the actual business of writing? Do you sharpen pencils like Hemingway, or anything like that to get the motor started?

MILLER: No, not generally, no, nothing of that sort. I generally go to work right after breakfast. I sit right down to the machine. If I find I'm not able to write, I quit. But no, there are no preparatory stages as a rule.

INTERVIEWER: Are there certain times of day, certain days when you work better than others?

MILLER: I prefer the morning now, and just for two or three hours. In the beginning I used to work after midnight until dawn, but that was in the very beginning. Even after I got to Paris I found it was much better working in the morning. But then I used to work long hours. I'd work in the morning, take a nap after lunch, get up and write again, sometimes write until midnight. In the last ten or fifteen years, I've found that it isn't necessary to work that much. It's bad, in fact. You drain the reservoir.

INTERVIEWER: Would you say you write rapidly? Perlès said in *My Friend Henry Miller* that you were one of the fastest typists he knew.

MILLER: Yes, many people say that. I must make a great clatter when I write. I suppose I do write rapidly. But then that varies. I can write rapidly for a while, then there come stages where I'm stuck, and I might spend an hour on a page. But that's rather rare, because when I find I'm being bogged down, I will skip a difficult part and go on, you see, and come back to it fresh another day.

INTERVIEWER: How long would you say it took you to write one of your earlier books once you got going?

MILLER: I couldn't answer that. I could never predict how long a book would take: even now when I set out to do something I couldn't say. And it's somewhat false to take the dates the author says he began and ended a book. It doesn't mean that he was writing the book constantly during that time. Take *Sexus*, or take the whole *Rosy Crucifixion*. I think I began that in 1940, and here I'm still on it. Well, it would be absurd to say that I've been working on it all this time. I haven't even thought about it for years at a time. So how can you talk about it?

INTERVIEWER: Well, I know that you rewrote *Tropic of Cancer* several times, and that work probably gave you more trouble than any other, but of course it was the beginning. Then too, I'm wondering if writing doesn't come easier for you now?

MILLER: I think these questions are meaningless. What does it matter how long it takes to write a book? If you were to ask that of Simenon, he'd tell you very definitely. I think it takes him from four to seven weeks. He knows that he can count on it. His books have a certain length usually. Then too, he's one of those rare exceptions, a man who when he says, "Now I'm going to start and write this book," gives himself to it completely. He barricades himself, he has nothing else to think about or do. Well, my life has never been that way. I've got everything else under the sun to do while writing.

INTERVIEWER: Do you edit or change much?

MILLER: That too varies a great deal. I never do any correcting or revising while in the process of writing. Let's say I write a thing out any old way, and then, after it's cooled off—I let it rest for a while, a month or two maybe—I see it with a fresh eye. Then I have a wonderful time of it. I just go to work on it with the ax. But not always. Sometimes it comes out almost like I wanted it.

INTERVIEWER: How do you go about revising?

MILLER: When I'm revising, I use a pen and ink to make changes, cross out, insert. The manuscript looks wonderful afterwards, like a Balzac. Then I retype, and in the process of retyping I make more changes. I prefer to retype everything myself, because even when I think I've made all the changes I want, the mere mechanical business of touching the keys sharpens my thoughts, and I find myself revising while doing the finished thing.

INTERVIEWER: You mean there is something going on between you and the machine?

MILLER: Yes, in a way the machine acts as a stimulus; it's a cooperative thing.

INTERVIEWER: In *The Books in My Life*, you say that most writers and painters work in an uncomfortable position. Do you think this helps?

MILLER: I do. Somehow I've come to believe that the last thing a writer or any artist thinks about is to make himself comfortable while he's working. Perhaps the *dis*comfort is a bit of an aid or stimulus. Men who can afford to work under better conditions often choose to work under miserable conditions.

INTERVIEWER: Aren't these discomforts sometimes psychological? You take the case of Dostoevski . . . .

MILLER: Well, I don't know. I know Dostoevski was always in a miserable state, but you can't say he deliberately chose psychological discomforts. No, I doubt that strongly. I don't think anyone chooses these things, unless unconsciously. I do think many writers have what you might call a demonic nature. They are always in trouble, you know, and not only while they're writing or because they're writing, but in every aspect of their lives, with marriage, love, business, money, everything. It's all tied together, all part and parcel of the same thing. It's an aspect of the creative personality. Not all creative personalities are this way, but some are.

INTERVIEWER: You speak in one of your books of "the dictation," of being almost possessed, of having this stuff spilling out of you. How does this process work?

MILLER: Well, it happens only at rare intervals, this dictation. Someone takes over and you just copy out what is being said. It occurred most strongly with the work on D. H. Lawrence, a work I never finished—and that was because I had to do too much thinking. You see, I think it's bad to think. A writer shouldn't think much. But this was a work which required thought. I'm not very good at thinking. I work from some deep down place; and when I write, well, I don't know just exactly what's going to happen. I know what I want to write about, but I'm not concerned too much with how to say it. But in that book I was grappling with ideas; it had to have some form and meaning, and what not. I'd been on it, I suppose, a good two years. I was saturated with it, and I got obsessed and couldn't drop it. I couldn't even sleep. Well, as I say, the dictation took over most strongly with that book. It occurred with *Capricorn* too, and with parts of other books. I think the passages stand out. I don't know whether others notice or not.

INTERVIEWER: Are these the passages you call cadenzas?

MILLER: Yes, I have used that expression. The passages I refer to are tumultuous, the words fall over one another. I could go on indefinitely. Of course I think that is the way one should write all the time. You see here the whole difference, the great difference, between Western and Eastern thinking and behavior and discipline. If, say, a Zen artist is going to do something, he's had a long preparation of discipline and meditation, deep quiet thought about it, and then no thought, silence, emptiness, and so on—it might be for months, it might be for years. Then, when he begins, it's like lightning, just what he wants—it's perfect. Well, this is the way I think all art should be done. But who does it? We lead lives that are contrary to our profession.

INTERVIEWER: Is there a particular conditioning that the writer can go through, like the Zen swordsman?

MILLER: Why, of course, but who does it? Whether he means to do it or not, however, every artist does discipline himself and condition himself in one way or another. Each man has his own way. After all, most writing is done away from the typewriter, away from the desk. I'd say it occurs in the quiet, silent moments, while you're walking or shaving or playing a game or whatever, or even talking to someone you're not vitally interested in. You're working, your mind is working, on this problem in the back of your head. So, when you get to the machine it's a mere matter of transfer.

INTERVIEWER: You said earlier there's something inside you that takes over.

MILLER: Yes, of course. Listen. Who writes the great books? It isn't we who sign our names. What is an artist? He's a man who has antennae, who knows how to hook up to the currents which are in the atmosphere, in the cosmos; he merely has the facility for hooking on, as it were. Who is original? Everything that we are doing, everything that we think, exists already, and we are only intermediaries, that's all, who make use of what is in the air. Why do ideas, why do great scientific discoveries often occur in different parts of the world at the same time? The same is true of the elements that go to make up a poem or a great novel or any work of art. They are already in the air, they have not been given voice, that's all. They need *the* man, *the* interpreter, to bring them forth. Well, and it's true too, of course, that some men are ahead of their time. But today, I don't think it's the artist who is so much ahead of his time as the man of science. The artist is lagging behind, his imagination is not keeping pace with the men of science.

INTERVIEWER: How do you account for the fact that certain men are creative? Angus Wilson says that the artist writes because of a kind of trauma, that he uses his art as a kind of therapy to overcome his neurosis. Aldous Huxley, on the other hand, takes quite the opposite view, and says that the writer is pre-eminently sane, that if he has a neurosis this only adds to his handicap as a writer. Do you have any views on this subject?

MILLER: I think this varies with the individual writer. I don't think you can make such statements about writers as a whole. A writer after all is a *man*, a man like other men; he may be neurotic or he may not. I mean his neurosis, or whatever it is that they say makes his personality, doesn't account for his writing. I think it's a much more mysterious thing than that and I wouldn't even try to put my finger on it. I said that a writer was a man who had antennae; if he really knew what he was, he would be very humble. He would recognize himself as a man who was possessed of a certain faculty which he was destined to use for the service of others. He has nothing to be proud of, his name means nothing, his ego is nil, he's only an instrument in a long procession.

INTERVIEWER: When did you find that you had this faculty? When did you first start writing?

MILLER: I must have begun while I was working for the Western Union. That's certainly when I wrote the first book, at any rate.

I wrote other little things at that time too, but the real thing happened after I quit the Western Union—in 1924—when I decided I would be a writer and give myself to it completely.

INTERVIEWER: So that means that you went on writing for a period of ten years before *Tropic of Cancer* appeared in print.

MILLER: Just about, yes. Among other things I wrote two or three novels during that time. Certainly I wrote two before I wrote the *Tropic of Cancer*.

INTERVIEWER: Could you tell me a little about that period?

MILLER: Well, I've told a good deal about it in *The Rosy Crucifixion: Sexus, Plexus,* and *Nexus* all deal with that period. There will be still more in the last half of *Nexus*. I've told all about my tribulations during this period—my physical life, my difficulties. I worked like a dog and at the same time—what shall I say?—I was in a fog. I didn't know what I was doing. I couldn't see what I was getting at. I was supposed to be working on a novel, writing this great novel, but actually I wasn't getting anywhere. Sometimes I'd not write more than three or four lines a day. My wife would come home late at night and ask, "Well, how is it going?" (I never let her see what was in the machine.) I'd say, "Oh, it's going along marvelously." "Well, where are you right now?" Now, mind you, maybe of all the pages I was supposed to have written maybe I had written only three or four, but I would talk as though I'd written a hundred or a hundred and fifty pages. I would go on talking about what I had done, composing the novel as I talked to her. And she would listen and encourage me, knowing damned well that I was lying. Next day she'd come back and say, "What about that part you spoke of the other day, how is that going?" And it was all a lie, you see, a fabrication between the two of us. Wonderful, wonderful. . . .

INTERVIEWER: When did you begin to conceive of all these autobiographical volumes as a whole?

MILLER: In the year 1927 when my wife went to Europe and I was left alone. I had a job for a while in the Park Department in Queens. One day, at the end of the day, instead of going home

I was seized with this idea of planning the book of my life, and I stayed up all night doing it. I planned everything that I've written to date in about forty or fifty typewritten pages. I wrote it in notes, in telegraphic style. But the whole thing is there. My whole work from *Capricorn* on through *The Rosy Crucifixion*—except *Cancer*, which was a thing of the immediate present—is about the seven years that I had lived with this woman, from the time I met her until I left for Europe. I didn't know then when I was leaving, but I knew I was going sooner or later. That was the crucial period of my life as a writer, the period just before leaving America.

INTERVIEWER: Durrell speaks of the writer's need to make the breakthrough in his writing, to hear the sound of his own voice. Isn't that your own expression, as a matter of fact?

MILLER: Yes, I think so. Anyway, it happened for me with *Tropic of Cancer*. Up until that point you might say I was a wholly derivative writer, influenced by everyone, taking on all the tones and shades of every other writer that I had ever loved. I was a *literary* man, you might say. And I became a *non*-literary man: I cut the cord. I said, I will do only what I can do, express what I am—that's why I used the first person, why I wrote about myself. I decided to write from the standpoint of my own experience, what I knew and felt. And that was my salvation.

INTERVIEWER: What were those earlier novels like?

MILLER: I imagine you would find, naturally you *must* find, some traces of my self in them. But I felt very keenly then that one should have some sort of story, a plot to unroll; I was more concerned then with the form and the manner of doing it than with the vital thing.

INTERVIEWER: That is what you mean by the "literary" approach?

MILLER: Yes, something that's outworn and useless, that you have to slough off. The literary man had to be killed off. Naturally you don't kill that man, he's a very vital element of your self as a writer, and certainly every artist is fascinated with technique. But the other thing in writing is *you*. The point I discovered is that the best technique is none at all. I never feel that I must adhere to any particular manner of approach. I try to remain open and flexible, ready to turn with the wind or with the current of thought. That's my stance, my technique, if you will, to be flexible and alert, to use whatever I think good at the moment.

INTERVIEWER: In "An Open Letter to Surrealists Everywhere" you say, "I was writing surrealistically in America before I ever heard the word." Now, what do you mean by surrealism?

MILLER: When I was living in Paris, we had an expression, a very American one, which in a way explains it better than anything else. We used to say, "Let's take the lead." That meant going off the deep end, diving into the unconscious, just obeying your instincts, following your impulses, of the heart, or the guts, or whatever you want to call it. But that's my way of putting it, that isn't really surrealist doctrine; that wouldn't hold water, I'm afraid, with an André Breton. However, the French standpoint, the doctrinaire standpoint, didn't mean too much to me. All I cared about was that I found in it another means of expression, an added one, a heightened one, but one to be used very judiciously. When the well-known surrealists employed this technique, they did it too deliberately, it seemed to me. It became unintelligible, it served no purpose. Once one loses all intelligibility, one is lost, I think.

INTERVIEWER: Is surrealism what you mean by the phrase "into the night life"?

MILLER: Yes, there it was primarily the dream. The surrealists make use of the dream, and of course that's always a marvelous fecund aspect of experience. Consciously or unconsciously, all writers employ the dream, even when they're not surrealists. The waking mind, you see, is the least serviceable in the arts. In the process of writing one is struggling to bring out what is unknown to himself. To put down merely what one is conscious of means nothing, really, gets one nowhere. Anybody can do that with a little practice, anybody can become that kind of writer.

INTERVIEWER: You have called Lewis Carroll a surrealist, and his name suggests the kind of jabberwocky which you use occasionally. . . .

MILLER: Yes, yes, of course Lewis Carroll is a writer I love. I would give my right arm to have written his books, or to be able to come anywhere near doing what he did. When I finish my project, if I continue writing, I would love to write sheer nonsense.

INTERVIEWER: What about dadaism? Did you ever get into that?

MILLER: Yes, dadaism was even more important to me than surrealism. The dadaist movement was something truly revolutionary. It was a deliberate conscious effort to turn the tables upside down, to show the absolute insanity of our present-day life, the worthlessness of all our values. There were wonderful men in the dadaist movement, and they all had a sense of humor. It was something to make you laugh, but also to make you think.

INTERVIEWER: It seems to me that in *Black Spring* you came pretty close to dadaism.

MILLER: No doubt. I was most impressionable then. I was open to everything that was going on when I reached Europe. Some things I already knew about in America, it's true. *Transition* came to us in America; Jolas was marvelous in selecting those strange bizarre writers and artists we had never heard of. Then I remember, for example, going to the Armory Show to see Marcel Duchamp's "Nude Descending a Staircase," and many other marvelous things. I was infatuated, intoxicated. All this was what I was looking for, it seemed so familiar to me.

INTERVIEWER: You've always been better understood and appreciated in Europe than in America or England. How do you account for this?

MILLER: Well, in the first place I didn't have much chance to be understood in America because my books weren't in print there. But aside from that, though I am one hundred per cent American (and I know it more and more every day), still I had better contact with Europeans. I was able to talk to them, express my thoughts more easily, be more quickly understood. I had a greater rapport with them than with Americans.

INTERVIEWER: In your book on Patchen you say that in America the artist will never be accepted unless he compromises himself. Do you still feel that way?

MILLER: Yes, more strongly than ever. I feel that America is essentially against the artist, that the enemy of America is the artist, because he stands for individuality and creativeness, and that's *un*-American somehow. I think that of all countries—we have to overlook the communist countries of course—America is the most mechanized, robotized, of all.

INTERVIEWER: What did you find in Paris in the thirties that you couldn't find in America?

MILLER: For one thing, I suppose I found a freedom such as I never knew in America. I found contact with people so much easier—that is, the people that I enjoyed talking to. I met more of my own kind there. Above all I felt that I was tolerated. I didn't ask to be understood or accepted. To be tolerated was enough. In America I never felt that. But then, Europe was a new world to me. I suppose it might have been good almost anywhere—just to be in some other, different world, an alien. Because all my life, really, and this is part of my psychological—what shall I say?—strangeness, I've liked only what is alien.

INTERVIEWER: In other words, if you'd gone to Greece in 1930 instead of 1940 you might have found the same thing?

MILLER: I might not have found the same thing, but I would have found the means of self-expression, of self-liberation there. I may not have become the kind of writer that I am now, but I feel I would have found myself. In America I was in danger of going mad, or committing suicide. I felt completely isolated.

INTERVIEWER: How about Big Sur? Did you find a congenial environment there?

MILLER: Oh, no, there was nothing there, except nature. I was alone, which was what I wanted. I stayed there because it was an isolated spot. I had already learned to write no matter where I lived. It was a wonderful change, Big Sur. I then definitely put the cities behind me. I'd had my fill of city life. Of course I never chose Big Sur, you understand. I was dumped on the road there one day by a friend. As he left me he said, "You go and see such and such a person, and she'll put you up for the night or a week. It's a wonderful country, I think you'll like it." And that's how I fell into it. I never had heard of Big Sur before. I knew of Point Sur because I'd read Robinson Jeffers. I read his *Women at Point Sur* in the Café Rotonde in Paris—I'll never forget it.

INTERVIEWER: Isn't it surprising that you should have gone out to nature that way, since you'd always been a city man?

MILLER: Well, you see, I have a Chinese nature. You know, in ancient China, when the artist or the philosopher began to get old, he retired to the country. To live and meditate in peace.

INTERVIEWER: But in your case it was something of a coincidence?

MILLER: Entirely. But, you see, everything of significance in my life has happened that way—by pure hazard. Of course I don't believe that either. I believe there always was a purpose, that it was destined to be that way. The explanation lies in my horoscope—that would be my frank answer. To me it's all quite clear.

INTERVIEWER: Why did you never go back to Paris to live?

MILLER: For several reasons. In the first place, I got married soon after I reached Big Sur; and then I had children; and then I had no money; and then too I fell in love with Big Sur. I had no desire to resume my Paris life, it was finished. Most of my friends were gone, the war had broken up everything.

INTERVIEWER: Gertrude Stein says that living in France purified her English because she didn't use the language in daily life, and this made her the stylist that she is. Did living in Paris have the same effect on you?

MILLER: Not exactly, but I understand what she meant. Of course I spoke much more English while there than Gertrude Stein did. Less French, in other words. Still, I was saturated with French all the time. Hearing another language daily sharpens your own language for you, makes you aware of shades and nuances you never suspected. Also, there comes a slight forgetting which makes you hunger to be able to recapture certain phrases and expressions. You become more conscious of your own language.

INTERVIEWER: Did you ever have anything to do with Gertrude Stein or her set?

MILLER: No, nothing whatever. Never met her, no, knew nobody belonging to her set. But then I didn't know much of any set, you might say. I was always a lone wolf, always against groups and sets and sects and cults and isms and so on. I knew a number of surrealists, but I never was a member of the surrealist group or any group.

INTERVIEWER: Didn't you know any American writers in Paris?

MILLER: I knew Walter Lowenfels, Samuel Putnam, Michael Fraenkel. Sherwood Anderson, Dos Passos, Steinbeck, and Saroyan I met later, in America. I met them only a few times, no more. I never had any real connection with them. Of all the American writers that I have met, Sherwood Anderson stands out as the one I liked most. Dos Passos was a warm, wonderful chap, but Sherwood Anderson—well, I had been in love with his work, his style, his language, from the beginning. And I liked him as a man—although we were completely at loggerheads about most things, especially America. He loved America, he knew it intimately, he loved the people and everything about America. I was the contrary. But I loved to hear what he had to say about America.

INTERVIEWER: Have you known many English writers? You've had a long-standing friendship, haven't you, with Durrell and Powys?

MILLER: Durrell, sure, but then I hardly think of him as an English writer. I think of him as *un*-British, completely. John Cowper Powys, of course, had the most tremendous influence on me; but then, I never knew him, never cultivated him. I didn't dare! I was a midget and he was a giant, you see. He was my god, my mentor, my idol. I had run across him when I was in my early twenties. He used to lecture then in Labor temples in New York, Cooper Union and such places. It cost only ten cents to hear him speak. Some thirty years later I went to see him in Wales, and found to my surprise that he knew my work. He seemed to have great respect for my work—which surprised me even more.

INTERVIEWER: You knew Orwell in those days too?

MILLER: Orwell I met maybe two or three times, on his visits to Paris. I wouldn't call him a friend, just a passing acquaintance. But I was crazy about his book *Down and Out in Paris and London*; I think it's a classic. For me it's still his best book. Though he was a wonderful chap in his way, Orwell, in the end I thought him stupid. He was like so many English people, an idealist, and, it seemed to me, a foolish idealist. A man of principle, as we say. Men of principle bore me.

INTERVIEWER: You don't have much use for politics?

MILLER: None whatever. I regard politics as a thoroughly foul, rotten world. We get nowhere through politics. It debases everything.

INTERVIEWER: Even political idealism of Orwell's sort?

MILLER: Especially that! The idealists in politics lack a sense of reality. And a politician must be a realist above all. These people with ideals and principles, they're all at sea, in my opinion. One has to be a lowbrow, a bit of a murderer, to be a politician, ready and willing to see people sacrificed, slaughtered, for the sake of an idea, whether a good one or a bad one. I mean, those are the ones who flourish.

INTERVIEWER: What about some of the great writers of the past that have particularly attracted you? You've done studies of Balzac and Rimbaud and Lawrence. Would you say there's a particular type of writer that draws you?

MILLER: That's hard to say, the writers I love are so diverse. They are the writers who are more than writers. They have this mysterious X quality which is metaphysical, occult, or what not— I don't know what term to use—this little extra something beyond the confines of literature. You see, people read to be amused, to pass the time, or to be instructed. Now I never read to pass the time, I never read to be instructed; I read to be taken out of myself, to become ecstatic. I'm always looking for the author who can lift me out of myself.

INTERVIEWER: Can you say why you never finished your book on D. H. Lawrence?

MILLER: Yes, it's very simple. The further I got into the book, the less I understood what I was doing. I found myself in a mass of contradictions. I found that I didn't really know who Lawrence was, I couldn't place him, I couldn't put my finger on him, I just couldn't cope with him after a while. I got completely bewildered. I'd got myself into a jungle, and I couldn't get out. So I abandoned the work.

INTERVIEWER: You didn't have this trouble with Rimbaud, though?

MILLER: No, oddly enough. He's more of an enigma as a personality, true. But then, I didn't do so much grappling with ideas in the Rimbaud book. Lawrence was entirely a man of ideas, and he hung his literature on the rack of these ideas.

INTERVIEWER: You don't necessarily subscribe to Lawrence's ideas, do you?

MILLER: No, not altogether, but I do admire his quest, his search, his struggle. And there are many things in Lawrence I agree with. On the other hand, there are many things I laugh about in Lawrence, things which seem absurd and stupid, foolish. I have a better perspective of him today, but I no longer find it important to say anything about him. Then he meant something to me, I was completely in his grip.

INTERVIEWER: Well, now, I suppose we have to go into this question of pornography and obscenity. I hope you don't mind. After all, you're considered an authority on the subject. Didn't you say somewhere, "I am for obscenity and against pornography"?

MILLER: Well, it's very simple. The obscene would be the forthright, and pornography would be the roundabout. I believe in saying the truth, coming out with it cold, shocking if necessary, not disguising it. In other words, obscenity is a cleansing process, whereas pornography only adds to the murk.

INTERVIEWER: Cleansing in what sense?

MILLER: Whenever a taboo is broken, something good happens, something vitalizing.

INTERVIEWER: All taboos are bad?

MILLER: Not among primitive peoples. There is reason for the taboo in primitive life, but not in our life, not in civilized communities. The taboo then is dangerous and unhealthy. You see, civilized peoples don't live according to moral codes or principles of any kind. We speak about them, we pay lip service to them, but nobody believes in them. Nobody practices these rules, they have no place in our lives. Taboos after all are only hangovers, the product of diseased minds, you might say, of fearsome people who hadn't the courage to live and who under the guise of morality and religion have imposed these things upon us. I see the world, the civilized world, as largely irreligious. The religion in force among civilized people is always false and hypocritical, the very opposite of what the initiators of any religion really meant.

INTERVIEWER: Still, you yourself have been called a very religious man.

MILLER: Yes, but without espousing any religion. What does that mean? That means simply having a reverence for life, being on the side of life instead of death. Again, the word "civilization" to my mind is coupled with death. When I use the word, I see civilization as a crippling, thwarting thing, a stultifying thing. For me it was always so. I don't believe in the golden ages, you see. What I mean is that it was a golden age for a very few people, for a select few, but the masses were always in misery, they were superstitious, they were ignorant, they were downtrodden, they were strangled by Church and State. I'm still a great believer in Spengler, and there you have it all. He makes the antithesis between culture and civilization. Civilization is the arteriosclerosis of culture.

INTERVIEWER: Now, Durrell in that article he wrote about you for *Horizon* about ten years ago speaks of obscenity as technique. Do you regard obscenity as a technique?

MILLER: I think I know what he meant. I think he meant a shock technique. Well, I may have used it thus unconsciously, but I never deliberately used it that way. I employed obscenity as naturally as I would any other way of speaking. It was like breathing, it was part of my whole rhythm. There were moments when you were obscene, and then there were other moments. I don't think obscenity is the most important element by any means. But it's a very important one, and it must not be denied, overlooked, or suppressed.

INTERVIEWER: It might also be exaggerated. . . .

MILLER: It could be, but what harm if it were? What are we so worried about, what is there to fear? Words, words—what is there to fear in them? Or in ideas? Supposing they are revolting, are we cowards? Haven't we faced all manner of things, haven't we been on the edge of destruction time and again through war, disease, pestilence, famine? What are we threatened with by the exaggerated use of obscenity? Where's the danger?

INTERVIEWER: You have commented that obscenity is mild by comparison to the sort of violence that is very common in American paperbacks.

MILLER: Yes, all this perverse sadistic writing is abhorrent to me. I've always said mine is healthy because it's joyous and natural. I never express anything that people are not saying and doing all the time. Where did I get it from? I didn't pick it out of a hat. It's all around us, we breathe it every day. People simply refuse to acknowledge it. Between the printed word and the spoken word—what difference? You know, we didn't always have this taboo. There was a time in English literature when most anything was permitted. It's only in the last two or three hundred years that we've had this queasy attitude.

INTERVIEWER: Well, even in Chaucer you won't find all the words you find in Henry Miller.

MILLER: But you do find plenty of joyous, healthy naturalism, plenty of freedom of speech.

INTERVIEWER: What do you think of the comment Durrell made in the interview he did for the *Paris Review*? He said that in retrospect he found parts of the *Black Book* too obscene now.

MILLER: Did he? Well, let me say that those are the parts I relish most. I thought they were marvelous when I first read them, and I still think so today. Maybe he was only spoofing, Durrell.

INTERVIEWER: Why have you written so much about sex? What does sex mean for you? Does it mean something special?

MILLER: That's hard to answer. You know, I think I have written as much of what my hostile critics call "flapdoodle"— that is, metaphysical nonsense—as I have about sex. Only they choose to look at the sex. No, I can't answer that question, except to say that it's played a great part in my life. I've led a good rich sexual life, and I don't see why it should be left out.

INTERVIEWER: Did it have anything to do with your break with the life you were leading in New York?

MILLER: No, I don't think so. But one becomes aware in France, after having lived in America, that sex pervades the air. It's there all around you, like a fluid. Now I don't doubt that Americans enter into sexual relations as strongly, deeply, and multifariously as any other people, but it's not in the atmosphere around you, somehow. Then too, in France woman plays a bigger role in man's life. She has a better standing there, she's taken into consideration, she's talked to like a person, not just as a wife or a mistress or whatnot. Besides the Frenchman prefers to be in the company of women. In England and America, men seem to enjoy being among themselves.

INTERVIEWER: Still, your life in the Villa Seurat was a very masculine kind of life.

MILLER: To be sure, but there were always women about. I had many friends, it's true, but I've had great friendships all through my life. That's another thing in my horoscope: I'm a man who is destined to make friends. That is probably the biggest factor in my life, and perhaps I ought to say something about it. When I started writing I began to realize how much I was indebted to others. I have been helped all my life, by friends and strangers too. What did I need money for, when I had friends? What does anyone want, if he has friends? I've had many friends, great friends, lifelong friends. I'm only now losing them through death.

INTERVIEWER: Let's leave sex and talk a little about painting. Now, you sensed this urge to write, about the middle of the twenties; did you start painting about the same time?

MILLER: Very shortly after. I think it was 1927 or –8 that I began. But not with the same seriousness, naturally. The desire to write was a big thing in my life, a very big thing. If I didn't begin writing till quite late—I was thirty-three when I definitely began—it wasn't that I had never thought about it. I had put it too far above me, I didn't think I had the ability, I didn't believe in myself as a writer, as an artist. I didn't dare to think I could be such a person, you see. Well, I didn't take to painting in that way. I discovered that there was another side of me that I could use. It gave me pleasure to paint, it was recreation, it was a rest from other things.

INTERVIEWER: Is it still a kind of game with you?

MILLER: Oh yes, nothing more.

INTERVIEWER: Don't you find some kind of fundamental connection, though, between the arts?

MILLER: Absolutely. If you're creative in one way, you're creative in another. Originally, you know, music was the biggest thing with me. I played the piano, I hoped to be a good pianist, but I didn't have the talent for it. Still, I was saturated with music. I might even say that music means more to me than writing or painting. It's there in the back of my head all the time.

INTERVIEWER: You were very keen on jazz at one time.

MILLER: So I was. I'm not so keen today. I think jazz quite

empty now. It's too limited. Just as I deplore what happened to the movies, so I deplore the fate of jazz. It becomes more and more automatic, it doesn't evolve enough, it's not enriching. It's like having a cocktail. I need wine and beer, champagne and brandy too.

INTERVIEWER: You wrote several essays in the thirties on the art of the film. Did you ever get a chance to practice that art?

MILLER: No, but I still hope to meet the man who will give me a chance. What I deplore most is that the medium of the film has never been properly exploited. It's a poetic medium with all sorts of possibilities. Just think of the element of dream and fantasy. But how often do we get it? Now and then a little touch of it, and we're agape. And think of all the technical devices at our command. But my God, we haven't even begun to use them. We could have incredible marvels, wonders, limitless joy and beauty. And what do we get? Sheer crap. The film is the freest of all media, you can do marvels with it. In fact I would welcome the day when the film would displace literature, when there'd be no more need to read. You remember faces in films, and gestures, as you never do when you read a book. If the film can hold you at all, you give yourself to it completely. Even when you listen to music, it's not like that. You go to the concert hall and the atmosphere is bad, the people are yawning, or falling asleep, the program is too long, it hasn't got the things you like, and so on. You know what I mean. But in the cinema, sitting there in the dark, the images coming and going, it's like a rain of meteorites hitting you.

INTERVIEWER: What's this about a film version of *Tropic of Cancer?*

MILLER: Well, there are rumors of it. There have been offers made, but I can't see how anyone could possibly make a film of that book.

INTERVIEWER: Would you like to do it yourself?

MILLER: No, I wouldn't because I think it's almost impossible to make a film of that book. I don't see the story there, for one thing. And then, so much depends on the language. Maybe one could get away with this tropical language in Japanese or Turkish. I can't see it being rendered in English, can you? The film is so definitely a dramatic, plastic medium, anyhow, a thing of images.

INTERVIEWER: You were a judge at the Cannes Film Festival, weren't you, last year?

MILLER: Yes, though I was rather a dubious choice. The French probably did it to show their appreciation of my work. Of course they knew I was a cineast, but when a reporter asked me if I still liked films, I had to say I hardly ever see them any more. For fifteen years now I've seen very few good movies. But sure, I'm still a cineast at heart.

INTERVIEWER: Well, now you've written a play. How do you feel about the medium?

MILLER: It's a medium I always wished to tackle, but I never had the courage. In *Nexus*, when I'm living that underground life and struggling to write, there's a description, a very vivid one, of how I tried to write a play about the life we were then living. I never finished it. I think I got as far as the first act. I had tacked an elaborate plan of it on the wall, and I could talk about it marvelously, but I couldn't bring it off. The play I've just written fell out of the hat, so to speak. I was in a peculiar state of mind: I had nothing to do, nowhere to go, nothing much to eat, everybody was away, and so I said why not sit down and try it? I had no idea what I was doing when I began, the words just came to me, I didn't struggle with it. There was hardly any effort involved.

INTERVIEWER: What's it all about?

MILLER: About everything and nothing. I don't think it matters much what it's about, really. It's a kind of farce or burlesque, with surrealistic elements. And there's music, incidental music, which comes from the jukebox and over the air. I don't think it has much importance. The most I can say about it is that you won't go to sleep if you see it.

INTERVIEWER: Do you think you'll go on and write more plays?

MILLER: I hope so, yes. The next one will be a tragedy, or a comedy to make one weep.

INTERVIEWER: What else are you writing now?

MILLER: I'm not writing anything else.

INTERVIEWER: Aren't you going on with volume two of *Nexus*?

MILLER: Yes, sure, that's what I *have* to do. But I haven't begun it yet. I made several attempts but gave up.

INTERVIEWER: You *have* to do it, you say?

MILLER: Well, yes, in a sense I must finish my project, the project I laid out in 1927. This is the end of it, you see. I think part of my delay in finishing it is that I don't want to bring the work to an end. It means that I will have to turn over, take a new tack, discover a new field, as it were. Because I no longer want to write about my personal experiences. I wrote all these autobiographical books not because I think myself such an important person but—this will make you laugh—because I thought when I began that I was telling the story of the most tragic suffering any man had endured. As I got on with it I realized that I was only an amateur at suffering. Certainly I had my full share of it, but I no longer think it was so terrible. That's why I called the trilogy *The Rosy Crucifixion*. I discovered that this suffering was good for me, that it opened the way to a joyous life, through acceptance of the suffering. When a man is crucified, when he dies to himself, the heart opens up like a flower. Of course you don't die, nobody dies, death doesn't exist, you only reach a new level of vision, a new realm of consciousness, a new unknown world. Just as you don't know where you came from, so you don't know where you're going. But that there is something there, before and after, I firmly believe.

INTERVIEWER: How does it feel to be a best-seller after enduring the plight of the creative artist all these years?

MILLER: I really have no feelings about it. It's unreal to me, the whole thing. I don't find myself involved. In fact I rather dislike it. It gives me no pleasure. All I see is more disruption in my life, more intrusions, more nonsense. People are concerned

about something which no longer concerns me. That book doesn't
mean anything to me any more. People think because they're all
worked up about it that I am too. They think it's a great thing
for me that I'm accepted at last. Well, I feel that I'd been accepted long before, at least by those I cared to be accepted by.
To be accepted by the mob doesn't mean a thing to me. In fact
it's rather painful. Because I'm being accepted for the wrong reasons. It's a sensational affair, it doesn't mean that I am appreciated for my true worth.

INTERVIEWER: But this is part of the recognition that you've
always known would come to you.

MILLER: Yes, of course. But then, don't you see, the only real
recognition comes from those who are on the same level with you,
from your peers. That's the only kind that matters, and I've had
that. I've had it for years now.

INTERVIEWER: Which of your books do you think came off
best?

MILLER: I always say *The Colossus of Maroussi*.

INTERVIEWER: The critics, most of them, say *Cancer* is your
great book.

MILLER: Well, on rereading *Cancer* I found that it was a much
better book than I had thought. I liked it. I was amazed, in fact.
I hadn't looked at it for many years, you know. I think it's a very
good book, that it has lasting qualities. But the *Colossus* was
written from some other level of my being. What I like about it
is that it's a joyous book, it expresses joy, it gives joy.

INTERVIEWER: What ever happened to *Draco and the Ecliptic*
which you announced many years ago?

MILLER: Nothing. That's been forgotten, though it is always
possible that I may one day write that book. My thought was to
write a very slim work, explaining what I had been trying to do in
writing all these books about my life. In other words, to forget
what I had written and try once again to explain what I had
hoped to do. In that way perhaps to give the significance of the
work from the author's standpoint. You see, the author's stand-

point is only one of many, and his idea of the significance of his own work is lost in the welter of other voices. Does he know his own work as well as he imagines? I rather think not. I rather think he's like a medium who, when he comes out of his trance, is amazed at what he's said and done.

GEORGE WICKES

8. *Aldous Huxley*

Aldous Huxley was born in Godalming, in Surrey, England, on July 26, 1894—the third son of Leonard Huxley (the eldest son and biographer of the scientist, Thomas Huxley) and Julia Arnold (Matthew Arnold's niece). He studied at Eton until he was forced to leave by an eye affliction (keratitis) which kept him nearly blind for several years. Equipped with a magnifying glass, he went to Oxford and took a degree in English literature. In 1919 he became associated with the *Athenaeum* and its editor, J. Middleton Murry. In this period Huxley began the writing of poems, essays, and historical pieces which he has continued throughout his literary career. But it was as a satirical novelist that he first caught the public fancy. *Crome Yellow* appeared in 1921, the first of an impressive output including *Antic Hay* (1923), *Those Barren Leaves* (1925), *Point Counter Point* (1928), *Brave New World* (1932), *Eyeless in Gaza* (1936), and *After Many a Summer Dies the Swan* (1939).

Mr. Huxley has written about the drug mescalin: *The Doors of Perception* (1954); the horrors of nuclear war: *Ape and Essence* (1948); and modern technology: *Science, Liberty and Peace* (1946). Recently he returned to the themes of his most popular book in *Brave New World Revisited* (1958) and *Island* (1962)—the work-in-progress that he speaks of in the interview. For many years he has lived in the United States.

"Attention," a voice began to call, and it was as though an

oboe had suddenly become articulate. "Attention," it repeated in the ~~the~~

same high, nasal monotone. "Attention. ~~Attention.~~"

Lying there like a corpse in the dead leaves, ~~his hair matted, and his~~ ~~his thin stony features~~ *his face grotesquely scarred and bruised,* ~~face~~ his clothes in rags and muddy Will Farnaby awoke with a start.

Molly had called him. Time to get up. Time to get dressed. Mustn't be

late at the office.

"Thank you, darling," he said and sat up. A sharp pain stabbed at

his right knee and there were other kinds of pain in his back, ~~and neck~~ *his arms, his fore-head*

"Attention," the voice insisted without the slightest change of

tone. Leaning on one elbow, Will looked about him and saw with bewilder-

ment, not ~~not~~ the ~~familiar~~ grey wallpaper and orange curtains of his ~~Lamb~~

~~&~~ London bedroom, but a glade among trees and the long shadows and

~~slanting lights of early morning in a forest. And~~ *And anyhow,*

~~"Attention. Attention."~~

~~And the voice wasn't Molly's~~ ~~was~~ *even* ~~Babs's: for the grey~~

re suddenly ~~he now remembered with a ~~pangxxxxxxxxxxx~~ that fa-~~

~~wallpaper and the orange curtains, xxxxxxxxxxxxxxxxxx~~

horribly sinking smel

anyhow the grey wallpaper & the orange ~~now at top familiar anxiety sinking~~ of guilt at the pit of his

curtains ~~stomach, were an anachronism. It was in~~ on Babs's shell-pink ~~bedroom that hax~~ ~~ma~~ ~~zx~~ ~~h~~

he had fearfully been opening his eyes in... ~~faxthaxhxxxxhxxxxxxxxx~~ ~~hought~~ ~~hxxhxxxxxxx~~ *it* *opening* ~~was~~ *had left him*

~~makingxxxxxxxxxxxx~~

~~he had been opening~~ ~~his eyes. And now. And now Babs had gone.~~

~~towards~~ ~~Babs~~ ~~sickening~~ an anguish about the heart,

warm To the guilt in the stomach was added ~~axxkmxpxnxnxxxx~~ ~~xpxxmxxxxxxxx~~

~~if the~~

thought ~~hxxxxx~~ constriction in the throat.

~~not that~~

"Attention. Attention."

~~"Attention. Attention."~~

~~Wat the devil? Was he still dreaming? Had he~~ ~~suddenly~~ ~~gone~~ ~~mad?~~

The arm that supported him began to tremble. Overcome with an annihilating

fatigue, he let himself fall back into the leaves Through the pain

on earth

and the weakness he wondered ~~vaguely,~~ confusedly where he was and how he

had got here. Not that it really ~~mattered.~~ At the moment nothing really

this

mattered ~~except~~ ~~his~~ miserable body ~~of his.~~ God, how it hurt! And he

~~was hungry, he was parched with thirst.~~ All the same, as a matter merely

Part of a manuscript by Aldous Huxley.

PAUL DARROW

Aldous Huxley

Among serious novelists, Aldous Huxley is surely the wittiest and most irreverent. Ever since the early twenties, his name has been a byword for a particular kind of social satire; in fact, he has immortalized in satire a whole period and a way of life. In addition to his ten novels, Huxley has written, during the course of an extremely prolific career, poetry, drama, essays, travel, biography, and history.

Descended from two of the most eminent Victorian families, he inherited science and letters from his grandfather T. H. Huxley and his great-uncle Matthew Arnold respectively. He absorbed both strains in an erudition so unlikely that it has sometimes been regarded as a kind of literary gamesmanship. (In conversation his learning comes out spontaneously, without the slightest hint of premeditation; if someone raises the topic of Victorian gastronomy, for example, Huxley will recite a typical daily menu of Prince Edward, meal by meal, course by course, down to the last crumb.) The plain fact is that Aldous Huxley is one of the most prodigiously learned writers not merely of this century but of all time.

After Eton and Balliol, he became a member of the postwar intellectual upper crust, the society he set out to vivisect and anatomize. He first made his name with such brilliant satires as Antic Hay *and* Point Counter Point, *writing in the process part of the social history of the twenties. In the thirties he wrote his most influential novel,* Brave New World, *combining satire and science fiction in the most successful of futuristic utopias. Since 1937, when he settled in Southern California, he has written fewer novels and turned his attention more to philosophy, history, and mysticism. Although remembered best for his early satires, he is still productive and provocative as ever.*

It is rather odd to find Aldous Huxley in a suburb of Los Angeles called Hollywoodland. He lives in an unpretentious hilltop house that suggests the Tudor period of American real-estate history. On a clear day he can look out across miles of cluttered, sprawling city at a broad sweep of the Pacific. Behind him dry brown hills rise to a monstrous sign that dominates the horizon, proclaiming HOLLYWOODLAND *in aluminum letters twenty feet high.*

Mr. Huxley is a very tall man—he must be six feet four—and, though lean, very broad across the shoulders. He carries his years lightly indeed; in fact he moves so quietly as to appear weightless, almost wraithlike. His eyesight is limited, but he seems to find his way about instinctively, without touching anything.

In manner and speech he is very gentle. Where one might have been led to expect the biting satirist or the vague mystic, one is impressed instead by how quiet and gentle he is on the one hand, how sensible and down-to-earth on the other. His manner is reflected in his lean, gray, emaciated face: attentive, reflective, and for the most part unsmiling. He listens patiently while others speak, then answers deliberately.

INTERVIEWERS: Would you tell us something first about the way you work?

HUXLEY: I work regularly. I always work in the mornings, and then again a little bit before dinner. I'm not one of those who work at night. I prefer to read at night. I usually work four or five hours a day. I keep at it as long as I can, until I feel myself going stale. Sometimes, when I bog down, I start reading—fiction or psychology or history, it doesn't much matter what—not to borrow ideas or materials, but simply to get started again. Almost anything will do the trick.

INTERVIEWERS: Do you do much rewriting?

HUXLEY: Generally, I write everything many times over. All my thoughts are second thoughts. And I correct each page a great deal, or rewrite it several times as I go along.

INTERVIEWERS: Do you keep a notebook, like certain characters in your novels?

HUXLEY: No, I don't keep notebooks. I have occasionally kept diaries for short periods, but I'm very lazy, I mostly don't. One should keep notebooks, I think, but I haven't.

INTERVIEWERS: Do you block out chapters or plan the over-all structure when you start out on a novel?

HUXLEY: No, I work away a chapter at a time, finding my way as I go. I know very dimly when I start what's going to happen. I just have a very general idea, and then the thing develops as I write. Sometimes—it's happened to me more than once—I will write a great deal, then find it just doesn't work, and have to throw the whole thing away. I like to have a chapter finished before I begin on the next one. But I'm never entirely certain what's going to happen in the next chapter until I've worked it out. Things come to me in driblets, and when the driblets come I have to work hard to make them into something coherent.

INTERVIEWERS: Is the process pleasant or painful?

HUXLEY: Oh, it's not painful, though it is hard work. Writing is a very absorbing occupation and sometimes exhausting. But

I've always considered myself very lucky to be able to make a living at something I enjoy doing. So few people can.

INTERVIEWERS: Do you ever use maps or charts or diagrams to guide you in your writing?

HUXLEY: No, I don't use anything of that sort, though I do read up a good deal on my subject. Geography books can be a great help in keeping things straight. I had no trouble finding my way around the English part of *Brave New World*, but I had to do an enormous amount of reading up on New Mexico, because I'd never been there. I read all sorts of Smithsonian reports on the place and then did the best I could to imagine it. I didn't actually go there until six years later, in 1937, when we visited Frieda Lawrence.

INTERVIEWERS: When you start out on a novel, what sort of a general idea do you have? How did you begin *Brave New World*, for example?

HUXLEY: Well, that started out as a parody of H. G. Wells' *Men Like Gods*, but gradually it got out of hand and turned into something quite different from what I'd originally intended. As I became more and more interested in the subject, I wandered farther and farther from my original purpose.

INTERVIEWERS: What are you working on now?

HUXLEY: At the moment I'm writing a rather peculiar kind of fiction. It's a kind of fantasy, a kind of reverse *Brave New World*, about a society in which real efforts are made to realize human potentialities. I want to show how humanity can make the best of both Eastern and Western worlds. So the setting is an imaginary island between Ceylon and Sumatra, at a meeting place of Indian and Chinese influence. One of my principal characters is, like Darwin and my grandfather, a young scientist on one of those scientific expeditions the British Admiralty sent out in the 1840s; he's a Scotch doctor, who rather resembles James Esdaile, the man who introduced hypnosis into medicine. And then, as in *News from Nowhere* and other utopias, I have another intruder from the outside world, whose guided tour provides a means of describing the society. Unfortunately, he's also the serpent in the garden, looking enviously at this happy, prosperous state. I haven't worked out the ending yet, but I'm afraid it must end with paradise lost —if one is to be realistic.

INTERVIEWERS: In the 1946 preface to *Brave New World* you make certain remarks that seem to prefigure this new utopia. Was the work already incubating then?

HUXLEY: Yes, the general notion was in the back of my mind at that time, and it has preoccupied me a good deal ever since— though not necessarily as the theme for a novel. For a long time I had been thinking a great deal about various ways of realizing human potentialities; then about three years ago I decided to write these ideas into a novel. It's gone very slowly because I've had to struggle with the fable, the framework to carry the expository part. I know what I want to say clearly enough; the problem is how to embody the ideas. Of course, you can always talk them out in dialogue, but you can't have your characters talking indef- initely without becoming transparent—and tiresome. Then there's always the problem of point of view: who's going to tell the story or live the experiences? I've had a great deal of trouble working out the plot and rearranging sections that I've already written. Now I think I can see my way clear to the end. But I'm afraid it's getting hopelessly long. I'm not sure what I'm going to do with it all.

INTERVIEWERS: Some writers hesitate to talk about their work in progress for fear they'll talk it away. You aren't afraid of that?

HUXLEY: No, I don't mind talking about my writing at all. In fact, it might be a good practice; it might give me a clearer notion of what I was trying to do. I've never discussed my writing with others much, but I don't believe it can do any harm. I don't think that there's any risk that ideas or materials will evaporate.

INTERVIEWERS: Some writers—Virginia Woolf, for example— have been painfully sensitive to criticism. Have you been much affected by your critics?

HUXLEY: No, they've never had any effect on me, for the simple reason that I've never read them. I've never made a point of writing for any particular person or audience; I've simply tried to do the best job I could and let it go at that. The critics don't interest me because they're concerned with what's past and done, while I'm concerned with what comes next. I've never reread my early novels, for example. Perhaps I should read them one of these days.

INTERVIEWERS: How did you happen to start writing? Do you remember?

HUXLEY: I started writing when I was seventeen, during a period when I was almost totally blind and could hardly do anything else. I typed out a novel by the touch system; I couldn't even read it. I've no idea what's become of it; I'd be curious to see it now, but it's lost. My aunt, Mrs. Humphry Ward, was a kind of literary godmother to me. I used to have long talks with her about writing; she gave me no end of sound advice. She was a very sound writer herself, rolled off her plots like sections of macadamized road. She had a curious practice: every time she started work on a new novel, she read Diderot's *Le Neveu de Rameau*. It seemed to act as a kind of trigger or release mechanism. Then later, during the war and after, I met a great many writers through Lady Ottoline Morrell. She used to invite all kinds of people out to her country house. I met Katherine Mansfield there, and Siegfried Sassoon, and Robert Graves, and all the Bloomsburies. I owe a great debt of gratitude to Roger Fry. Listening to his talk about the arts was a liberal education. At Oxford I began writing verse. I had several volumes of verse published before I turned to writing stories. I was very lucky; I never had any difficulty getting published. After the war, when I came down from Oxford, I had to make my living. I had a job on the *Athenaeum*, but that paid very little, not enough to live on; so in spare moments I worked for the Condé Nast publications. I worked for *Vogue* and *Vanity Fair*, and for *House and Garden*. I used to turn out articles on everything from decorative plaster to Persian rugs. And that wasn't all. I did dramatic criticism for the *Westminster Review*. Why—would you believe it?—I even did music criticism. I heartily recommend this sort of journalism as an apprenticeship. It forces you to write on everything under the sun, it develops your facility, it teaches you to master your material quickly, and it makes you look at things. Fortunately, though, I didn't have to keep at it very long. After *Crome Yellow*—that was 1921—I didn't have to worry so much about making a living. I was already married, and we were then able to live on the Continent—in Italy until the Fascists made life unpleasant, then in France. We had a little house outside Paris, where I could write without being disturbed. We'd be in London part of every year, but there was always too much going on; I couldn't get much writing done there.

INTERVIEWERS: Do you think that certain occupations are more conducive to creative writing than others? In other words, does the work you do or the company you keep affect your writing?

HUXLEY: I don't believe there is an ideal occupation for the writer. He could write under almost any circumstance, even in complete isolation. Why, look at Balzac, locked up in a secret room in Paris, hiding from his creditors, and producing the *Comédie Humaine*. Or think of Proust in his cork-lined room (although of course he had plenty of visitors). I suppose the best occupation is just meeting a great many different kinds of people and seeing what interests them. That's one of the disadvantages of getting older; you're inclined to make intimate contacts with fewer people.

INTERVIEWERS: What would you say makes the writer different from other people?

HUXLEY: Well, one has the urge, first of all, to order the facts one observes and to give meaning to life; and along with that goes the love of words for their own sake and a desire to manipulate them. It's not a matter of intelligence; some very intelligent and original people don't have the love of words or the knack to use them effectively. On the verbal level they express themselves very badly.

INTERVIEWERS: What about creativeness in general?

HUXLEY: Yes, what about it? Why is it that in most children education seems to destroy the creative urge? Why do so many boys and girls leave school with blunted perceptions and a closed mind? A majority of young people seem to develop mental arteriosclerosis forty years before they get the physical kind. Another question: why do some people remain open and elastic into extreme old age, whereas others become rigid and unproductive before they're fifty? It's a problem in biochemistry and adult education.

INTERVIEWERS: Some psychologists have claimed that the creative urge is a kind of neurosis. Would you agree?

HUXLEY: Most emphatically not. I don't believe for a moment that creativity is a neurotic symptom. On the contrary, the neurotic who succeeds as an artist has had to overcome a tremendous handicap. He creates in spite of his neurosis, not because of it.

INTERVIEWERS: You've never had much use for Freud, have you?

HUXLEY: The trouble with Freudian psychology is that it is based exclusively on a study of the sick. Freud never met a healthy human being—only patients and other psychoanalysts. Then too, Freudian psychology is only concerned with the past. Other systems of psychology, that concern themselves with the present state of the subject or his future potentialities, seem to me to be more realistic.

INTERVIEWERS: Do you see any relation between the creative process and the use of such drugs as lysergic acid?

HUXLEY: I don't think there is any generalization one can make on this. Experience has shown that there's an enormous variation in the way people respond to lysergic acid. Some people probably could get direct aesthetic inspiration for painting or poetry out of it. Others I don't think could. For most people it's an extremely significant experience, and I suppose in an indirect way it could help the creative process. But I don't think one can sit down and say, "I want to write a magnificent poem, and so I'm going to take lysergic acid." I don't think it's by any means certain that you would get the result you wanted—you might get almost any result.

INTERVIEWERS: Would the drug give more help to the lyric poet than the novelist?

HUXLEY: Well, the poet would certainly get an extraordinary view of life which he wouldn't have had in any other way, and this might help him a great deal. But, you see (and this is the most significant thing about the experience), during the experience you're really not interested in doing anything practical—even writing lyric poetry. If you were making love to a woman, would you be interested in writing about it? Of course not. And during the experience you're not particularly interested in words, because the experience transcends words and is quite inexpressible in terms of words. So the whole notion of conceptualizing what is happening seems very silly. *After* the event, it seems to me quite possible that it might be of great assistance; people would see the universe around them in a very different way and would be inspired, possibly, to write something about it.

INTERVIEWERS: But is there much carry-over from the experience?

HUXLEY: Well, there's always a complete memory of the experience. You remember something extraordinary having happened. And to some extent you can relive the experience, particularly the transformation of the outside world. You get hints of this, you see the world in this transfigured way now and then—not to the same pitch of intensity, but something of the kind. It does help you to look at the world in a new way. And you come to understand very clearly the way that certain specially gifted people have seen the world. You are actually introduced into the kind of world that Van Gogh lived in, or the kind of world that Blake lived in. You begin to have a direct experience of this kind of world while you're under the drug, and afterwards you can remember and to some slight extent recapture this kind of world, which certain privileged people have moved in and out of, as Blake obviously did all the time.

INTERVIEWERS: But the artist's talents won't be any different from what they were before he took the drug?

HUXLEY: I don't see why they should be different. Some experiments have been made to see what painters can do under the influence of the drug, but most of the examples I have seen are very uninteresting. You could never hope to reproduce to the full extent the quite incredible intensity of color that you get under the influence of the drug. Most of the things I have seen are just rather tiresome bits of expressionism, which correspond hardly at all, I would think, to the actual experience. Maybe an immensely gifted artist—someone like Odilon Redon (who probably saw the world like this all the time, anyhow)—maybe such a man could profit by the lysergic-acid experience, could use his visions as models, could reproduce on canvas the external world as it is transfigured by the drug.

INTERVIEWERS: Here this afternoon, as in your book, *The Doors of Perception*, you've been talking chiefly about the visual experience under the drug, and about painting. Is there any similar gain in psychological insight?

HUXLEY: Yes, I think there is. While one is under the drug one has penetrating insights into the people around one, and also into one's own life. Many people get tremendous recalls of buried material. A process which may take six years of psychoanalysis happens in an hour—and considerably cheaper! And the experience can be very liberating and widening in other ways. It shows that the world one habitually lives in is merely a creation of this conventional, closely conditioned being which one is, and that there are quite other kinds of worlds outside. It's a very salutary thing to realize that the rather dull universe in which most of us spend most of our time is not the only universe there is. I think it's healthy that people should have this experience.

INTERVIEWERS: Could such psychological insight be helpful to the fiction writer?

HUXLEY: I doubt it. After all, fiction is the fruit of sustained effort. The lysergic-acid experience is a revelation of something outside of time and the social order. To write fiction, one needs a whole series of inspirations about people in an actual environment, and then a whole lot of hard work on the basis of those inspirations.

INTERVIEWERS: Is there any resemblance between lysergic acid, or mescalin, and the "soma" of your *Brave New World?*

HUXLEY: None whatever. Soma is an imaginary drug, with three different effects—euphoric, hallucinant, or sedative—an impossible combination. Mescalin is the active principle of the peyote cactus, which has been used for a long time by the Indians of the Southwest in their religious rites. It is now synthesized. Lysergic acid diethylamide (LSD-25) is a chemical compound with effects similar to mescalin; it was developed about twelve years ago, and it is only being used experimentally at present. Mescalin and lysergic acid transfigure the external world and in some cases produce visions. Most people have the sort of positive and enlightening experience I've described; but the visions may be infernal as well as celestial. These drugs are physiologically innocuous, except to people with liver damage. They leave most people with no hangover, and they are not habit-forming. Psychiatrists have found that, skillfully used, they can be very helpful in the treatment of certain kinds of neuroses.

INTERVIEWERS: How did you happen to get involved in experiments with mescalin and lysergic acid?

HUXLEY: Well, I'd been interested in it for some years, and I had been in correspondence with Humphrey Osmond, a very gifted young British psychiatrist working in Canada. When he started testing its effects on different kinds of people, I became one of his guinea pigs. I've described all this in *The Doors of Perception.*

INTERVIEWERS: To return to writing, in *Point Counter Point* you have Philip Quarles say, "I am not a congenital novelist." Would you say the same of yourself?

HUXLEY: I don't think of myself as a congenital novelist—no. For example, I have great difficulty in inventing plots. Some people are born with an amazing gift for storytelling; it's a gift which I've never had at all. One reads, for example, Stevenson's accounts of how all the plots for his stories were provided in dreams by his subconscious mind (what he calls the "Brownies" working for him), and that all he had to do was to work up the material they had provided. I've never had any Brownies. The great difficulty for me has always been creating situations.

INTERVIEWERS: Developing character has been easier for you than creating plots?

HUXLEY: Yes, but even then I'm not very good at creating people; I don't have a very wide repertory of characters. These are difficult things for me. I suppose it's largely a question of temperament. I don't happen to have the right kind of temperament.

INTERVIEWERS: By the phrase "congenital novelist" we thought you meant one who is only interested in writing novels.

HUXLEY: I suppose this is another way of saying the same thing. The congenital novelist doesn't have other interests. Fiction for him is an absorbing thing which fills up his mind and takes all his time and energy, whereas someone else with a different kind of mind has these other, extracurricular activities going on.

INTERVIEWERS: As you look back on your novels, which are you most happy with?

HUXLEY: I personally think the most successful was *Time Must Have a Stop*. I don't know, but it seemed to me that I integrated what may be called the essay element with the fictional element better there than in other novels. Maybe this is not the case. It just happens to be the one that I like best, because I feel that it came off best.

INTERVIEWERS: As you see it, then, the novelist's problem is to fuse the "essay element" with the story?

HUXLEY: Well, there are lots of excellent storytellers who are simply storytellers, and I think it's a wonderful gift, after all. I suppose the extreme example is Dumas: that extraordinary old gentleman, who sat down and thought nothing of writing six volumes of *The Count of Monte Cristo* in a few months. And my God, *Monte Cristo* is damned good! But it isn't the last word. When you can find storytelling which carries at the same time a kind of parable-like meaning (such as you get, say, in Dostoevski or in the best of Tolstoi), this is something extraordinary, I feel. I'm always flabbergasted when I reread some of the short things of Tolstoi, like *The Death of Ivan Ilyich*. What an astounding work that is! Or some of the short things of Dostoevski, like *Notes from Underground.*

INTERVIEWERS: What other novelists have especially affected you?

HUXLEY: It's awfully difficult for me to answer such a question. I read individual books that I like and take things from and am stimulated by. . . . As a very young man, as an undergraduate, I used to read a lot of French novels. I was very fond of a novelist who is now very much out-of-date—Anatole France. I haven't read him now for forty years; I don't know what he's like. Then I remember reading the first volume of Proust in 1915 and being tremendously impressed by it. (I reread it recently and was curiously disappointed.) Gide I read at that time too.

INTERVIEWERS: Several of your early novels, *Point Counter Point* especially, appear to have been written under the influence of Proust and Gide. Is this so?

HUXLEY: I suppose some of my early novels are faintly Proustian. I don't think I shall ever experiment again with the kind of treatment of time and remembrance of things past that I used in *Eyeless in Gaza*, shifting back and forth in time to show the pressure of the past on the present.

INTERVIEWERS: Then in some of those early novels you also make use of musical effects, much as Gide does.

HUXLEY: The marvelous thing about music is that it does so easily and rapidly what can be done only very laboriously in words, or really can't be done at all. It's futile to even attempt to write musically. But I've tried in some of my essays—in *Themes and Variations*, for instance. Then I've used the equivalent of musical variations in some of my stories, where I take certain traits of character and treat them seriously in one personage and comically, in a sort of parody, in another.

INTERVIEWERS: Were you much taken with Joyce?

HUXLEY: Never very much—no. I never got very much out of *Ulysses*. I think it's an extraordinary book, but so much of it consists of rather lengthy demonstrations of how a novel ought *not* to be written, doesn't it? He does show nearly every conceivable way it should not be written, and then goes on to show how it might be written.

INTERVIEWERS: What do you think of Virginia Woolf's fiction?

HUXLEY: Her works are very strange. They're very beautiful, aren't they? But one gets such a curious feeling from them. She sees with incredible clarity, but always as though through a sheet of plate glass; she never touches anything. Her books are not immediate. They're very puzzling to me.

INTERVIEWERS: How about Henry James? Or Thomas Mann?

HUXLEY: James leaves me very cold. And I find Mann a little boring. He's obviously an admirable novelist. You know, I used to go every summer to the place described in *Mario and the Magician*, and it seemed to me that I never got any sense of the place out of Mann. I knew it very well: the coast where Shelley was washed up, under the mountains of Carrara, where the marble comes from. It was an incredibly beautiful place then. Now, needless to say, it's all become like Coney Island, with millions of people there.

INTERVIEWERS: Speaking of places, do you think your own writing was affected when you transplanted yourself from England to America?

HUXLEY: I don't know—I don't think so. I never strongly felt that the place where I lived had great importance to me.

INTERVIEWERS: Then you don't think the social climate makes much difference to fiction?

HUXLEY: Well, what is "fiction"? So many people talk about "fiction" or "the writer" as though you could generalize about them. There are always many diverse members of the group; and fiction is a genus of which there are many species. I think that certain species of fiction quite clearly call for a certain locale. It's impossible that Trollope could have written except where he did write. He couldn't have gone off to Italy like Byron or Shelley. He required the English middle-class life. But then look at Lawrence. At the beginning you would have said that he had to stay in the Midlands of England, near the coal mines. But he could write anywhere.

INTERVIEWERS: Now, thirty years later, would you care to say what you think of Lawrence as a novelist and as a man?

HUXLEY: I occasionally reread some of his books. How good he is! Especially in the short stories. And the other day I read part of *Women in Love*, and that again seemed very good. The vividness, the incredible vividness of the descriptions of nature is amazing in Lawrence. But sometimes one doesn't know what he's getting at. In *The Plumed Serpent*, for instance, he'll glorify the Mexican Indians with their dark life of the blood on one page, and then on the next he'll damn the lazy natives like a British colonel in the days of Kipling. That book is a mass of contradictions. I was very fond of Lawrence as a man. I knew him very well the last four years of his life. I had met him during the First World War and saw him a certain amount then, but I didn't get to know him really well till 1926. I was a little disturbed by him. You know, he *was* rather disturbing. And to a conventionally brought up young bourgeois he was rather difficult to understand. But later on I got to know and like him. My first wife became very friendly with him and understood him and they got on very well together. We saw the Lawrences often during those last four years; they stayed with us in Paris, then we were together in Switzerland, and we visited them at the Villa Mirenda near Florence. My wife typed out the manuscript of *Lady Chatterley's Lover* for him, even though she was a bad typist and had no patience with English spelling—she was a Belgian, you know. Then she didn't always appreciate the nuances of the language she was typing. When she started using some of those four-letter words in conversation, Lawrence was profoundly shocked.

INTERVIEWERS: Why did Lawrence keep moving around so much?

HUXLEY: One reason he was forever moving on is that his relations with people would become so complicated that he'd have to get away. He was a man who loved and hated too intensely; he both loved and hated the same people at the same time. Then, like a great many tubercular people, he was convinced that climate had a great effect on him—not only the temperature, but the direction of the wind, and all sorts of atmospheric conditions. He had invented a whole mythology of climate. In his last years he wanted to go back to New Mexico. He had been very happy there on the ranch in Taos. But he wasn't strong enough to make the trip. By all the rules of medicine he should have been dead; but he lived on, supported by some kind of energy that seemed to be independent of his body. And he kept on writing to the end. . . . We were there, in Vence, when he died. . . . He actually died in my first wife's arms. After his death his wife Frieda was utterly helpless and didn't know what to do with herself. Physically she was very strong, but in the practical affairs of life she depended on Lawrence entirely. For instance, when she went back to London after his death to settle his affairs, she stayed in a particularly dreary old hotel, simply because she had stayed there once with him and didn't feel secure in any other place.

INTERVIEWERS: Certain characters in your novels seem to have been based on people you knew—on Lawrence and Norman Douglas and Middleton Murry, for instance. Is this true? And how do you convert a real person into a fictional character?

HUXLEY: I try to imagine how certain people I know would behave in certain circumstances. Of course I base my characters partly on the people I know—one can't escape it—but fictional characters are oversimplified; they're much less complex than the people one knows. There is something of Murry in several of my characters, but I wouldn't say I'd put Murry in a book. And there is something of Norman Douglas in old Scogan of *Crome Yellow*. I knew Douglas quite well in the twenties in Florence. He was a remarkably intelligent and highly educated man, but he had deliberately limited himself to the point where he would talk about almost nothing but drink and sex. He became quite boring after a time. Did you ever see that collection of pornographic limericks that he had privately printed? It was the only way, poor fellow, that he could make some money. It was a terribly unfunny book. I didn't see him at all in his later years.

INTERVIEWERS: Lawrence and Frieda are represented in Mark and Mary Rampion of *Point Counter Point*, aren't they? You even follow the story of the Lawrences quite closely in many particulars.

HUXLEY: Yes, I suppose so, but only a small part of Lawrence is in that character. Isn't it remarkable how everyone who knew Lawrence has felt compelled to write about him? Why, he's had more books written about him than any writer since Byron!

INTERVIEWERS: How do you name your characters? Do you pick them at random, like Simenon, out of telephone directories? Or are the names meant to convey something? Some of your characters in *After Many a Summer Dies the Swan* have odd names; do these have any particular significance?

HUXLEY: Yes, names are very important, aren't they? And the most unlikely names keep turning up in real life, so one must be careful. I can explain some of the names in *After Many a Summer*. Take Virginia Maunciple. That name was suggested to me by Chaucer's manciple. What is a manciple, anyhow? a kind of steward. It's the sort of a name that a movie starlet would choose, in the hope of being unique, custom-made. She's called Virginia because she appears so virginal to Jeremy, and so obviously isn't in fact; also because of her devotion to the Madonna. Dr. Sigmund Obispo: here the first name obviously refers to Freud, and Obispo I took from San Luis Obispo for local color and because it has a comical sound. And Jeremy Pordage. There's a story connected with that name. When I was an undergraduate at Oxford, Professor Walter Raleigh (who was a marvelous teacher) had me do a piece of research on the literature connected with the Popish

Plot. One of the authors mentioned by Dryden under the name of "lame Mephibosheth" was called Pordage. His poetry, when I read it at the Bodleian, turned out to be unbelievably bad. But the name was a treasure. As for Jeremy, that was chosen for the sound; combined with Pordage it has a rather spinsterish ring. Propter came from the Latin for "on account of"—because, as a wise man, he is concerned with ultimate causes. Another reason why I chose the name was its occurrence in a poem of Edward Lear, "Incidents in the Life of My Uncle Arly." Let's see, how does it go now?

> *Like the ancient Medes and Persians,*
> *Always by his own exertions*
>   *He subsisted on those hills;*
> *Whiles, by teaching children spelling,*
> *Or at times by merely yelling,*
> *Or at intervals by selling*
>   *"Propter's Nicodemus Pills."*

Pete Boone doesn't mean anything in particular. It's just a straight-forward American name that suits the character. Jo Stoyte, too—the name simply means what it sounds like.

INTERVIEWERS: You seem to have turned away from satire in recent years. What do you think of satire now?

HUXLEY: Yes, I suppose I have changed in that respect. But I'm all for satire. We need it. People everywhere take things much too seriously, I think. People are much too solemn about things. I'm all for sticking pins into episcopal behinds, and that sort of thing. It seems to me a most salutary proceeding.

INTERVIEWERS: Were you fond of Swift as a young man?

HUXLEY: Oh, yes, I was very fond of Swift. And of another book, a wonderfully funny book, one of the few old books that have stayed funny: *The Letters of Obscure Men*, the *Epistolae Obscurorum Virorum*. I'm sure Swift must have read it; it is so much his method. In general, I get a great deal out of the eighteenth century: Hume, Law, Crébillon, Diderot, Fielding, Pope—

though I'm old-fashioned enough to think the Romantics are better poets than Pope.

INTERVIEWERS: You praised Fielding long ago in your essay "Tragedy and the Whole Truth." Do you still believe that fiction can give a fuller view of life than tragedy?

HUXLEY: Yes, I still believe that tragedy is not necessarily the highest form. The highest form does not yet exist, perhaps. I can conceive of something much more inclusive and yet equally sublime, something which is adumbrated in the plays of Shakespeare. I think that in some way the tragic and comic elements can be more totally fused. I don't know how. Don't ask me how. If we get another Shakespeare one of these days—as I hope we will— perhaps we'll see. As I say in that essay, Homer has a kind of fusion of these elements, but on a very simple-minded level. But, my goodness, how good Homer is, anyhow! And there's another really sublime writer who has this quality—Chaucer. Why, Chaucer invented a whole psychology out of absolutely nothing: an incredible achievement. It's one of the great misfortunes of English literature that Chaucer wrote at a time when his language was to become incomprehensible. If he had been born two or three hundred years later I think the whole course of English literature would have been changed. We wouldn't have had this sort of Platonic mania—separating mind from body and spirit from matter.

INTERVIEWERS: Then, even though you have been writing fewer novels in recent years, you don't think less highly of the art of fiction than you used to?

HUXLEY: Oh, no, no, no. I think fiction, and biography and history, are *the* forms. I think one can say much more about general abstract ideas in terms of concrete characters and situations, whether fictional or real, than one can in abstract terms. Several of the books I like best of what I've written are historical and biographical things: *Grey Eminence*, and *The Devils of Loudun*, and the biography of Maine de Biran, the "Variations on a Philosopher." These are all discussions of what are to me important general ideas in terms of specific lives and incidents. And I must say I think that probably *all* philosophy ought to be written in this form; it would be much more profound and much more edifying. It's awfully easy to write abstractly, without attaching much meaning to the big words. But the moment you have to express ideas in the light of a particular context, in a particular set of circumstances, although it's a limitation in some ways, it's also an invitation to go much further and much deeper. I think that fiction and, as I say, history and biography are *immensely* important, not only for their own sake, because they provide a picture of life now and of life in the past, but also as vehicles for the expression of general philosophic ideas, religious ideas, social ideas. My goodness, Dostoevski is six times as profound as Kierkegaard, because he writes *fiction*. In Kierkegaard you have this Abstract Man going on and on—like Coleridge—why, it's *nothing* compared with the really profound Fictional Man, who has always to keep these tremendous ideas *alive* in a concrete form. In fiction you have the reconciliation of the absolute and the relative, so to speak, the expression of the general in the particular. And this, it seems to me, is the exciting thing—both in life and in art.

GEORGE WICKES
RAY FRAZER

9. Ernest Hemingway

Ernest Hemingway was born in Oak Park, Illinois, on July 21, 1899, and began his writing career as a reporter for the *Kansas City Star* when he was eighteen. In 1921 he became a roving correspondent for the *Toronto Star Weekly*, and in December of that year sailed for Europe, where he covered the Graeco-Turkish war and the subsequent Lausanne peace conference. It was during this period that a suitcase containing all the poems and stories he had written—with the exception of one story, "My Old Man," which was making the rounds of the magazines—was lost on a train trip, and he had to start over again.

Hemingway's first book, *Three Stories and Ten Poems*, was published in an edition of three hundred in 1923. *In Our Time*, a collection of short stories, came next, in 1924. He published *Torrents of Spring*, a satire, in 1926, and the fall of the same year saw publication of his novel *The Sun Also Rises*. Another volume of short stories, *Men without Women*, was published in October 1927; this collection contained "The Killers" and "The Undefeated," two stories which are considered to be among the best examples of modern short-story writing. It was the publication of *A Farewell To Arms* in 1929 that brought him full recognition as one of the foremost writers of our time. Hemingway's stories were published in collected form as *The First Forty-Nine* in 1938.

In 1940 he completed *For Whom the Bell Tolls*, his long novel about the Spanish Civil War. Ten years later *Across the River and Into the Trees* appeared, and in 1952 *The Old Man and the Sea*. In 1954 Hemingway was the recipient of the Nobel Prize for literature, an honor which has come to only six other writers of American birth. The award citation said: "For his powerful and style-forming mastery of the art of modern narration. . . ."

Ernest Hemingway lived in Cuba for many years. His last days were spent in Ketchum, Idaho, where he died on July 2, 1961.

"I could take it," the man said. "Don't you think I could take it, Kid?"

"You bet."

"They all bust their hands on me," the little man said "They couldn't hurt me."

He looked at Nick.

"Set down," he said. "Want to eat?"

"Yeah." ~~Starts to back~~ "Nick said. "I'm hungry"

"Listen," the man said, "Call me Ad"

"Sure."

"Listen," the ~~man~~ little man said. "I'm not quite right."

"What's the matter?"

"I'm crazy."

He put on his cap. Nick felt like laughing "You're all right," he said.

"No I'm not. I'm crazy. Listen, you ever been crazy?"

"No," Nick said. "How does it get you?"

"I don't know," Ad said, "When you got it you don't know about it. You know me don't you?"

"No."

"I'm ad Francis."

"Really?"

Manuscript page from Ernest Hemingway's short story, "The Battler."

BEE W. DABNEY

Ernest Hemingway

HEMINGWAY: *You go to the races?*

INTERVIEWER: *Yes, occasionally.*

HEMINGWAY: *Then you read the* Racing Form. . . . *There you have the true art of fiction.*

—Conversation in a Madrid café, May 1954

Ernest Hemingway writes in the bedroom of his house in the Havana suburb of San Francisco de Paula. He has a special work-room prepared for him in a square tower at the southwest corner of the house, but prefers to work in his bedroom, climbing to the tower room only when "characters" drive him up there.

The bedroom is on the ground floor and connects with the main room of the house. The door between the two is kept ajar by a heavy volume listing and describing The World's Aircraft Engines. *The bedroom is large, sunny, the windows facing east and south* letting in the day's light on white walls and a yellow-tinged tile floor.

The room is divided into two alcoves by a pair of chest-high bookcases that stand out into the room at right angles from opposite walls. A large and low double bed dominates one section, oversized slippers and loafers neatly arranged at the foot, the two bedside tables at the head piled seven-high with books. In the other alcove stands a massive flat-top desk with a chair at either side, its surface an ordered clutter of papers and mementos. Beyond it, at the far end of the room, is an armoire with a leopard skin draped across the top. The other walls are lined with white-painted bookcases from which books overflow to the floor, and are piled on top among old newspapers, bullfight journals, and stacks of letters bound together by rubber bands.

It is on the top of one of these cluttered bookcases—the one against the wall by the east window and three feet or so from his bed—that Hemingway has his "work desk"—a square foot of cramped area hemmed in by books on one side and on the other by a newspaper-covered heap of papers, manuscripts, and pamphlets. There is just enough space left on top of the bookcase for a typewriter, surmounted by a wooden reading board, five or six pencils, and a chunk of copper ore to weight down papers when the wind blows in from the east window.

A working habit he has had from the beginning, Hemingway stands when he writes. He stands in a pair of his oversized loafers on the worn skin of a Lesser Kudu—the typewriter and the reading board chest-high opposite him.

When Hemingway starts on a project he always begins with a pencil, using the reading board to write on onionskin typewriter paper. He keeps a sheaf of the blank paper on a clipboard to the left of the typewriter, extracting the paper a sheet at a time from under a metal clip which reads "These Must Be Paid." He places the paper slantwise on the reading board, leans against the board with his left arm, steadying the paper with his hand, and fills the paper with handwriting which through the years has become *larger, more boyish, with a paucity of punctuation, very few capitals, and often the period marked with an x. The page completed, he clips it face-down on another clipboard which he places off to the right of the typewriter.*

Hemingway shifts to the typewriter, lifting off the reading board, only when the writing is going fast and well, or when the writing is, for him at least, simple: dialogue, for instance.

He keeps track of his daily progress—"so as not to kid myself"—on a large chart made out of the side of a cardboard packing case and set up against the wall under the nose of a mounted gazelle head. The numbers on the chart showing the daily output of words differ from 450, 575, 462, 1250, back to 512, the higher figures on days Hemingway puts in extra work so he won't feel guilty spending the following day fishing on the Gulf Stream.

A man of habit, Hemingway does not use the perfectly suitable desk in the other alcove. Though it allows more space for writing, it too has its miscellany: stacks of letters, a stuffed toy lion of the type sold in Broadway nighteries, a small burlap bag full of carnivore teeth, shotgun shells, a shoehorn, wood carvings of lion, rhino, two zebras, and a wart-hog—these last set in a neat row across the surface of the desk—and, of course, books: piled on the desk, beside tables, jamming the shelves in indiscriminate order—novels, histories, collections of poetry, drama, essays. A look at their titles shows their variety. On the shelf opposite Hemingway's knee as he stands up to his "work desk" are Virginia Woolf's The Common Reader, *Ben Ames Williams'* House Divided, The Partisan Reader, *Charles A. Beard's* The Republic, *Tarle's* Napoleon's Invasion of Russia, How Young You Look *by Peggy Wood, Alden Brooks'* Will Shakespeare and the Dyer's Hand, *Baldwin's* African Hunting, *T. S. Eliot's* Collected Poems, *and two books on General Custer's fall at the battle of the Little Big Horn.*

The room, however, for all the disorder sensed at first sight, indicates on inspection an owner who is basically neat but cannot bear to throw anything away—especially if sentimental value is attached. One bookcase top has an odd assortment of mementos:

a giraffe made of wood beads, a little cast-iron turtle, tiny models of a locomotive, two jeeps and a Venetian gondola, a toy bear with a key in its back, a monkey carrying a pair of cymbals, a miniature guitar, and a little tin model of a U.S. Navy biplane (one wheel missing) resting awry on a circular straw place mat—the quality of the collection that of the odds-and-ends which turn up in a shoe-box at the back of a small boy's closet. It is evident, though, that these tokens have their value, just as three buffalo horns Hemingway keeps in his bedroom have a value dependent not on size but because during the acquiring of them things went badly in the bush which ultimately turned out well. "It cheers me up to look at them," he says.

Hemingway may admit superstitions of this sort, but he prefers not to talk about them, feeling that whatever value they may have can be talked away. He has much the same attitude about writing. Many times during the making of this interview he stressed that the craft of writing should not be tampered with by an excess of scrutiny—"that though there is one part of writing that is solid and you do it no harm by talking about it, the other is fragile, and if you talk about it, the structure cracks and you have noth-ing."

As a result, though a wonderful raconteur, a man of rich humor, and possessed of an amazing fund of knowledge on subjects which interest him, Hemingway finds it difficult to talk about writing—not because he has few ideas on the subject, but rather that he feels so strongly that such ideas should remain unexpressed, that to be asked questions on them "spooks" him (to use one of his favorite expressions) to the point where he is almost inarticulate. Many of the replies in this interview he preferred to work out on his reading board. The occasional waspish tone of the answers is also part of this strong feeling that writing is a private, lonely oc-cupation with no need for witnesses until the final work is done.

This dedication to his art may suggest a personality at odds with the rambunctious, carefree, world-wheeling Hemingway-at-play of popular conception. The fact is that Hemingway, while obviously enjoying life, brings an equivalent dedication to every-thing he does—an outlook that is essentially serious, with a horror of the inaccurate, the fraudulent, the deceptive, the half-baked.

Nowhere is the dedication he gives his art more evident than in the yellow-tiled bedroom—where early in the morning Heming-way gets up to stand in absolute concentration in front of his reading board, moving only to shift weight from one foot to an-other, perspiring heavily when the work is going well, excited as a boy, fretful, miserable when the artistic touch momentarily van-ishes—slave of a self-imposed discipline which lasts until about noon when he takes a knotted walking stick and leaves the house for the swimming pool where he takes his daily half-mile swim.

INTERVIEWER: Are these hours during the actual process of writing pleasurable?

HEMINGWAY: Very.

INTERVIEWER: Could you say something of this process? When do you work? Do you keep to a strict schedule?

HEMINGWAY: When I am working on a book or a story I write every morning as soon after first light as possible. There is no one to disturb you and it is cool or cold and you come to your work and warm as you write. You read what you have written and, as you always stop when you know what is going to happen next, you go on from there. You write until you come to a place where you still have your juice and know what will happen next and you stop and try to live through until the next day when you hit it again. You have started at six in the morning, say, and may go on until noon or be through before that. When you stop you are as empty, and at the same time never empty but filling, as when you have made love to someone you love. Nothing can hurt you, nothing can happen, nothing means anything until the next day when you do it again. It is the wait until the next day that is hard to get through.

INTERVIEWER: Can you dismiss from your mind whatever project you're on when you're away from the typewriter?

HEMINGWAY: Of course. But it takes discipline to do it and this discipline is acquired. It has to be.

INTERVIEWER: Do you do any rewriting as you read up to the place you left off the day before? Or does that come later, when the whole is finished?

HEMINGWAY: I always rewrite each day up to the point where I stopped. When it is all finished, naturally you go over it. You get another chance to correct and rewrite when someone else types it, and you see it clean in type. The last chance is in the proofs. You're grateful for these different chances.

INTERVIEWER: How much rewriting do you do?

HEMINGWAY: It depends. I rewrote the ending to *Farewell to Arms*, the last page of it, thirty-nine times before I was satisfied.

INTERVIEWER: Was there some technical problem there? What was it that had stumped you?

HEMINGWAY: Getting the words right.

INTERVIEWER: Is it the rereading that gets the "juice" up?

HEMINGWAY: Rereading places you at the point where it *has* to go on, knowing it is as good as you can get it up to there. There is always juice somewhere.

INTERVIEWER: But are there times when the inspiration isn't there at all?

HEMINGWAY: Naturally. But if you stopped when you knew what would happen next, you can go on. As long as you can start, you are all right. The juice will come.

INTERVIEWER: Thornton Wilder speaks of mnemonic devices that get the writer going on his day's work. He says you once told him you sharpened twenty pencils.

HEMINGWAY: I don't think I ever owned twenty pencils at one time. Wearing down seven number two pencils is a good day's work.

INTERVIEWER: Where are some of the places you have found most advantageous to work? The Ambos Mundos hotel must have been one, judging from the number of books you did there. Or do surroundings have little effect on the work?

HEMINGWAY: The Ambos Mundos in Havana was a very good place to work in. This Finca is a splendid place, or was. But I have worked well everywhere. I mean I have been able to work as well as I can under varied circumstances. The telephone and visitors are the work destroyers.

INTERVIEWER: Is emotional stability necessary to write well? You told me once that you could only write well when you were in love. Could you expound on that a bit more?

HEMINGWAY: What a question. But full marks for trying. You can write any time people will leave you alone and not interrupt you. Or rather you can if you will be ruthless enough about it. But the best writing is certainly when you are in love. If it is all the same to you I would rather not expound on that.

INTERVIEWER: How about financial security? Can that be a detriment to good writing?

HEMINGWAY: If it came early enough and you loved life as much as you loved your work it would take much character to resist the temptations. Once writing has become your major vice and greatest pleasure only death can stop it. Financial security then is a great help as it keeps you from worrying. Worry destroys the ability to write. Ill health is bad in the ratio that it produces worry which attacks your subconscious and destroys your reserves.

INTERVIEWER: Can you recall an exact moment when you decided to become a writer?

HEMINGWAY: No, I always wanted to be a writer.

INTERVIEWER: Philip Young in his book on you suggests that the traumatic shock of your severe 1918 mortar wound had a great influence on you as a writer. I remember in Madrid you talked briefly about his thesis, finding little in it, and going on to say that you thought the artist's equipment was not an acquired characteristic, but inherited, in the Mendelian sense.

HEMINGWAY: Evidently in Madrid that year my mind could not be called very sound. The only thing to recommend it would be that I spoke only briefly about Mr. Young's book and his trauma theory of literature. Perhaps the two concussions and a skull fracture of that year had made me irresponsible in my statements. I do remember telling you that I believed imagination could be the result of inherited racial experience. It sounds all right in good jolly post-concussion talk, but I think that is more or less where it belongs. So until the next liberation trauma, let's leave it there. Do you agree? But thanks for leaving out the names of any relatives I might have implicated. The fun of talk is to explore, but much of it and all that is irresponsible should not be written. Once written you have to stand by it. You may have said it to see whether you believed it or not. On the question you raised, the effects of wounds vary greatly. Simple wounds which do not break bone are of little account. They sometimes give confidence. Wounds which do extensive bone and nerve damage are not good for writers, nor anybody else.

INTERVIEWER: What would you consider the best intellectual training for the would-be writer?

HEMINGWAY: Let's say that he should go out and hang himself because he finds that writing well is impossibly difficult. Then he should be cut down without mercy and forced by his own self to write as well as he can for the rest of his life. At least he will have the story of the hanging to commence with.

INTERVIEWER: How about people who've gone into the academic career? Do you think the large numbers of writers who hold teaching positions have compromised their literary careers?

HEMINGWAY: It depends on what you call compromise. Is the usage that of a woman who has been compromised? Or is it the compromise of the statesman? Or the compromise made with your grocer or your tailor that you will pay a little more but will pay it later? A writer who can both write and teach should be able to do both. Many competent writers have proved it could be done. I could not do it, I know, and I admire those who have been able to. I would think though that the academic life could put a period to outside experience which might possibly limit growth of knowledge of the world. Knowledge, however, demands more responsibility of a writer and makes writing more difficult.

Trying to write something of permanent value is a full-time job even though only a few hours a day are spent on the actual writing. A writer can be compared to a well. There are as many kinds of wells as there are writers. The important thing is to have good water in the well and it is better to take a regular amount out than to pump the well dry and wait for it to refill. I see I am getting away from the question, but the question was not very interesting.

INTERVIEWER: Would you suggest newspaper work for the young writer? How helpful was the training you had with the *Kansas City Star*?

HEMINGWAY: On the *Star* you were forced to learn to write a simple declarative sentence. This is useful to anyone. Newspaper work will not harm a young writer and could help him if he gets out of it in time. This is one of the dustiest clichés there is and I apologize for it. But when you ask someone old tired questions you are apt to receive old tired answers.

INTERVIEWER: You once wrote in the *Transatlantic Review* that the only reason for writing journalism was to be well paid. You said: "And when you destroy the valuable things you have by writing about them, you want to get big money for it." Do you think of writing as a type of self-destruction?

HEMINGWAY: I do not remember ever writing that. But it sounds silly and violent enough for me to have said it to avoid having to bite on the nail and make a sensible statement. I certainly do not think of writing as a type of self-destruction, though journalism, after a point has been reached, can be a daily self-destruction for a serious creative writer.

INTERVIEWER: Do you think the intellectual stimulus of the company of other writers is of any value to an author?

HEMINGWAY: Certainly.

INTERVIEWER: In the Paris of the twenties did you have any sense of "group feeling" with other writers and artists?

HEMINGWAY: No. There was no group feeling. We had respect for each other. I respected a lot of painters, some of my own age, others older—Gris, Picasso, Braque, Monet, who was still alive then—and a few writers: Joyce, Ezra, the good of Stein. . . .

INTERVIEWER: When you are writing, do you ever find yourself influenced by what you're reading at the time?

HEMINGWAY: Not since Joyce was writing *Ulysses*. His was not a direct influence. But in those days when words we knew were barred to us, and we had to fight for a single word, the influence of his work was what changed everything, and made it possible for us to break away from the restrictions.

INTERVIEWER: Could you learn anything about writing from the writers? You were telling me yesterday that Joyce, for example, couldn't bear to talk about writing.

HEMINGWAY: In company with people of your own trade you ordinarily speak of other writers' books. The better the writers the less they will speak about what they have written themselves. Joyce was a very great writer and he would only explain what he was doing to jerks. Other writers that he respected were supposed to be able to know what he was doing by reading it.

INTERVIEWER: You seem to have avoided the company of writers in late years. Why?

HEMINGWAY: That is more complicated. The further you go in writing the more alone you are. Most of your best and oldest friends die. Others move away. You do not see them except rarely, but you write and have much the same contact with them as though you were together at the café in the old days. You exchange comic, sometimes cheerfully obscene and irresponsible letters, and it is almost as good as talking. But you are more alone because that is how you must work and the time to work is shorter all the time and if you waste it you feel you have committed a sin for which there is no forgiveness.

INTERVIEWER: What about the influence of some of these people —your contemporaries—on your work? What was Gertrude Stein's contribution, if any? Or Ezra Pound's? Or Max Perkins'?

HEMINGWAY: I'm sorry but I am no good at these post-mortems. There are coroners literary and non-literary provided to deal with such matters. Miss Stein wrote at some length and with considerable inaccuracy about her influence on my work. It was necessary for her to do this after she had learned to write dialogue from a book called *The Sun Also Rises*. I was very fond of her and thought it was splendid she had learned to write conversation. It was no new thing to me to learn from everyone I could, living or dead, and I had no idea it would affect Gertrude so violently. She already wrote very well in other ways. Ezra was extremely intelligent on the subjects he really knew. Doesn't this sort of talk bore you? This backyard literary gossip while washing out the dirty clothes of thirty-five years ago is disgusting to me. It would be different if one had tried to tell the whole truth. That would have some value. Here it is simpler and better to thank Gertrude for everything I learned from her about the abstract relationship of words, say how fond I was of her, reaffirm my loyalty to Ezra as a great poet and a loyal friend, and say that I cared so much for Max Perkins that I have never been able to accept that he is dead. He never asked me to change anything I wrote except to remove certain words which were not then publishable. Blanks were left, and anyone who knew the words would know what they were. For me he was not an editor. He was a wise friend and a wonderful companion. I liked the way he wore his hat and the strange way his lips moved.

INTERVIEWER: Who would you say are your literary forebears—those you have learned the most from?

HEMINGWAY: Mark Twain, Flaubert, Stendhal, Bach, Turgenev, Tolstoi, Dostoevski, Chekhov, Andrew Marvell, John Donne, Maupassant, the good Kipling, Thoreau, Captain Marryat, Shakespeare, Mozart, Quevedo, Dante, Vergil, Tintoretto, Hieronymus Bosch, Brueghel, Patinir, Goya, Giotto, Cézanne, Van Gogh, Gauguin, San Juan de la Cruz, Góngora—it would take a day to remember everyone. Then it would sound as though I were claiming an erudition I did not possess instead of trying to remember all the people who have been an influence on my life and work. This isn't an old dull question. It is a very good but a solemn question and requires an examination of conscience. I put in painters, or started to, because I learn as much from painters about how to write as from writers. You ask how this is done? It would take another day of explaining. I should think what one learns from composers and from the study of harmony and counterpoint would be obvious.

INTERVIEWER: Did you ever play a musical instrument?

HEMINGWAY: I used to play cello. My mother kept me out of school a whole year to study music and counterpoint. She thought I had ability, but I was absolutely without talent. We played chamber music—someone came in to play the violin; my sister played the viola, and mother the piano. That cello—I played it worse than anyone on earth. Of course, that year I was out doing other things too.

INTERVIEWER: Do you reread the authors of your list? Twain, for instance?

HEMINGWAY: You have to wait two or three years with Twain. You remember too well. I read some Shakespeare every year, *Lear* always. Cheers you up if you read that.

INTERVIEWER: Reading, then, is a constant occupation and pleasure.

HEMINGWAY: I'm always reading books—as many as there are. I ration myself on them so that I'll always be in supply.

INTERVIEWER: Do you ever read manuscripts?

HEMINGWAY: You can get into trouble doing that unless you know the author personally. Some years ago I was sued for plagiarism by a man who claimed that I'd lifted *For Whom the Bell Tolls* from an unpublished screen scenario he'd written. He'd read this scenario at some Hollywood party. I was there, he said, at least there was a fellow called "Ernie" there listening to the reading, and that was enough for him to sue for a million dollars. At the same time he sued the producers of the motion pictures *Northwest Mounted Police* and the *Cisco Kid*, claiming that these, as well, had been stolen from that same unpublished scenario. We went to court and, of course, won the case. The man turned out to be insolvent.

INTERVIEWER: Well, could we go back to that list and take one of the painters—Hieronymus Bosch, for instance? The nightmare symbolic quality of his work seems so far removed from your own.

HEMINGWAY: I have the nightmares and know about the ones other people have. But you do not have to write them down. Anything you can omit that you know you still have in the writing and its quality will show. When a writer omits things he does not know, they show like holes in his writing.

INTERVIEWER: Does that mean that a close knowledge of the works of the people on your list helps fill the "well" you were speaking of a while back? Or were they consciously a help in developing the techniques of writing?

HEMINGWAY: They were a part of learning to see, to hear, to think, to feel and not feel, and to write. The well is where your "juice" is. Nobody knows what it is made of, least of all yourself. What you know is if you have it, or you have to wait for it to come back.

INTERVIEWER: Would you admit to there being symbolism in your novels?

HEMINGWAY: I suppose there are symbols since critics keep finding them. If you do not mind I dislike talking about them and being questioned about them. It is hard enough to write books and stories without being asked to explain them as well. Also it deprives the explainers of work. If five or six or more good explainers can keep going why should I interfere with them? Read anything I write for the pleasure of reading it. Whatever else you find will be the measure of what you brought to the reading.

INTERVIEWER: Continuing with just one question on this line: One of the advisory staff editors wonders about a parallel he feels he's found in *The Sun Also Rises* between the dramatis personae of the bull ring and the characters of the novel itself. He points out that the first sentence of the book tells us Robert Cohn is a boxer; later, during the *desencajonada*, the bull is described as using his horns like a boxer, hooking and jabbing. And just as the bull is attracted and pacified by the presence of a steer, Robert Cohn defers to Jake who is emasculated precisely as is a steer. He sees Mike as the picador, baiting Cohn repeatedly. The editor's thesis goes on, but he wondered if it was your conscious intention to inform the novel with the tragic structure of the bullfight ritual.

HEMINGWAY: It sounds as though the advisory staff editor was a little bit screwy. Who ever said Jake was "emasculated precisely as is a steer"? Actually he had been wounded in quite a different way and his testicles were intact and not damaged. Thus he was capable of all normal feelings as a *man* but incapable of consummating them. The important distinction is that his wound was physical and not psychological and that he was not emasculated.

INTERVIEWER: These questions which inquire into craftsmanship really are an annoyance.

HEMINGWAY: A sensible question is neither a delight nor an annoyance. I still believe, though, that it is very bad for a writer to talk about how he writes. He writes to be read by the eye and no explanations or dissertations should be necessary. You can be sure that there is much more there than will be read at any first reading and having made this it is not the writer's province to explain it or to run guided tours through the more difficult country of his work.

INTERVIEWER: In connection with this, I remember you have also warned that it is dangerous for a writer to talk about a work-in-progress, that he can "talk it out" so to speak. Why should this be so? I only ask because there are so many writers—Twain, Wilde, Thurber, Steffens come to mind—who would seem to have polished their material by testing it on listeners.

HEMINGWAY: I cannot believe Twain ever "tested out" *Huckleberry Finn* on listeners. If he did they probably had him cut out good things and put in the bad parts. Wilde was said by people who knew him to have been a better talker than a writer. Steffens talked better than he wrote. Both his writing and his talking were sometimes hard to believe, and I heard many stories change as he grew older. If Thurber can talk as well as he writes he must be one of the greatest and least boring talkers. The man I know who talks best about his own trade and has the pleasantest and most wicked tongue is Juan Belmonte, the matador.

INTERVIEWER: Could you say how much thought-out effort went into the evolvement of your distinctive style?

HEMINGWAY: That is a long-term tiring question and if you spent a couple of days answering it you would be so self-conscious that you could not write. I might say that what amateurs call a style is usually only the unavoidable awkwardnesses in first trying to make something that has not heretofore been made. Almost no new classics resemble other previous classics. At first people can see only the awkwardness. Then they are not so perceptible. When they show so very awkwardly people think these awkwardnesses are the style and many copy them. This is regrettable.

INTERVIEWER: You once wrote me that the simple circumstances under which various pieces of fiction were written could be instructive. Could you apply this to "The Killers"—you said that you had written it, "Ten Indians," and "Today Is Friday" in one day —and perhaps to your first novel *The Sun Also Rises?*

HEMINGWAY: Let's see. *The Sun Also Rises* I started in Valencia on my birthday, July twenty-first. Hadley, my wife, and I had gone to Valencia early to get good tickets for the Feria there which started the twenty-fourth of July. Everybody my age had written a novel and I was still having a difficult time writing a paragraph. So I started the book on my birthday, wrote all through the Feria, in bed in the morning, went on to Madrid and wrote there. There was no Feria there, so we had a room with a table and I wrote in great luxury on the table and around the corner from the hotel in a beer place in the Pasaje Alvarez where it was cool. It finally got too hot to write and we went to Hendaye. There was a small cheap hotel there on the big long lovely beach and I worked very well there and then went up to Paris and finished the first draft in the apartment over the sawmill at 113 rue Notre-Dame-des-Champs six weeks from the day I started it. I showed the first draft to Nathan Asch, the novelist, who then had quite a strong accent, and he said, "Hem, vaht do you mean saying you wrote a novel? A novel huh. Hem you are riding a travhel büch." I was not too discouraged by Nathan and rewrote the book, keeping in the travel (that was the part about the fishing trip and Pamplona) at Schruns in the Vorarlberg at the Hotel Taube.

The stories you mention I wrote in one day in Madrid on May sixteenth when it snowed out the San Isidro bullfights. First I wrote "The Killers," which I'd tried to write before and failed. Then after lunch I got in bed to keep warm and wrote "Today Is Friday." I had so much juice I thought maybe I was going crazy and I had about six other stories to write. So I got dressed and walked to Fornos, the old bullfighters' café, and drank coffee and then came back and wrote "Ten Indians." This made me very sad and I drank some brandy and went to sleep. I'd forgotten to eat and one of the waiters brought me up some *bacalao* and a small steak and fried potatoes and a bottle of Valdepeñas.

The woman who ran the Pension was always worried that I did not eat enough and she had sent the waiter. I remember sitting up in bed and eating, and drinking the Valdepeñas. The waiter said he would bring up another bottle. He said the Señora wanted to know if I was going to write all night. I said no, I thought I would lay off for a while. Why don't you try to write just one more, the waiter asked. I'm only supposed to write one, I said. Nonsense, he said. You could write six. I'll try tomorrow, I said. Try it tonight, he said. What do you think the old woman sent the food up for?

I'm tired, I told him. Nonsense, he said (the word was not nonsense). You tired after three miserable little stories. Translate me one.

Leave me alone, I said. How am I going to write it if you don't leave me alone? So I sat up in bed and drank the Valdepeñas and thought what a hell of a writer I was if the first story was as good as I'd hoped.

INTERVIEWER: How complete in your own mind is the conception of a short story? Does the theme, or the plot, or a character change as you go along?

HEMINGWAY: Sometimes you know the story. Sometimes you make it up as you go along and have no idea how it will come out. Everything changes as it moves. That is what makes the movement which makes the story. Sometimes the movement is so slow it does not seem to be moving. But there is always change and always movement.

INTERVIEWER: Is it the same with the novel, or do you work out the whole plan before you start and adhere to it rigorously?

HEMINGWAY: *For Whom the Bell Tolls* was a problem which I carried on each day. I knew what was going to happen in principle. But I invented what happened each day I wrote.

INTERVIEWER: Were *The Green Hills of Africa, To Have and Have Not*, and *Across the River and Into the Trees* all started as short stories and developed into novels? If so, are the two forms so similar that the writer can pass from one to the other without completely revamping his approach?

HEMINGWAY: No, that is not true. *The Green Hills of Africa* is not a novel but was written in an attempt to write an absolutely true book to see whether the shape of a country and the pattern of a month's action could, if truly presented, compete with a work of the imagination. After I had written it I wrote two short stories, "The Snows of Kilimanjaro" and "The Short Happy Life of Francis Macomber." These were stories which I invented from the knowledge and experience acquired on the same long hunting trip one month of which I had tried to write a truthful account of in *The Green Hills. To Have and Have Not* and *Across the River and Into the Trees* were both started as short stories.

INTERVIEWER: Do you find it easy to shift from one literary project to another or do you continue through to finish what you start?

HEMINGWAY: The fact that I am interrupting serious work to answer these questions proves that I am so stupid that I should be penalized severely. I will be. Don't worry.

INTERVIEWER: Do you think of yourself in competition with other writers?

HEMINGWAY: Never. I used to try to write better than certain dead writers of whose value I was certain. For a long time now I have tried simply to write the best I can. Sometimes I have good luck and write better than I can.

INTERVIEWER: Do you think a writer's power diminishes as he grows older? In *The Green Hills of Africa* you mention that American writers at a certain age change into Old Mother Hubbards.

HEMINGWAY: I don't know about that. People who know what they are doing should last as long their heads last. In that book you mention, if you look it up, you'll see I was sounding off about American literature with a humorless Austrian character who was forcing me to talk when I wanted to do something else. I wrote an accurate account of the conversation. Not to make deathless pronouncements. A fair per cent of the pronouncements are good enough.

INTERVIEWER: We've not discussed character. Are the characters of your work taken without exception from real life?

HEMINGWAY: Of course they are not. *Some* come from real life. Mostly you invent people from a knowledge and understanding and experience of people.

INTERVIEWER: Could you say something about the process of turning a real-life character into a fictional one?

HEMINGWAY: If I explained how that is sometimes done, it would be a handbook for libel lawyers.

INTERVIEWER: Do you make a distinction—as E. M. Forster does —between "flat" and "round" characters?

HEMINGWAY: If you describe someone, it is flat, as a photograph is, and from my standpoint a failure. If you make him up from what you know, there should be all the dimensions.

INTERVIEWER: Which of your characters do you look back on with particular affection?

HEMINGWAY: That would make too long a list.

INTERVIEWER: Then you enjoy reading over your own books— without feeling there are changes you would like to make?

HEMINGWAY: I read them sometimes to cheer me up when it is hard to write and then I remember that it was always difficult and how nearly impossible it was sometimes.

INTERVIEWER: How do you name your characters?

HEMINGWAY: The best I can.

INTERVIEWER: Do the titles come to you while you're in the process of doing the story?

HEMINGWAY: No. I make a list of titles *after* I've finished the story or the book—sometimes as many as a hundred. Then I start eliminating them, sometimes all of them.

INTERVIEWER: And you do this even with a story whose title is supplied from the text—"Hills Like White Elephants," for example?

HEMINGWAY: Yes. The title comes afterwards. I met a girl in Prunier where I'd gone to eat oysters before lunch. I knew she'd had an abortion. I went over and we talked, not about that, but on the way home I thought of the story, skipped lunch, and spent that afternoon writing it.

INTERVIEWER: So when you're not writing, you remain constantly the observer, looking for something which can be of use.

HEMINGWAY: Surely. If a writer stops observing he is finished. But he does not have to observe consciously nor think how it will be useful. Perhaps that would be true at the beginning. But later everything he sees goes into the great reserve of things he knows or has seen. If it is any use to know it, I always try to write on the principle of the iceberg. There is seven-eighths of it underwater for every part that shows. Anything you know you can eliminate and it only strengthens your iceberg. It is the part that doesn't show. If a writer omits something because he does not know it then there is a hole in the story.

The Old Man and the Sea could have been over a thousand pages long and had every character in the village in it and all the processes of how they made their living, were born, educated, bore children, etc. That is done excellently and well by other writers. In writing you are limited by what has already been done satisfactorily. So I have tried to learn to do something else. First I have tried to eliminate everything unnecessary to conveying experience to the reader so that after he or she has read something it will become a part of his or her experience and seem actually to have happened. This is very hard to do and I've worked at it very hard.

Anyway, to skip how it is done, I had unbelievable luck this time and could convey the experience completely and have it be one that no one had ever conveyed. The luck was that I had a good man and a good boy and lately writers have forgotten there still are such things. Then the ocean is worth writing about just as man is. So I was lucky there. I've seen the marlin mate and know about that. So I leave that out. I've seen a school (or pod) of more than fifty sperm whales in that same stretch of water and once harpooned one nearly sixty feet in length and lost him. So I left that out. All the stories I know from the fishing village I leave out. But the knowledge is what makes the under-water part of the iceberg.

INTERVIEWER: Archibald MacLeish has spoken of a method of conveying experience to a reader which he said you developed while covering baseball games back in those *Kansas City Star* days. It was simply that experience is communicated by small details, intimately preserved, which have the effect of indicating the whole by making the reader conscious of what he had been aware of only subconsciously. . . .

HEMINGWAY: The anecdote is apocryphal. I never wrote baseball for the *Star*. What Archie was trying to remember was how I was trying to learn in Chicago in around 1920 and was searching for the unnoticed things that made emotions, such as the way an outfielder tossed his glove without looking back to where it fell, the squeak of resin on canvas under a fighter's flat-soled gym shoes, the gray color of Jack Blackburn's skin when he had just come out of stir, and other things I noted as a painter sketches. You saw Blackburn's strange color and the old razor cuts and the way he spun a man before you knew his history. These were the things which moved you before you knew the story.

INTERVIEWER: Have you ever described any type of situation of which you had no personal knowledge?

HEMINGWAY: That is a strange question. By personal knowledge do you mean carnal knowledge? In that case the answer is positive. A writer, if he is any good, does not describe. He invents or *makes* out of knowledge personal and impersonal and sometimes he seems to have unexplained knowledge which could come from forgotten racial or family experience. Who teaches the homing pigeon to fly as he does; where does a fighting bull get his bravery, or a hunting dog his nose? This is an elaboration or a condensation on that stuff we were talking about in Madrid that time when my head was not to be trusted.

INTERVIEWER: How detached must you be from an experience before you can write about it in fictional terms? The African air crashes you were involved in, for instance?

HEMINGWAY: It depends on the experience. One part of you sees it with complete detachment from the start. Another part is very involved. I think there is no rule about how soon one should write about it. It would depend on how well adjusted the individual was and on his or her recuperative powers. Certainly it is valuable to a trained writer to crash in an aircraft which burns. He learns several important things very quickly. Whether they will be of use to him is conditioned by survival. Survival, with honor, that outmoded and all-important word, is as difficult as ever and as all important to a writer. Those who do not last are always more beloved since no one has to see them in their long, dull, unrelenting, no-quarter-given-and-no-quarter-received, fights that they make to do something as they believe it should be done before they die. Those who die or quit early and easy and with every good reason are preferred because they are understandable and human. Failure and well-disguised cowardice are more human and more beloved.

INTERVIEWER: Could I ask you to what extent you think the writer should concern himself with the socio-political problems of his times?

HEMINGWAY: Everyone has his own conscience, and there should be no rules about how a conscience should function. All you can be sure about in a political-minded writer is that if his work should last you will have to skip the politics when you read it. Many of the so-called politically enlisted writers change their politics frequently. This is very exciting to them and to their political-literary reviews. Sometimes they even have to rewrite their viewpoints . . . and in a hurry. Perhaps it can be respected as a form of the pursuit of happiness.

INTERVIEWER: Has the political influence of Ezra Pound on the segregationalist Kasper had any effect on your belief that the poet ought to be released from St. Elizabeth's Hospital? *

HEMINGWAY: No. None at all. I believe Ezra should be released and allowed to write poetry in Italy on an undertaking by him to abstain from any politics. I would be happy to see Kasper jailed as soon as possible. Great poets are not necessarily girl guides nor scoutmasters nor splendid influences on youth. To name a few: Verlaine, Rimbaud, Shelley, Byron, Baudelaire, Proust, Gide should not have been confined to prevent them from being aped in their thinking, their manners or their morals by local Kaspers. I am sure that it will take a footnote to this paragraph in ten years to explain who Kasper was.

INTERVIEWER: Would you say, ever, that there is any didactic intention in your work?

HEMINGWAY: Didactic is a word that has been misused and has spoiled. *Death in the Afternoon* is an instructive book.

INTERVIEWER: It has been said that a writer only deals with one

---

* In 1958 a Federal court in Washington, D.C., dismissed all charges against Pound, clearing the way for his release from St. Elizabeth's.

or two ideas throughout his work. Would you say your work reflects one or two ideas?

HEMINGWAY: Who said that? It sounds much too simple. The man who said it possibly *had* only one or two ideas.

INTERVIEWER: Well, perhaps it would be better put this way: Graham Greene said that a ruling passion gives to a shelf of novels the unity of a system. You yourself have said, I believe, that great writing comes out of a sense of injustice. Do you consider it important that a novelist be dominated in this way—by some such compelling sense?

HEMINGWAY: Mr. Greene has a facility for making statements that I do not possess. It would be impossible for me to make generalizations about a shelf of novels or a wisp of snipe or a gaggle of geese. I'll try a generalization though. A writer without a sense of justice and of injustice would be better off editing the Year Book of a school for exceptional children than writing novels. Another generalization. You see; they are not so difficult when they are sufficiently obvious. The most essential gift for a good writer is a built-in, shock-proof, shit detector. This is the writer's radar and all great writers have had it.

INTERVIEWER: Finally, a fundamental question: namely, as a creative writer what do you think is the function of your art? Why a representation of fact, rather than fact itself?

HEMINGWAY: Why be puzzled by that? From things that have happened and from things as they exist and from all things that you know and all those you cannot know, you make something through your invention that is not a representation but a whole new thing truer than anything true and alive, and you make it alive, and if you make it well enough, you give it immortality. That is why you write and for no other reason that you know of. But what about all the reasons that no one knows?

GEORGE PLIMPTON

10. S. J. Perelman

S. J. Perelman was born February 1, 1904, in Brooklyn. He attended Brown University, where he was a contemporary of Nathanael West, whose sister, Laura, he later married. In 1934 he started writing for *The New Yorker* and has been closely associated with that magazine ever since.

In addition to his voluminous output of short pieces, Mr. Perelman has worked extensively in both the theater and films, having written several of the early Marx Brothers classics and *Around the World in Eighty Days.* In 1943 he collaborated with Ogden Nash to produce the musical comedy *One Touch of Venus.* His play, *The Beauty Part,* opened in New York late in 1962.

S. J. Perelman is generally considered, along with the late James Thurber, to be among the greatest humorists American literature has produced. He is the author of *Dawn Ginsbergh's Revenge* (1929), and his most recent published work, in book form, includes the following: *Strictly from Hunger* (1937), *Crazy Like a Fox* (1944), *Westward Ha!* (1948), *Listen to the Mocking Bird* (1949), *The Swiss Family Perelman* (1950), *The Ill-Tempered Clavichord* (1953), *The Road to Miltown* (1957), *The Most of S. J. Perelman* (1958), *The Rising Gorge* (1961).

2-

pity, when I beheld a poster that ~~thankfully banished those dark humors~~ *mercifully*
~~and~~ set me off on quite another tangent. "Win a fabulous week for two at
the Stardust in Las Vegas plus $2500. in cash!" it trumpeted. "Play ~~Eagle~~ Magle
Pencil Company's Quality Control Game!" I never ascertained whether I was
some magic
to watch for ~~a~~ serial numbers or to hawk the pencils from door to
door. In the next breath, I was ejected to the platform, and there super-
imposed~~itself~~ on my mind a memory ~~of~~ this self-same Stardust, fabulous
short
indeed, as I saw it during a ~~enforced~~ visit to Las Vegas a year ago.

My trip to the ~~gambling Mecca~~ ~~was no casual stop-over between~~ it
planes; I flew there from Rome, ~~a matter of~~ ~~Seven thousand odd miles, to~~
~~honor~~ ~~le an actor,~~ ~~impending film property;~~
~~and I undertook the journey with the direst~~
misgivings. ~~The circumstances were roughly~~ as follows. Several months
film
before, an Italian ~~producer~~ ~~named Riccardo~~ had engaged me to devise a
tenor   it might be prudent to call
vehicle for a meteoric ~~singer~~ whom ~~Riccardo~~ ~~Harry Fauntleroy. The~~
~~latter,~~
~~whose~~ ~~and his recent personal appearances, had, scored a phe-~~ *Sigur Bombasi*
~~nomenal success in the United States and Europe; his presence in a picture,~~
it was universally felt, would make it a bonanza; and, ~~Riccardo,~~ from the
moment I began work in Rome, declared himself ready to go to any lengths
to win ~~Fauntleroy's~~ approval of our story. I soon found out what he meant.
which is to say the
Shortly after finishing the treatment, ~~the~~ narrative outline of the ~~scenario,~~
a composite of Congreve, Pirandello, and ~~Norman Mailer~~, and
I was ~~summoned~~ ~~to my employee,~~ hailed as ~~the most scintillating, warm-~~
Renaissance   affirmed ~~Riccardo~~
~~hearted to convey the inexhaustible in person to Fauntleroy.~~ Nobody else could
adequately interpret its gusto and sparkle, its rippling mirth and delicious
nuances. My expostulations, my protests that I was anathema to performers,
went for naught; in a supplication ~~that would have reduced Ralph Henry~~
Bombasi
~~Barbour to tears,~~ ~~Riccardo~~ entreated me, for the sake of the
team if not my own future, to comply. Seven hours later, I ~~hedged~~
~~the~~ Ciampino West Airdrome.

---

* (And nobody else in the ~~entire~~ organization spoke even rudimentary
English, he might well have added.)

---

*Manuscript page from S. J. Perelman's "Revulsion in the Desert" (from The Rising
Gorge).*

AL HIRSCHFELD

S. J. Perelman

S. J. Perelman has an eighty-acre farm in Bucks County, Pennsylvania (where the house is "shingled with second-hand wattles"), a Greenwich Village apartment, and a no-nonsense, one-room office, also in the Village. It was there that the interview took place. The office is furnished like a slightly luxuriant monk's cell: a few simple chairs, a desk, a cot. On the walls are a Stuart Davis water color and photographs of James Joyce, Somerset Maugham, and the late Gus Lobrano, a New Yorker editor and close friend of the author. The only bizarre touch is David Niven's hat from Around the World in Eighty Days, mounted on a pedestal.

Mr. Perelman, trim and well-tailored, is of medium build. His hair is gently receding, and graying at the temples. He wears old-fashioned steel-rimmed spectacles, bought in Paris many years ago. He is soft-spoken and reserved, sometimes chilling, and gives the impression that he does not suffer "nudniks" gladly. He cares about

words in their proper places; in his speech each sentence emerges
whole and well-balanced, and each generally contains one or two
typically Perelmanesque words. He is impatient with obvious
questions—those that he has been asked over and over again in
hundreds of interviews—but lights up when talking about his days
in Hollywood, or telling anecdotes about his friend Robert Benchley. As The Listener put it, reporting on a television interview,
"Mr. Perelman knew all the answers and gave such as he chose."

INTERVIEWER: We've always been intrigued that when your first
book, Dawn Ginsbergh's Revenge, appeared in '29, there was no
author's name on the title page. Why?

PERELMAN: Well, it was really an oversight of my own. I was so
exalted at being collected for the first time that, in correcting the
galleys, I completely overlooked the fact that there was no author's
name on the title page. Unless one happened to look at the spine
of the book, there would be every implication that it was written
by its publisher, Horace Liveright.

INTERVIEWER: Do you look back on your work with pleasure?
How long is it since you've re-examined Dawn Ginsbergh's
Revenge?

PERELMAN: I haven't actually looked on it for some time. As far
as deriving any pleasure, it would be quite the reverse.

INTERVIEWER: Is that true of all your pieces?

PERELMAN: Well, there are a couple of them I consider verbal
zircons if not gems. In Raymond Chandler Speaking, a recently-
published collection of his letters, I ran across a very flattering
reference he made to a parody of his work I had done, "Farewell,
My Lovely Appetizer." So I reread a few pages of that to see
whether the praise was merited. I prefer not to say whether I think
so or not. Otherwise, let me assure you I don't sit in the chimney
corner cackling over what I've written.

INTERVIEWER: Is that because of the effort you put into each
piece?

PERELMAN: Possibly. I very much doubt whether I work harder than any other writer, but this particular kind of sludge is droned over while working so that it becomes incantatory and quite sickening for me, at least, to reread.

INTERVIEWER: So much of it is pure art and skill, I should think one would say, "My God, how did I make that association, that connection?"

PERELMAN: I don't know whether I approve of the picture you suggest of me, lounging about admiring myself in a hand mirror.

INTERVIEWER: Well, in those rare instances when you reread something after a few years, do you get the feeling you should have done something else to a sentence, to a phrase?

PERELMAN: No, I generally feel astonished at whatever I put down in the first place. The effort of writing seems more arduous all the time. Unlike technicians who are supposed to become more proficient with practice, I find I've grown considerably less articulate.

INTERVIEWER: Is that because you are increasingly more selective?

PERELMAN: Could be. Also the variety of subjects is restricted the longer I stay at this dodge.

INTERVIEWER: Why?

PERELMAN: Well, principally through sheer ennui on my part. I've sought material, for example, in the novels I read in my youth, the movies I saw, my Hollywood years, and in advertising. Ultimately, I began to regard these matters as boring. I always grieve for the poor souls who have to grind out a daily humorous column or a weekly piece—people like H. I. Phillips who are obligated to be comical on whatever topic. I remember Benchley did a column three times a week at one time and ran into deep trouble. It's just not possible, in my view.

INTERVIEWER: There were more of those columns back in the twenties and thirties when Don Marquis was working that way, and F.P.A.

PERELMAN: Well, Marquis fortunately had Archie, his cockroach, and the Old Soak. When you create character it's much easier, because you can keep that spinning. In Frank Adams's case, let's not overlook the extensive help he got from contributors —Ira Gershwin, Sam Hoffenstein, Arthur Kober, Yip Harburg— a pretty respectable roster of names.

INTERVIEWER: In the introduction to *The Most of S. J. Perelman* Dorothy Parker referred to you as a "humorist writer." Do you think of yourself as a humorist writer?

PERELMAN: I may be doing Mrs. Parker an injustice, but I think the linotyper had one drink too many, and that "humorous" was what was intended. In my more pompous moments I like to think of myself as a writer rather than a humorist, but I suppose that's merely the vanity of advancing age.

INTERVIEWER: Mrs. Parker has said that there aren't any humorists any more . . . except for Perelman. She went on to say, "There's no need for them. Perelman must be very lonely." Are there humorists? Is there a need for them, and are you lonely?

PERELMAN: Well, it must be thoroughly apparent how many more people wrote humor for the printed page in the twenties. The form seems to be passing, and there aren't many practitioners left. The only magazine nowadays that carries any humor worthy of the name, in my estimation, is *The New Yorker*. Thirty years ago, on the other hand, there were *Judge, Life, Vanity Fair, College Humor*, and one or two others. I think the explanation for the paucity of written humor is simply that very few fledgling writers deign to bother with it. If someone has a flair for comedy, he usually goes into television or what remains of motion pictures. There's far more loot in those fields, and while it's ignominious to be an anonymous gagman, perhaps, eleven hundred dollars a week can be very emollient to the ego. The life of the free-lance writer of humor is highly speculative and not to be recommended as a vocation. In the technical sense, the comic writer is a cat on a hot tin roof. His invitation to perform is liable to wear out at any moment; he must quickly and constantly amuse in a short span, and the first smothered yawn is a signal to get lost. The fiction writer, in contrast, has much more latitude. He's allowed to side-slip into exposition, to wander off into interminable byways and browse around endlessly in his characters' heads. The development of a comic idea has to be swift and economical; consequently, the pieces are shorter than conventional fiction and fetch a much smaller stipend.

INTERVIEWER: Is this the reason so few comic novels are written?

PERELMAN: Well, the comic novel, I feel, is perhaps the most difficult form a writer can attempt. I can think of only three or four successful ones—*Cakes and Ale, Count Bruga,* and *Lucky Jim. Zuleika Dobson* is often held forth, but the sad fact is that it falls apart two-thirds of the way through, ending rather lamely with the mass suicide at Oxford.

INTERVIEWER: Would you call *The Ginger Man* a comic novel?

PERELMAN: Rather terrifying. I think it's funny in spots, but many people boggle at certain scabrous passages early in the book. In a way, it's a pity the author should have retained them, because they add little and, on the whole, constrict the fun. . . . The name of F. Anstey, rarely heard nowadays, deserves honorable mention when comic novels are discussed. He edited *Punch* in the late nineties and was also a very successful playwright. He worked for the most part in the realm of fantasy and turned out some very diverting stories—*Vice Versa, The Brass Bottle,* and specifically *The Tinted Venus,* which Ogden Nash and I used as the basis for a musical we wrote called *One Touch of Venus.*

INTERVIEWER: Was Anstey an influence on you? Would you talk a little about your admirations?

PERELMAN: I stole from the very best sources. I was, and still remain, a great admirer of George Ade, who flourished in this country between 1905 and 1915, and who wrote a good many fables in slang that enjoyed a vogue in my youth. I was also a devotee of Stephen Leacock and, of course, Ring Lardner, who at his best was the nonpareil; nobody in America has ever equaled him. One day, I hope, some bearded Ph.D. will get around—

belatedly—to tracing the indebtedness of John O'Hara and a couple other of my colleagues to Lardner. In addition to Ade, Leacock, and Lardner, I was also an earnest student of Benchley, Donald Ogden Stewart, and Frank Sullivan—and we mustn't forget Mencken. At the time I was being forcefully educated, in the early twenties, Mencken and Nathan had a considerable impact, and many of us undergraduates modeled our prose styles on theirs.

INTERVIEWER: How would you describe the form you work in? You've called it "the sportive essay" in a previous interview.

PERELMAN: I classify myself as a writer of what the French call *feuilletons*—that is, a writer of little leaves. They're comic essays of a particular type.

INTERVIEWER: Are there any devices you use to get yourself going on them?

PERELMAN: No, I don't think so. Just anguish. Just sitting and staring at the typewriter and avoiding the issue as long as possible. Raymond Chandler and I discussed this once, and he admitted to the most bitter reluctance to commit anything to paper. He evolved the following scheme: he had a tape recorder into which he spoke the utmost nonsense—a stream of consciousness which was then transcribed by a secretary and which he then used as a basis for his first rough draft. Very laborious. He strongly advised me to do the same . . . in fact became so excited that he kept plying me with information for months about the machine that helped him.

INTERVIEWER: Hervey Allen, the author of *Anthony Adverse*, apparently had the voices of his ancestors to help him. All he had to do was lie on a bed, close his eyes, and they went to work for him.

PERELMAN: I fully believe it, judging from my memory of his work.

INTERVIEWER: How many drafts of a story do you do?

PERELMAN: Thirty-seven. I once tried doing thirty-three, but something was lacking, a certain—how shall I say?—*je ne sais quoi*. On another occasion, I tried forty-two versions, but the final effect was too lapidary—you know what I mean, Jack? What the hell are you trying to extort—my trade secrets?

INTERVIEWER: . . . merely to get some clue to the way you work.

PERELMAN: With the grocer sitting on my shoulder. The only thing that matters is the end product, which must have *brio*—or, as you Italians put it, vivacity.

INTERVIEWER: Speaking of vivacity, you have been quoted as saying that the Walpurgisnacht scene in *Ulysses* is the greatest single comic achievement in the language.

PERELMAN: I was quoted accurately. And here's something else to quote. Joyce was probably one of the most careful writers who ever lived. I have been studying the work you mentioned for nigh on thirty-five years, and I still choke up with respect.

INTERVIEWER: Your writing—like Joyce's, in fact—presupposes a great deal of arcane knowledge on the part of your reader. There are references to cultural figures and styles long past, obsolete words, architectural oddities—reverberations that not everybody will catch. Do you agree that you're writing for a particularly cultured audience?

PERELMAN: Well, I don't know if that grocer on my shoulder digs all the references, but other than him, I write pretty much for myself. If, at the close of business each evening, I myself can understand what I've written, I feel the day hasn't been totally wasted.

INTERVIEWER: Perhaps you would talk about the incongruity that turns up so often in your use of language.

PERELMAN: And then perhaps I would not. Writers who pontificate about their own use of language drive me right up the wall. I've discovered that this is an occupational disease of those ladies with three-barreled names one meets at the Authors' League, the P.E.N. Club, and so forth. In what spare time I have, I read the expert opinions of V. S. Pritchett and Edmund Wilson, who are to my mind the best-qualified authorities on the written English language. Vaporizing about one's own stylistic intricacies strikes me as being visceral, and, to be blunt, inexcusable.

INTERVIEWER: In your own writing, when you're at work, thinking hard, and a particularly felicitous expression or phrase comes to mind, do you laugh?

PERELMAN: When I was young I used to literally roll over and over on the floor with delight, marveling at the intricacy of the mind that had wrought such gems. I've become much less supple in late middle age.

INTERVIEWER: It's often said—or taught, anyway—that what seems at first blush funny is usually not. Would that be a good maxim in writing humor?

PERELMAN: In writing anything, sweetie. The old apothegm that easy writing makes hard reading is as succinct as ever. I used to know several eminent writers who were given to boasting of the speed with which they created. It's not a lovable attribute, to put it mildly, and I'm afraid our acquaintanceship has languished.

INTERVIEWER: The country's comics can't write a book or even a piece of any value at all. Why is that?

PERELMAN: You're confusing comedians—that is to say, performers—with writers. The two have entirely different orientations. How many writers do you know who can run around a musical-comedy stage like Groucho Marx, or, for that matter, talk collectedly into a microphone? Only a genius like David Susskind can do everything.

INTERVIEWER: I'd like to ask about the frequent use of Yiddish references and expressions throughout your writing. Words like "nudnik" and "schlepp" and "tzimmas" come in frequently enough.

PERELMAN: Your pronunciation of "nudnik," by the way, is appalling. It's "nudnik," not "noodnik." As to why I occasionally use the words you indicate, I like them for their invective content. There are nineteen words in Yiddish that convey gradations of disparagement from a mild, fluttery helplessness to a state of downright, irreconcilable brutishness. All of them can be usefully employed to pin-point the kind of individuals I write about.

INTERVIEWER: Almost all the humorous writers of your period have worked in Hollywood. How do you look back on the time you served there?

PERELMAN: With revulsion. I worked there sporadically from 1931 to 1942, and I can say in all sincerity that I would have spent my time to better advantage on Tristan da Cunha.

INTERVIEWER: Does that include your association with the Marx Brothers, for whom you worked on *Monkey Business* and *Horsefeathers?*

PERELMAN: I've dealt exhaustively with this particular phase of my life: to such a degree, in fact, that the mere mention of Hollywood induces a condition in me like breakbone fever. It was a hideous and untenable place when I dwelt there, populated with few exceptions by Yahoos, and now that it has become the chief citadel of television, it's unspeakable. Could we seguy into some other subject?

INTERVIEWER: Yes, but before we do, might we stimulate your memory of any colleagues of yours—writers humorous or otherwise—who functioned in Hollywood during the time you spent there?

PERELMAN: Well, of course everyone imaginable worked there at one time or another, and the closest analogy I can draw to describe the place is that it strikingly resembled the Sargasso Sea— an immense, turgidly revolving whirlpool in which literary hulks encrusted with verdigris moldered until they sank. It was really quite startling, at those buffet dinners in Beverly Hills, to encounter some dramatist or short-story writer out of your boyhood, or some one-shot lady novelist who'd had a flash success, who was now grinding out screenplays about the Cisco Kid for Sol Wurtzel. I remember, one day on the back lot at M-G-M, that a pallid wraith of a man erupted from a row of ramshackle dressing rooms and embraced me as though we had encountered each other in the Empty Quarter of Arabia. He was a geezer I'd known twelve years before on *Judge* magazine, a fellow who ran some inconsequential column full of Prohibition jokes. When I asked him what he was doing, he replied that he had been writing a screenplay of "Edwin Drood" for the past two years. He confessed quite candidly that he hadn't been able as yet to devise a finish, which, of course, wasn't too surprising inasmuch as Charles Dickens couldn't do so either.

INTERVIEWER: Surely you must have drawn some comfort from the presence of writers like Robert Benchley, Dorothy Parker, and Donald Ogden Stewart?

PERELMAN: It goes without saying, but since you've said it, I can only agree most emphatically. You happen to have mentioned a remarkable trio, all of them people who had no more connection with the screen-writing fraternity than if they'd been Martians. Benchley and Mrs. Parker differed from Stewart in the sense that neither of them ever made an accommodation with Hollywood. Stewart did; he was a highly paid screenwriter for many years, made a great deal of loot there, and managed to get it out. The last is quite a trick, because that fairy money they paid you had a way of evaporating as you headed east through the Cajon Pass. But whereas Stewart was a consecrated scenarist, Mrs. Parker and Benchley viewed Hollywood with utter accuracy, is my belief.

INTERVIEWER: Which was what?

PERELMAN: As a dreary industrial town controlled by hoodlums of enormous wealth, the ethical sense of a pack of jackals, and taste so degraded that it befouled everything it touched. I don't mean to sound like a boy Savonarola, but there were times, when I drove along the Sunset Strip and looked at those buildings, or when I watched the fashionable film colony arriving at some premiere at Grauman's Egyptian, that I fully expected God in his wrath to obliterate the whole shebang. It was—if you'll allow me to use a hopelessly inexpressive word—*dégoutant*.

INTERVIEWER: Feeling as you assert Mrs. Parker and Mr. Benchley did, and as you plainly did, how could you manage to remain there for even limited periods?

PERELMAN: We used to ask each other that with great frequency. The answer, of course, was geetus—gelt—scratch. We all badly needed the universal lubricant, we all had dependents and insurance policies and medical bills, and the characters who ran the celluloid factories were willing to lay it on the line. After all, it was no worse than playing the piano in a whorehouse.

INTERVIEWER: Do you feel that Hollywood evolved any writers of consequence, men and women who did important and memorable work in the medium?

PERELMAN: Oh, certainly—Frances Goodrich and Albert Hackett, Robert Riskin, and one or two others—but actually, it was a director's medium rather than a writer's. Men like W. S. Van Dyke, Frank Capra, George Cukor, Mitchell Leisen, William Wyler, and John Huston were the real film-makers, just as their predecessors in the silent era had been. I always felt that the statement attributed to Irving Thalberg, the patron saint at Metro-Goldwyn-Mayer, beautifully summed up the situation: "The writer is a necessary evil." As a sometime employee of his, I consider that a misquotation. I suspect he said "weevil."

INTERVIEWER: Haven't there been writers who originated in films and then went on to make a contribution on Broadway?

PERELMAN: Well, after scratching my woolly poll for half an hour, I can think of three—Dore Schary, Norman Krasna, and Leonard Spigelgass—but I believe I am in my legal rights in refusing to assess their contribution. We shall have to leave that to the verdict of history, and meanwhile permit me to soothe my agitated stomach with this Gelusil tablet.

INTERVIEWER: Do you ever revisit Hollywood?

PERELMAN: Every few years, and never out of choice. The place has become pretty tawdry by now; there was a time, back in the early thirties, when all the stucco and the Georgian shop fronts were fresh, and, while the architecture was hair-raising, there was enough greenery to soften it. But they've let the place go down nowadays—Hollywood proper is cracked and crazed, the gilt's peeling, and the whole thing has a depressing bargain-basement air. Beverly Hills, except for a few streets, is a nightmare; the entrance to it, which used to be a field of poinsettias, now sports a bank that must be the single most horrendous structure in the world. Of course, I except the Guggenheim Museum on Fifth Avenue.

INTERVIEWER: In short, then, you experience almost no feelings of nostalgia when you return to Southern California?

PERELMAN: Sir, you are a master of understatement.

INTERVIEWER: Nathanael West lived in Hollywood, and wrote a remarkable book about it, *The Day of the Locust*. He was your brother-in-law. And you are his literary executor?

PERELMAN· Whatever that implies. In my case it takes the form of being the recipient of a lot of slush mail from ambitious people working toward a degree, usually a doctorate. The curious thing is that every single one of them nurses the delusion that he has discovered Nathanael West, and that with his thesis West will receive the recognition he's entitled to. It keeps the incinerator going full time.

INTERVIEWER: You knew F. Scott Fitzgerald in Hollywood?

PERELMAN: Yes—in a period of his life that must have been one of his most trying. The anxieties and pressures of his private life, combined with the decline of his reputation, had nearly overwhelmed him, and he was seeking to re-establish himself as a writer for films. He didn't succeed, and I don't believe he ever would have. He was pathetically innocent about the kind of hypocrisy and the infighting one had to practice to exist in the industry.

INTERVIEWER: Did you ever see Faulkner out there?

PERELMAN: Very infrequently. Sometimes, of a Sunday morning, he used to stroll by a house I occupied in Beverly Hills. I noticed him only because the sight of anybody walking in that environment stamped him as an eccentric, and indeed, it eventually got him into trouble. A prowl car picked him up and he had a rather sticky time of it. The police were convinced he was a finger man for some jewelry mob planning to knock over one of the fancy residences.

INTERVIEWER: Your reluctance to discuss Hollywood is so manifest that we will change the venue to a more metropolitan one. *The New Yorker* is known as the most closely edited magazine of all time. What can you tell us of its interior structure?

PERELMAN: No more than you would have gleaned from Thurber's disquisitions on the subject. Personally, I thought that in *The Years with Ross* he made the paper and its staff sound prankish, like a bunch of schoolboys playing at journalism. But one must remember that Thurber's entire life was bound up in *The New Yorker* and that on occasion he was inclined to deify it. At a gathering one evening during the mid-thirties, when he was extolling its glories and parenthetically his major share in creating them, I mildly suggested that a sense of moderation was indicated and that it was merely another fifteen-cent magazine. Thurber sprang on me, and, had it not been for the intercession of several other contributors, unquestionably would have garrotted me.

INTERVIEWER: How often did Ross or *The New Yorker* come up with an idea or a suggestion for a piece?

PERELMAN: Not too often. Most of the suggestions I get originate in mysterious quarters. They drift in from kindly readers, or I spot something—

INTERVIEWER: There are kindly readers?

PERELMAN: There are, and I'm continually heartened by the fact that people take the time to forward a clipping or a circular they feel might inspire me.

INTERVIEWER: Does it worry you, since you often pick very contemporary subjects to write about, that your work may become outdated?

PERELMAN: Sir, the answer to that is that I regard myself as a species of journalist, and that questions of imperishability are at best idle. At my most euphoric, I don't expect to outlast Mount Rushmore.

INTERVIEWER: Have you ever considered a serious book?

PERELMAN: It may surprise you to hear me say—and I'll thank you not to confuse me with masters of the paradox like Oscar Wilde and G. K. Chesterton—that I regard my comic writing as serious. For the past thirty-four years, I have been approached almost hourly by damp people with foreheads like Rocky Ford melons who urge me to knock off my frivolous career and get started on that novel I'm burning to write. I have no earthly intention of doing any such thing. I don't believe in the importance of scale; to me the muralist is no more valid than the miniature painter. In this very large country, where size is all and where Thomas Wolfe outranks Robert Benchley, I am content to stitch away at my embroidery hoop. I think the form I work can have its own distinction, and I would like to surpass what I have done in it.

WILLIAM COLE
GEORGE PLIMPTON

11. Lawrence Durrell

Lawrence Durrell, a British citizen of Irish parents, was born in the Himalayas on February 27, 1912. He went to school in India until he was ten, when he transferred to St. Edmund's in Canterbury. He was one of four children, all of whom, when still young, were taken by their mother to live on the island of Corfu in the Mediterranean. His book on Corfu is entitled *Prospero's Cell* (1945), and *Reflections on a Marine Venus* (1953) is about nearby Rhodes.

Twice divorced, he has two daughters, one with the unusual name of Sappho-Jane, with whom he lived for a while the life of a recluse on the island of Cyprus. *Bitter Lemons* (1957) is an impressionistic study of the moods and atmosphere of these troubled years (1953–1956) on Cyprus, as, of course, are many passages in *Justine*. Durrell owned a small house there, where he wrote in the late hours. When necessity arose, he taught English at the local *gymnasium*. Then he found himself in the middle of a revolutionary situation, and he spent two years as a senior government official.

Durrell has also had a diplomatic career as a press attaché in Athens, Alexandria, Cairo, Rhodes, and Belgrade, and has been a lecturer in Argentina and Greece. He has satirized many of his government and travel experiences in *Esprit de Corps* (1957) and *Stiff Upper Lip* (1959).

Prior to his "Alexandria Quartet" (*Justine, Balthazar, Mountolive, Clea,* 1957–1960), Durrell had published three other novels, *Panic Spring* (1937), *The Black Book* (1938), and *Cefalu* (1947, republished as *The Dark Labyrinth* in 1958). *The Black Book,* first published in Paris, was hailed by T. S. Eliot as "the first piece of work by a new English writer to give me any hope for the future of prose fiction." Mr. Durrell has also published *Collected Poems* (1960), *Art and Outrage* (critical essays with Alfred Perlès, 1959), and *Sappho* (1950), a verse play.

Here at least there was nothing to quarrel memory, for it was all exactly as I remembered it. I had stepped back into Clea's room as one might step back into a favourite picture. The crowded bookshelves and the heavy candlesticks drawing-boards, the tiny cottage piano, the cluttered desk with its papers in disorder. Against the wall a bundle of canvases with showing their backs. I went and turned a few round. "My god you've gone abstract"

"I know. Balthazar hates them! I expect it is just a phase I am going through. It's a different way of mobilising one's feelings about things. Do you hate them?"

"No. They're stranger than the last I saw."

"Hum. Candlelight is flattering them with false Chiaroscuro."

"Perhaps"

"Come, sit down and drink."

As if by common consent we sat facing each other on the carpet as we had so often done in the past, cross legged like "Armenian tailors" as she once said; to drink our nightcap by the rosy light of the candles which ~~burned~~ stood unwinking in the still air. Here too we at last embraced into — how shall one say — a momentous calm, the reward of silence, as if the cup of language had silently overflowed into these eloquent kisses which annealed the heart. They were not aberrant, but like soft clear forms of a novel innocence

Manuscript page from Lawrence Durrell's novel Clea.

D. RASSMUSSON

Lawrence Durrell

The interview took place at Durrell's home in the Midi. It is a peasant cottage with four rooms to which he has added a bathroom and a lavatory. He writes in a room without windows, with notices of his work in foreign languages he cannot understand pinned to the bookcase. The sitting room, where the interview was held, has a large fireplace and a french window leading onto a terrace constructed by Durrell himself. From the terrace one has a view of the small valley at the end of which he lives. It is a bare rocky district, full of twisted olive trees, destroyed in a blight a few years back.

Lawrence Durrell is a short man, but in no sense a small one. Dressed in jeans, a tartan shirt, a navy-blue pea-jacket, he looks like a minor trade-union official who has successfully absconded with the funds. He is a voluble, volatile personality, who talks fast and with enormous energy. He is a gift for an interviewer,

turning quite stupid questions into apparently intelligent ones by
assuming that the interviewer meant something else. Though he
was rather distrustful of the tape recorder, he acquiesced in its use.
He smokes heavily, Gauloises bleues. *When at rest he looks like*
Laurence Olivier; at other times his face has all the ferocity of a
professional wrestler's.

The interview was recorded on April 23, 1959, the birthday of
William Shakespeare and Scobie of Durrell's quartet. Beginning
after lunch and continuing that evening, it commenced with
Durrell reviewing his early life, his schooling at Canterbury, and
his failure to enter Cambridge.

INTERVIEWERS: What did you do after Cambridge turned you down?

DURRELL: Well, for a time I had a small allowance. I lived in London. I played the piano in a night club—the "Blue Peter" in St. Martin's Lane, of all places—until we were raided by the police. I worked as an estate agent in Leytonstone and had to collect rents, and was badly bitten by dogs. I tried everything, including the Jamaica police. I have been driven to writing by sheer ineptitude. I wanted to write, of course, always. I did a certain amount of stuff but I couldn't get anything published—it was too bad. I think writers today learn so much more quickly. I mean, I could no more write as well at their age than fly.

INTERVIEWERS: Had you written anything before *Pied Piper of Lovers?*

DURRELL: Oh yes, since the age of eight I have been madly scribbling.

INTERVIEWERS: How long did you stay in London before you decided to leave?

DURRELL: In my parents' view, only Colonial Office jobs or the Army were then respectable; their dream was to see me as an Indian Civil Servant. Thank God I escaped it, but I manfully did my best to try all these things. I think I must have failed more examinations in about three years than probably anyone of my weight, height, size, and religion. But my parents, who were unwisely sending me quite large sums of money, didn't realize that I was putting it all into night clubs and fast cars and living a perfectly stupid puppy-clubman sort of life, do you see? I think the first breath of Europe I got was when I went on a reading party for one final cram for something—I think it was for Cambridge again, which I must have tried about eight times, I suppose. Mathematics—three, two, one, nought—it was always this damn thing. I was taken to Switzerland, you see, which gave me a glimpse of Paris on the way, and I went to a reading party which was conducted by a very deaf old scholar, and instead of reading I suddenly had a look at Lausanne, Vevey, and the lakes there, and on the way back managed to get three days in Paris which converted me to Europe as such. And then after this whole question of being educated failed and faded out, I made my way immediately for Paris.

INTERVIEWERS: Was it then that you met Henry Miller?

DURRELL: Oh, no, that was much later. I went to Paris for a brief period and then I came back and convinced my family, who were dying of catarrh, that it was necessary to get out of England for a breath of air and see some new landscapes and places. And it was then that I persuaded them that Greece was a good idea, which my brother has recounted in his book on Greece.* So then I went ahead and they all followed about a year later, and then began this wonderful period in Corfu of—oh, what? I suppose five or six years?—really until the outbreak of the war. In the meantime I'd got married and, you know, I was trying everything.

INTERVIEWERS: It seems that your writing very much improved when you got to Corfu. For instance, *Panic Spring* is very much better than *Pied Piper of Lovers*.

---

* Gerald Durrell, *My Family and Other Animals*.

DURRELL: Yes. It's still a damn bad book. There's quite a gap in between there, you know. *Panic Spring* I think I wrote there, actually. I used all the color material I could get from Corfu, there's no doubt.

INTERVIEWERS: And since then you have never lived in England at all, have you?

DURRELL: Well, no, I haven't, really. I have not been domiciled in England. I have had the odd six months at a time, I mean, which is just about the length of time I enjoy England for. It gives you time to see your friends, get all the free meals you can, and everyone is glad to see you, to begin with, and so on. But I must confess that I've been a European since I was eighteen, and I think it is a grave national defect that we aren't Europeans any more. We were talking today at lunch about Kingsley Amis. I was thinking about the anti-living-abroad trend or something— which implies a sort of unpatriotic attitude on my part—but, you see, my heroes of my generation, the Lawrences, the Norman Douglases, the Aldingtons, the Eliots, the Graveses, their ambition was always to be a European. It didn't qualify their Englishness in any way, but it was recognized that a touch of European fire was necessary, as it were, to ignite the sort of dull sodden mass that one became, living in an unrestricted suburban way. Things would have been vastly different if I had had a very large private income, been a member of the gentry, had a charming country house and a flat in town and the ability to live four months of the year in Europe: I should certainly have been domiciled in London. But when you're poor and you have to face shabby boarding houses and all the dreariness of South Ken or Bayswater or Woburn Place, with only the chance of seeing Europe in snippets of a month at a time, you have to make the vital decision as to whether you live in Europe and visit England, or whether you live in England and visit Europe.

INTERVIEWERS: There is still quite a lot of violent anti-bourgeois England in your early things.

DURRELL: I think part of it I may have got from my heroes of that time—Lawrence, as I said, and Aldington, and so on—but it's more than just a fashionable thing. I think that, as I say, in England, living as if we are not part of Europe, we are living against the grain of what is nourishing to our artists, do you see? There seems to be an ingrown psychological thing about it, I don't know why it is. You can see it reflected even in quite primitive ways like this market business now—the European Common Market. It's purely psychological, the feeling that we are too damned superior to join this bunch of continentals in anything they do. And I think that's why it is so vitally important for young artists to identify more and more with Europe. As for me, I have joined the Common Market, as it were. But, mind you, that doesn't qualify one's origins or one's attitudes to things. I mean if I'm writing, I'm writing for England—and so long as I write English it will be for England that I have to write.

INTERVIEWERS: You show a great respect for England in many of your things—for instance, the General Uncebunke poems.

DURRELL: Well, of course, yes. You mustn't forget that I'm a mixed-up son of a failed B.A. colonial of Benares University. And to a certain extent, being a colonial, you have these wild romantic dreams about "Home." I mean, Roy Campbell is another example of a mixed-up kid from another colony.

INTERVIEWERS: You didn't find it difficult to write in England, did you?

DURRELL: No, I think it's a most creative landscape. It's a *violently* creative landscape. I think the only thing that's wrong is the way we're living in it.

INTERVIEWERS: Can you summarize what's wrong with the way we're living in it?

DURRELL: The things one notices immediately are petty—it's the construction of a sort of giant pin-table of inhibitions and restrictive legislation and ignoble, silly defenses against feeling, really. That's what it amounts to. Of course there may be other mitigating factors which one leaves out when one is talking jolly glibly. If you put a writer in the pontiff's seat, God knows what you might expect out of his mouth—you know, there may be economic conditions. It may be just that England is too over-crowded to be able to live in a joyous—

INTERVIEWERS: Mediterranean way?

DURRELL: No, not necessarily Mediterranean. One of the writers I reread every two or three years is Surtees, and I very much hoped that England was going to be Surtees' England—a vulgar, jolly, roistering England, not especially aesthetic or cultivated or delicate in any sense, but something with its vulgar roots in food, sex, and good living. By which I don't mean fine living or refinement of values, because those are just the top dressing. It is at the roots that something's wrong.

INTERVIEWERS: It is the whole attitude towards living in England that's wrong, then?

DURRELL: One says that, but what I want to say is that it is wrong for me only. I don't wish to correct it. I am not a prose-lytizer. I wouldn't know if you asked me tomorrow how I'd go about making that English nation over into something nearer my heart's desire. I am simply trying to explain to you why one is always an English orphan, as a writer, as an artist; and one goes to Europe because, like a damn cuckoo, one has to lay these eggs in someone else's nest. Here in France, in Italy, and Greece, you have the most hospitable nests, you see, where there's very little chi-chi about writing or artists as such, but which provide the most extraordinarily congenial frames in which a job of work can be done. Here one feels on a par with a good or bad cheese—the attitude to art of a Frenchman is the attitude to what is viable—eatable, so to speak. It is a perfectly down to earth *terre à terre* thing, you see. Yet they don't treat camembert with less reverence than they treat Picasso when he comes to Arles; they are in the same *genre* of things. But in England everyone is worried to death about moral uplift and moral downfall, and they never seem to go beyond that problem, simply because they feel separated from the artists. It's the culture that separates, you see, and turns the artist into a sort of refugee. It's not a question of residence. Even the home artist has to fight for recognition; instantly, people don't recognize that he is as good as good cheddar. It's a different category to them.

INTERVIEWERS: Who would you say was the first Englishman who felt this particularly?

DURRELL: It goes back all the way. The last bunch were the Romantics. And what about Shelley, Keats, and Byron and Company? They all needed Europe. And now, this sinister decision on the part of the young—I sympathize with them personally—Kingsley Amis and John Wain, admirable writers both—shut up all through the war years in England, with Europe all plowed up anyhow, and by the end of the war Europe really didn't mean anything to them.

INTERVIEWERS: Do you think the war made it worse?

DURRELL: Oh, yes. And also the financial restrictions on getting to Europe. I mean this wretched travel-allowance thing. The whole complex of "Stay out of Europe," as it were. Which is so sad. I wouldn't go so far as to say we caused the last two world wars by our indifference to Europe, but certainly Hitler wouldn't have taken six years to mow down if we'd been very much earlier on the ball and helped Europe put him down. And perhaps that might go for the 1914 thing. The Europeans themselves see us as people absolutely ready at any moment to draw stumps and clear out. I am not talking simply of politics now, I'm also talking about art.

INTERVIEWERS: Do you think a young writer in England today should get out and join the Europeans?

DURRELL: Well, after all, it's possible to write *Wuthering Heights* without leaving England, except for a weekend at Brussels. In fact I write perfectly well in England, but I'm always being foxed because the pubs are shut. It's just a petty symbol of the kind of limitless obstruction which is put in people's way.

INTERVIEWERS: What do you find are the best conditions for writing?

DURRELL: I've never had really comfy conditions to write under.

This last time I came to France I had four hundred pounds, with all kinds of impending debts like school fees and so on; I had been waiting fifteen years for this quartet of novels to form up and get ready, and when I got the signal saying the bloody thing was there and I only had to write it out, it was at the very worst period of my life, when I had no job, a tiny gratuity, and it literally was a choice—I suspected I would be driven from France and back to funds in two months, but thank God the Americans and Germans saved me.

INTERVIEWERS: Do you plan to go to America?

DURRELL: I haven't really made any plans. You know I'm so travel-stained with fifteen or sixteen years of it—the great anxiety of being shot at in Cyprus, being bombed, being tormented by the Marxists in Yugoslavia—that now for the first time I've a yen for my tiny roof. Staying put is so refreshing that it's almost anguish to go into town for a movie. I haven't seen a movie for eighteen months now, and I'm only eighteen minutes away from one. So while on one hand I'd like to go to America I feel it's an experience I should preserve for my late fifties. Experiences of continents are much bigger than experiences of small countries. Since both America and Russia between them are going to determine the shape of our future, one is obliged as a traveler in visiting those countries to stop traveling and start thinking. It's different from going to Italy, say, where it's pure pleasure. But to go either to America or Russia means going at absolute concert pitch because you'll have to bring away some sort of judgment on the whole future of humanity from both those countries. Besides, if I went to America I'd immediately start falling in love with American girls—which would blind my vision. So I'll have to go there when all my passion is spent. No, but you see what I mean. I'd like to look at it slightly detached. An official flight across America under auspices which would demand lectures and so forth is not the way I'd want to do it. I'd rather like to meet someone like Henry Miller secretly on the coast in a broken-down jalopy and take America as an anonymous person, an immigrant.

INTERVIEWERS: How do you write, in fact?

DURRELL: On a typewriter.

INTERVIEWERS: And are you like Darley in *Balthazar*, who finds writing so difficult? He says, for instance, "I write so slowly, with such pain . . . landlocked in spirit as all writers are . . . like a ship in a bottle sailing nowhere." Is this what you feel at all?

DURRELL: Oh, no. Well, let me tell you. In the last three years, during this awful financial trouble, I wrote *Bitter Lemons* in six weeks, and sent it off with only the typescript corrected. It was published as it stood. *Justine* was held up by bombs, but she took about four months—really a year, because the whole middle period I dropped in order to deal with the Cyprus job. I finished it in Cyprus just before leaving. I wrote *Balthazar* in six weeks in Sommières, I wrote *Mountolive* in two months in Sommières, and finished *Clea* in about seven weeks in all. You see, the beauty of it is, that when you are really frantic and worried about money, you find that if it's going to be a question of writing to live, why, you just damn well buckle to and do it. Now none of these manuscripts have been altered, apart from *Mountolive*—the construction gave me some trouble, and I let in a hemstitch here, a gusset there—but apart from them, the bloody things have gone out of the house to the printer—apart from typing errors.

INTERVIEWERS: In fact, you find writing very easy.

DURRELL: Yes. I only pray that I can do it and nothing else.

INTERVIEWERS: Your prose seems so highly worked. Does it just come out like that?

DURRELL: It's too juicy. Perhaps I need a few money terrors and things to make it a bit clearer—less lush. I always feel I am overwriting. I am conscious of the fact that it is one of my major difficulties. It comes of indecision when you are not sure of your target. When you haven't drawn a bead on it, you plaster the whole damn thing to make sure. And that leads to overwriting. For instance, a lot of poems of my middle period got too corpulent.

INTERVIEWERS: Do you take longer over your poems than your prose?

Durrell: Yes—except the lucky ones which seem to come out on the back of an envelope when you are not ready for it. It's rather like spilling egg on your tie. They're written straight out, but I'm afraid they are terribly rare—about a fifth of the total amount. And the rest—I do them in handwriting—I do go over a good deal.

Interviewers: It's impossible to write a poem on a typewriter, isn't it?

Durrell: Well, the only amazing exception to the rule is George Barker, who always composes on a typewriter. In London he used to slip in and borrow mine, and I thought he was writing letters to his family. But no, he was composing.

Interviewers: Have you written a lot of anonymous and pseudonymous stuff?

Durrell: I've done hundreds and thousands of words of feature articles, all buried in remote periodicals. Some under my own name, some under initials. In Cairo I ran a comic column. And then I've written millions of words of Foreign Office dispatches— a much harder job than any foreign correspondent's because I was the buffer state between, say, four and four hundred correspondents in a situation where a statement of policy was expected on a split-second basis and so water-tight that it wouldn't fall apart under analysis. Of course, to make that kind of statement you have to have a policy, and in most of the places where I worked we didn't. In fact, I was selling a pig in a poke most of the time, living on my wits. Or, as Sir Henry Wotton said, "lying abroad for my country." But I mean it's an incomparable training, and by rubbing shoulders with a vast variety of journalists I learned most of the tricks of the trade—most of them rather shabby tricks, mind you, and magpie tricks and easy to learn. But one of the lessons, writing as you do under pressure in the journalistic world, is that you learn concision, which is invaluable, and you also learn to work for a deadline. Whenever the deadline is you've got to do it and you've got to have the will to do it. Well, you do it. Of course, the element of luck is very great. I might have written all my things and not had a publisher, or I might not have written them well enough to sell them. . . . I have to admit in my heart of hearts that I could have written books twice as good as the quartet and not have sold three hundred copies. The element of luck is absolutely mixed up with the whole thing.

INTERVIEWERS: Do you regard any of your writing as potboiling?

DURRELL: I have had to do a lot of potboiling in my career. Let me say this: if one stays absolutely sincere and honest towards a form—even when I'm writing this Antrobus nonsense, I'm writing it with a reverence to P. G. Wodehouse. I mean every form thoroughly exploited and honestly dealt with is not shameful. So that potboiling as an idea of someone writing with a typewriter in his cheek or something—I can't say I do that. I mean I put as much hard work into a dull Antrobus story, which may or may not come off, as I put into the next chapter of the book I have to get on with.

INTERVIEWERS: Why did you publish *Panic Spring* under a pseudonym?

DURRELL: The appallingly bad trade record of my first novel. It was so hideously bad that when I shifted publishers from Cassells to Faber, Faber made it a condition to wipe out my past and start me off with a new name. They had the grace after they saw *The Black Book* to say that I was a good enough writer to deserve having my own name, and allowed me to go back to it.

INTERVIEWERS: Do you consider *The Black Book* important to the evolution of the Justine series?

DURRELL: Only in the sense that it was important for my evolution, you know, my inside evolution. It was my first breakthrough. I don't regard it as a good book. In fact, I wince at it a bit, and there are parts of it which I think probably are a bit too obscene and which I wouldn't have written that way now . . . but, how shall I say, I turned myself inside out in that book. Mr. Eliot is kind enough to praise it very highly, and what he is praising is not the book—which is more a curiosity of literature than a contribution to it—but that as a boy of twenty-four I had to undergo a sort of special crisis even to write the book at all and *that* was what was truthful, not the book itself, not the paper with stuff on it. It was the act of making the breakthrough and suddenly hearing your own tone of voice, like being reborn, like cracking the egg all of a sudden. And that's what it was for me. I cracked the crust in that book and the lava was there, and I had only to find a way of training the lava so it didn't spill over everything and burn everything up. I had to canalize it. That was the problem of the next ten years. Poetry turned out to be an invaluable mistress. Because poetry is form, and the wooing and seduction of form is the whole game. You can have all the apparatus in the world, but what you finally need is something like a—I don't know what—a lasso . . . a very delicate thing, for catching wild deer. Oh, no, I'll give you an analogy for it. To write a poem is like trying to catch a lizard without its tail falling off. Did you know that? In India when I was a boy they had great big green lizards there, and if you shouted or shot them their tails would fall off. There was only one boy in the school who could catch lizards intact. No one knew quite how he did it. He had a special soft way of going up to them, and he'd bring them back with their tails on. That strikes me as the best analogy I can give you. To try and catch your poem without its tail falling off.

INTERVIEWERS: Which of your books do you like most? Which are you most satisfied with?

DURRELL: [*Pause*] I suffer from terrible nausea about my own work, purely physical nausea. It sounds stupid, but the fact is I write at a terrific speed, and . . . you cross inner resistances like you cross a shoal of transmitters when you are fiddling with the dial on a radio. By the time the thing is in typescript, it is really with physical nausea that I regard it. When the proofs come back I have to take an aspirin before I can bring myself really to read it through. Occasionally when I'm asked to correct or edit a version, I always ask someone to do it for me. I don't know why. I just have a nausea about it. Perhaps when one day I get something I really do like, I won't have to take aspirin.

INTERVIEWERS: Once you've finished one thing you want to get on with the next?

DURRELL: Well, yes. It is sort of peeled skin, you see, and anything you let into that skin is just patching something already thrown aside. It's rather like assaulting the damn thing once and for all. If it comes off, well, you're in luck. If it's a failure, no amount of niggling is going to do it any good. That's how I feel. I know it's a wrong attitude, because some people can, with patience, resurrect and retailor things. But I can't. I write very fast, I throw away.

INTERVIEWERS: Have you thrown away a lot?

DURRELL: Hundreds of books, yes. No, that's an exaggeration. No, I mean hundreds of passages. What I do is try and write a slab of ten thousand words, and if it doesn't come off, I do it again.

INTERVIEWERS: How long does it take you to write ten thousand words?

DURRELL: Ten thousand? Two pages a thousand, twenty pages . . . oh, two days. It varies, of course, according to different circumstances, but in general, when one is in good form one can really pour it out.

INTERVIEWERS: Have you written any short stories?

DURRELL: I have, yes, three or four, but the length worries me. There are two things which feel uncomfortable and awkward to me . . . like a wooden leg. One is the short story of about four thousand words, and the other is the feature for the *Times*. I could easily give them five thousand words or eight thousand words, but I'm damned if I can do anything under one thousand. So what I have to do is overwrite, give them eight thousand, and let them cut it down to their required size. As for the short story, I've done, as I say, several, but I've never felt happy in the form. Either I've felt it should be another forty pages, in which case it becomes a junior novel, a concertina novel, or else I've felt it should be two pages . . . O. Henry and finish, you know. I admire the form, but it doesn't come easily to me.

INTERVIEWERS: You said you had fifteen years waiting for your quartet to arrive. You said you had signals saying it was coming. Could you explain that a little?

DURRELL: Well, it's simply a sort of premonitory sense that one day one was going to put one's whole shoulder behind a particular punch. But one had to be patient and wait and let it form up, and not catch it in the early jelly stage before it had set properly, and ruin it by a premature thing. That explains why I have hung around in the Foreign Service for so long—keeping the machine running by writing other sorts of things, but waiting patiently, and now I suddenly felt this was it, and this was the moment, and bang—at least I hope, bang.

INTERVIEWERS: You seem to use the same kind of material, and often the same characters again and again, in your novels, in your poems and in the travel books. One of your critics has said, "Durrell has never made any proper distinction in his writing between real people and imaginary persons." Would you agree with that?

DURRELL: Yes, certainly.

INTERVIEWERS: Are these characters that reappear personae or real people?

DURRELL: No, they are personae, I think. They are not real people. There is hardly a snatch of autobiography. Most of the autobiography is in places and scenes and *ambiances*. I think it is not understood to what a limited extent artists have any experience at all, you know. People imagine them to have absolutely boundless experience. In fact I think that they are as nearsighted as moles, and if you limit your field to your own proper capabilities it is astonishing how little you know about life. It sounds a paradox, but I think it's true. I think the magnification of gifts magnifies the defects as well. One of the things I have strongly is the defect of vision. For example I can't remember any of the wild flowers that I write about so ecstatically in the Greek islands, I have to look them up. And Dylan Thomas once told me that poets only know two kinds of birds at sight; one is a robin and the other a seagull, he said, and the rest of them he had to look up, too. So I'm not alone in the defect of vision. I have to check my own impressions all the time.

INTERVIEWERS: In spite of that I understand you're also a painter.

DURRELL: Yes, but I'm a dauber.

INTERVIEWERS: Well, it's always seemed to me that you have a very visual imagination. Even if you don't remember things accurately, at least you imagine them very vividly.

DURRELL: I think that's the juggling quality I have. This gentleman who has just been dissecting me astrologically tells me that, apart from the evasion and the flight and noncomprehension of what I really am and what I really feel, I am the supreme trickster. Which is probably why my unkinder critics always seize on something like "sleight-of-hand" or "illusionist," which are actually the words this chap uses. But fortunately I'm not to blame. I gather it's something to do with the Fishes, to which I belong. In other words he says quite plainly that Pisceans are a bunch of liars, and when you add to that an Irish background, you have got some pretty hefty liar.

INTERVIEWERS: Wouldn't you say this was true of all artists probably—that they lie all the time?

DURRELL: Well, they fabricate, I suppose. They're all egotists, you see, fundamentally, I suppose. It's a form of self-aggrandizement, writing at all, isn't it?

INTERVIEWERS: Do you pay any attention to what your critics say?

DURRELL: No. Because then I get blocks. This won't sound very reasonable to you, either; I have discovered quite recently that the characteristic Freudian resistances to confessions of any sort, which are very well represented in all the writing blocks one goes through—the dizzy fits, the nauseas, and so on and so forth, which almost every writer has recorded—are a standard pattern for all kinds of creative things. They are simply forms of egotism. And egotism can be inflamed very easily by a good review, or a bad review for that matter, and you can get a nice tidy block which will cost you two days of work. And when you've got to get the money for the work, you can't afford it. So I don't read reviews unless they're sent to me. Usually they go to my agent because they help to sell foreign rights. And it sounds very pompous, but really I think they have a bad influence on one, and even the good ones make you a bit ashamed. In fact I think the best regimen is to get up early, insult yourself a bit in the shaving mirror, and then pretend you're cutting wood, which is really just about all the hell you are doing—if you see what I mean. But all the Jungian guilt about the importance of one's message, and all that sort of thing—well, you get a nice corpulent ego standing in the way there, telling you that you're so damn clever that you're almost afraid to write it down, it's so wonderful. And the minute you get that, where are your checks going to come from for next month's gas, light, and heat? You can't afford it.

INTERVIEWERS: What a splendidly pragmatic view of writing.

DURRELL: I'm forced to it, you see; I'm writing for a living.

INTERVIEWERS: Are you conscious of any specific influence in your writing?

DURRELL: You know, I'm not quite sure about the word, because I copy what I admire. I pinch. When you say "influences" it suggests an infiltration of someone else's material into yours, semiconsciously. But I read not only for pleasure, but as a journey-man, and where I see a good effect I study it, and try to repro-duce it. So that I am probably the biggest thief imaginable. I steal from people—my seniors, I mean. And in fact, *Panic Spring*, which you said was a respectable book, seemed to me dreadful, because it was an anthology, you see, with five pages of Huxley, three pages of Aldington, two pages of Robert Graves, and so on —in fact all the writers I admire. But they didn't influence me. I pinched effects, I was learning the game. Like an actor will study a senior character and learn an effect of make-up or a particular slouchy walk for a role he's not thought of himself. He doesn't regard that as being particularly influenced by the actor, but as a trick of the trade which he owes it to himself to pick up.

INTERVIEWERS: It has been said that in your poetry you were considerably influenced by Auden.

DURRELL: Well, there again I pinched. Yes, of course. He is a great master of colloquial effects which no one before him dared to use.

INTERVIEWERS: Did you consciously develop your own style of writing, or did it just come naturally?

DURRELL: I don't think anyone can, you know, develop a style consciously. I read with amazement, for example, of old Maugham solemnly writing out a page of Swift every day when he was trying to learn the job, in order to give himself a stylistic purchase, as it were. It struck me as something I could never do. No. When you say "consciously" I think you're wrong. I mean, it's like "Do you consciously dream?" One doesn't know very much about these processes at all. I think the writing itself grows you up, and you grow the writing up, and finally you get an amalgam of everything you have pinched with a new kind of personality which is your own, and then you are able to pay back these socking debts with a tiny bit of interest, which is the only honorable thing for a writer to do—at least a writer who is a thief like me.

INTERVIEWERS: You said you admired Norman Douglas?

DURRELL: I admire him because he was a European.

INTERVIEWERS: But stylistically?

DURRELL: Both as a man *and* a stylist. His was a writing personality that I admired and still admire very much. You see, he was unsnobbish, and yet he was the extreme stylist of the silver age . . . and in my day it is a very rare quality to have someone who is a good stylist without being snobbish. The delicacy and tact and the stylish gentlemanly thing was so well matched in Douglas that it carried no affectations; he was not trying to be pompous or anything. He is the happy example of the style perfectly married to the man. I never met him, but I'm sure his speaking tone was exactly like his writing tone. That easy informal Roman silver-age style is something everyone should be able to enjoy and appreciate. It wouldn't do if you were going to tackle a large-scale work like

War and Peace, or the later Dostoevski, or even the sort of thing that Henry Miller is doing. It would just not be adaptable enough for it. It's a finished, delicate thing. It's like chamber music. But style is in a separate box, you know. I have never really been a stylist deliberately. The stylists have taught me economy, which is what I very badly needed. Being naturally over-efflorescent, I have always probably learned more from the sort of writers I have never really imitated. They taught me just as feature journalism told me to put the most important fact in the first sentence—a simple gimmick, as it were. You can learn from Lytton Strachey, for example, to write something balanced and pointed, as shortly as possible. It is condensation I admired in them.

INTERVIEWERS: Do you regard your quartet as your *magnum opus?*

DURRELL: It is for *me,* so to speak. It's as high up the ladder as I can climb at this moment, you know, and it cost a good deal of effort to write. I am particularly proud of it because I have been able to write it under these difficulties. It gives me more pleasure for that reason, even though I probably won't ever read it again. Of its relative importance, I don't know. The most interesting thing about it for me is the form, and those ideas are not mine.

INTERVIEWERS: You say at the beginning of *Balthazar* that the central topic of the book is an investigation of modern love.

DURRELL: Yes.

INTERVIEWERS: *Justine* and *Balthazar* bear this out, but there is a complete change of focus in *Mountolive.*

DURRELL: It was simply a shift from subjective to objective. *Mountolive* is an account of the thing by an invisible narrator, as, opposed to somebody engaged in the action.

INTERVIEWERS: One critic has said, "The novel is only half secretly about art, the great subject of modern artists." How do you feel about that?

DURRELL: The theme of art is the theme of life itself. This artificial distinction between artists and human beings is precisely what we are all suffering from. An artist is only someone unrolling and digging out and excavating the areas normally accessible to normal people everywhere, and exhibiting them as a sort of scarecrow to show people what can be done with themselves.

INTERVIEWERS: You have got a lot of writers in your books—Pursewarden, Darley, Arnauti, Balthazar, the author of *Mountolive*—which does seem to show a particular concern with the artist's view of things.

DURRELL: I see what you mean, but I think it comes from this artificial distinction of artists as something qualitatively different from ordinary human beings.

INTERVIEWERS: How do you feel about Proust's name being mentioned in most critics' analyses of the *Justine* series?

DURRELL: It's tremendously flattering, but I don't think I've done anything to cause the comparisons to be made. But the Proustian comparison does interest me from another standpoint. He seems to have summed up a particular air pocket, a particular cosmology really, and one of the things I was trying to get at was this: it seems to me in every age we are all trying . . . we're all, as artists, attacking as a battalion on a very broad front. Individual and temperamental personalities are incidental to the general attack and what we as artists are trying to do is to sum up in a sort of metaphor the cosmology of a particular moment in which we are living. When an artist does that completely and satisfactorily he creates a crisis in the form. The artists immediately following him become dissatisfied with the existing forms and try to invent or grope around for new forms. Proust, I think, in his work exemplified the Bergsonian universe—the universe of his time—and then you find a complete breakdown in the form. The big artists who followed him, Joyce, Lawrence, and Virginia Woolf, went off hunting frantically for a new form. . . . I mean, Joyce even goes so far as Homer, it's ridiculous, why Homer? Anyway you see forms becoming psychic. *Finnegans Wake* begins and ends with the same words. The word cycles became obsessional, and in Joyce, of course, there is such an emphasis on time as to literally block the drains: if you get too much time into works of art you stop the process—so that the focus in the works of Joyce, Woolf, and the rest seems like a colossal blown-up image of an incident, which, of course, *is* the Bergsonian eternity.

Now, *I* oppose to this the Einsteinian concept, trying to see if I can't apply Einsteinian time instead of Bergsonian time. A mathematical friend of mine says I'm crazy, an idiot, that you can't create a continuum of words. Of course it sounds crazy, doesn't it? I mean you can't apply scientific hypothesis to the novel. On the other hand, is it so crazy? Just as I see artists as a great battalion moving through paint, words, music towards cosmological interpretation, I see them linked on the right and left hand by the pure scientists. Ideas are sort of biological entities to me. Now, my mathematical friend says that the Einsteinian concept of welding time to matter is purely mathematical and cannot be expressed in any other way; if you try you're simply violating the concept. That to me seems the reverse of Keats drinking damnation to Newton because he explained the rainbow. And, besides, I don't pretend what I'm doing is a continuum exactly. What I'm saying is that Mercator's projection is not a sphere but it does give you a very good impression of what a sphere is like. It serves its purpose, and that's how I regard this continuum idea of mine. It may be that I'm violating sacred territory, and indeed that I'm seeing the whole thing in the wrong set of terms, but for the moment it seems valid. If in the quartet my people tend, as some people complain, to be dummies, it's because I'm trying to light them from several different angles. I'm trying to give you stereoscopic narrative with stereophonic personality, and if that doesn't mean anything to anybody at least it should be of interest to radio engineers.

INTERVIEWERS: Can you say how some of these ideas are motivated in the quartet?

DURRELL: Well, let me think. Let me explain it to you this way: the ideas behind this thing, which have nothing whatsoever to do with the fun of it as reading matter, are roughly these. Eastern and Western metaphysics are coming to a point of confluence in the most interesting way. It seems unlikely in a way, but nevertheless the two major architects of this breakthrough have been Einstein and Freud. Einstein torpedoed the old Victorian material universe—in other words, the view of matter—and Freud torpedoed the idea of the stable ego so that personality began to diffuse. Thus in the concept of the space-time continuum you've got an absolutely new concept of what reality might be, do you see? Well, this novel is a four-dimensional dance, a relativity poem. Of course, ideally, all four volumes should be read simultaneously, as I say in my note at the end; but as we lack four-dimensional spectacles the reader will have to do it imaginatively, adding the part of time to the other three, and holding the whole lot in solution in his skull. I call it a continuum, though in fact it can't be quite accurate in the sense that Mercator's projection represents a sphere; it's a continuum but *isn't* one, if you see what I mean. So that really this is only a kind of *demonstration* of a possible continuum. But the thoughts which followed from it, and which I hope will be sort of—*visible*, as it were, in the construction of the thing, will be first of all, the ego as a series of masks, which Freud started, a depersonalization which was immediately carried over the border by Jung and Groddek and company to end up—where . . . but in Hindu metaphysics? In other words, the non-personality attitude to the human being is a purely Eastern one; it is a confluence that is now approaching in psychology. Simultaneously, this fascinating theory of indeterminacy—which I'm told you can't demonstrate except mathematically—is precisely the same thing in space-time physics, so to speak. So that I regard those two things as the cosmological touchpoints, as it were, of our attitude to reality today. In other words, I see Eastern and Western metaphysics getting jolly close together. And while I'm not trying to write a thesis—I'm just trying to write a series of novels which are good fun whether you look deep or shallow, but which keep their end up as an honest job of work—nevertheless, basically that's the sort of mix, that's the sort of soup mix, I'm at. And I'm just as much in the dark as the reader, in the sense that I undertook this thing in good faith, I didn't know what the results would be, and I still don't know. It might be a muck-up, do you see? But those are the ideas I would have liked to indicate, without writing a thesis on them or expressing them in any more clarified form.

INTERVIEWERS: Don't you think that, in publishing *Justine* first, you gave a false impression of the series as a whole?

DURRELL: Ideally, had I not been short of money, I would have written the four, and matched them properly, because there are still quite a lot of discrepancies which will have to be tidied up if the thing is gathered. But shortage of money made me compose them one after the other. There is also another thing I must confess to you: while I was tackling this idea, I didn't know whether it was possible, humanly possible, to do. I didn't know whether I was barking up the wrong tree, and I was quite prepared to abandon the whole series as a failure, at any point, if I felt I couldn't compass them, or if I felt they were coming out wrong, and the thing was an abortion. I simply approached the three sides of space and one of time as a cook will open a recipe-book and say "Let's cook this gigot." I had no idea what sort of gigot was going to come out of it. I still haven't, and we won't have until the critics get a chance to have a look at the four, and tear them all apart. But sometimes you have to take these colossal chances when you see a ray of light that beckons to you particularly.

INTERVIEWERS: How far in advance do you plot your novels?

DURRELL: Very little deliberate plotting as such. I have a certain amount of data, but the great danger of this sort of thing is a mechanical exercise in a form: and having a clear form in mind, I wanted the books to be as alive as possible. So that I was prepared at any moment to throw all the data overboard and let it live its own life, you see. So that I should say only about a third of the incidental matter was advance plotting. It's like driving a few stakes in the ground; you haven't got to that point in the construction yet, so you run ahead fifty yards, and you plank a stake in to show roughly the direction your road is going, which helps to give you your orientation. But they are very far from planned in the exact sense.

INTERVIEWERS: Where do you go from *Clea*, or, more comprehensively, from the Justine series?

DURRELL: I haven't any clear idea of what I'm going to do, but whatever I do will depend upon trying to crack forms. You see, I have a feeling about forms that they are up in the air in the Shelleyan way. If the damn things would come down like soap bubbles and settle on my head I'd be very grateful. If the form comes off, everything comes off.

INTERVIEWERS: I understand you're also contemplating a comic novel.

DURRELL: I have an idea for one. I see some amusing characters in the shadows, but if I attack the book I don't want to attack it in an inhibited frame of mind which might make it "pawky"— do you have that word? It means a kind of schoolmasterish, donnish intent to be funny. That I want to avoid like the plague. But one of the problems is that it is hardly permissible for me to be as vulgar as I would like. You see, I don't really think a comic novel is any good unless it's as vulgar as it is satiric. It's only with great vulgarity that you can achieve real refinement, only out of bawdry that you can get tenderness. For example, if you rule out bawdry entirely, it's astonishing how anemic your love lyric becomes. It wouldn't please me at all to write a mildly smiling book which was just witty, though, of course, there have been astonishing strides in that vein: Evelyn Waugh's *The Loved One* is a masterpiece that Swift would have been proud to write had he lived in our age. But I want to stay nearer Rabelais; I want to be coarse and vulgarly funny. Like the Jacobeans. I don't know whether that's permissible, whether it would come off, or whether the results might be in appalling bad taste with no redeeming feature. I'd have to face all those problems. But then again, for me they're problems of form. The exciting thing would be to conquer them inside a form or frame. Yes, that's a project I have for this winter. And also I'd like to write another play. I'm a fated dramatist in a sense. My only play was such a shambles. It's taken about fifteen years to find people who can cut it up and put it on the stage. Now for the first time the Germans are going to give me a chance to see what it looks like. Until you've had that experience you can't really become a dramatist. It's possible I shall be so disgusted that I shall never write another one, but on the other hand it's possible I shall be so fired up watching someone play it that I may fall passionately in love with the play as a form and go on to write much better plays.

INTERVIEWERS: You mentioned form again. That is your primary interest, isn't it, whatever the art?

DURRELL: Yes, I think so. More than most people. It may be that I haven't as much personality to deploy. My interest in form might be—I'm talking seriously now, not modestly—an indication of a second-rate talent. So one has to face these things. It doesn't really matter whether you're first rate, second rate, or third rate, but it's of vital importance that the water finds its own level and that you do the very best you can with the powers that are given you. It's idle to strive for things out of your reach, just as it's utterly immoral to be slothful about the qualities you have. You see, I'm not fundamentally interested in the artist. I use him to try to become a happy man, which is a good deal harder for me. I find art easy. I find life difficult.

JULIAN MITCHELL
GENE ANDREWSKI

12. Mary McCarthy

Mary McCarthy was born in Seattle, Washington, on June 21, 1912, and was raised by grandparents, uncles, and aunts after her parents died of influenza in 1918. At the age of eight she won a state prize for an article entitled "The Irish in American History." She was educated at the Forest Ridge Convent in Seattle, Annie Wright Seminary in Tacoma, and Vassar College, where she was graduated in 1933. At Vassar she was elected to Phi Beta Kappa in her senior year.

After her graduation from college she began to write book reviews for the *Nation* and the *New Republic*. In 1936 and 1937 she was an editor for Covici Friede, and from 1937 to 1948 she was an editor and theater critic for the *Partisan Review*. During this period she wrote articles, stories, and finally novels.

She has one son, Reuel Wilson, who was born in 1938. After she was divorced from Edmund Wilson, she taught for a short time at Bard College and at Sarah Lawrence. She was a Guggenheim Fellow during 1949 and 1950, and again in 1959 and 1960. In 1949 she received the *Horizon* prize, and in 1957 a National Institute grant.

Her books include *The Company She Keeps* (1942), *The Oasis* (1949), *Cast a Cold Eye* (1950), *The Groves of Academe* (1952), *A Charmed Life* (1955), *Sights and Spectacles* (1956), *Venice Observed* (1956), *Memories of a Catholic Girlhood* (1957), *The Stones of Florence* (1959), *On the Contrary* (1962).

who would advise me about budgeting and not letting friends make long-distance calls on my wire. But all that was normal; it was happening to everybody and nobody could feel it as a profound or permanent change, for it was like the life of a college student prolonged; middle-class college students always overspent their allowances and ran up bills that scared them because they couldn't pay. ######## The thirties proper, which I was inducted into in about 1936, were somethin<u>in a way</u> harsher. They were Armageddon. This panel itself is rather thirtyish. The idea behind it is that we (or you) are sitting in judgment on a period of history. The thirties ## <u>are</u> being presented as a choice. Are you for them or against them, and as you answer, so will you be defined. The rhetorical form that best expresses the thirties is the debate. Today, perhaps, it is the panel, which recognizes the possibility of shades of opinion; in the thirties, the meetings of this sort that I remember ######## featured only a pair of antagonists. People used to tell about a debate, so called, at the University of Chicago, when President Hutchin represented Aristotle, Mortimer Adler represented Aquinas, and a student wearing a dunce-cap (yes, literally) represented Hume. Thus the debate shaded into the trial, and in the thirties the weaker member of a pair of debaters found himself, always, on trial. This state of war, of incessant belligerency, was not confined to politics. It infected literature, education, psychiatry, art. The word, re-
conciliation, which was often used at that time, testifies to the state of belli-
gerency. Certain mediators were always trying to "reconcile" Freud with Marx, or,
a little later, Freud with religion. A common form of speech was "How do you re-
concile what you say with---?" In practice, there were were some very strange reconciliations. The tiara at the Waldorf strike; the gold evening dress to go to Madrid in the Spanish Civil War. Those women were trying to reconcile the twenties (fun) with the thirties. There was a strong affinity in the thirties <u>(unconscious)</u> for the absurd. Looking back, people remember grotesque and unbelievable events#, events that flew, as they say, in the face of Nature. But I will come back to that in a minute.

The thirties are presented now, nostalgically, as a time of freedom. Not so.

Manuscript page from an article by Mary McCarthy.

HANS BECK

Mary McCarthy

The interview took place in the living room of the apartment in Paris where Miss McCarthy was staying during the winter of 1961. It was a sunny, pleasant room, not too large, with long windows facing south toward the new buildings going up along the Avenue Montaigne. A dining-cum-writing table stood in an alcove at one end; on it were a lamp, some books and papers, and a rather well-worn portable typewriter. At the other end of the room were several armchairs and a low sofa where Miss McCarthy sat while the interview was recorded. On this early spring afternoon (it was March 16), the windows were open wide, letting in a warm breeze and the noise of construction work nearby. An enormous pink azalea bloomed on the balcony, and roses graced a small desk in one corner.

Miss McCarthy settled down on the sofa and served coffee. She was wearing a simple beige dress with little jewelry—a large and rather ornate ring was her one elaborate ornament. She is of medium height, dark, with straight hair combed back from a

center part into a knot at the nape of her neck; this simple
coiffure sets off a profile of beautiful, almost classic regularity.
Her smile is a generous one, flashing suddenly across her face,
crinkling up her wide-set eyes. She speaks not quickly, but with
great animation and energy, gesturing seldom, and then only with
a slight casual motion of her wrists and hands. Her sentences are
vigorously punctuated with emphatic verbal stresses and short
though equally emphatic pauses. In general, she impresses one
as a woman who combines a certain gracefulness and charm with
positively robust and somewhat tense assurance; it is typical of
her that she matches the tremendously elegant carriage of her
arms and neck and handsomely poised head with a deliberate,
almost jerky motion in taking a step.

While Miss McCarthy's conversation was remarkably fluent
and articulate, she would nevertheless often interrupt herself,
with a kind of nervous carefulness, in order to reword or qualify
a phrase, sometimes even impatiently destroying it and starting
again in the effort to express herself as exactly as possible. Several
times during the interview she seized upon a question in such a
way that one felt she had decided upon certain things she wanted
to say about herself and would willy-nilly create the opportunity
to do so. At other moments, some of them hilarious—her gifts
for pitiless witticism are justifiably celebrated—she would indulge
in unpremeditated extravagances of description or speculation that
she would then laughingly censor as soon as the words were out
of her mouth. She was extremely generous in the matter of silly
or badly worded questions, turning them into manageable ones
by the nature of her response. In all, her conversation was marked
by a scrupulous effort to be absolutely fair and honest, and by a
kind of natural and exuberant enjoyment of her own intellectual
powers.

INTERVIEWER: Do you like writing in Europe?

McCARTHY: I don't really find much difference. I think if you stayed here very long, you'd begin to notice a little difficulty about language.

INTERVIEWER: Did you write about Europe when you first came here after the war?

McCARTHY: Only in that short story, "The Cicerone." That was in the summer of 1946. We were just about the only tourists because you weren't allowed to travel unless you had an official reason for it. I got a magazine to give me some sort of *carnet*.

INTERVIEWER: Did the old problem, the American in Europe, interest you as a novelist?

McCARTHY: I suppose at that time, at least in that story somewhat, it did. But no, not further. For one thing, I don't know whether I cease to feel so much like an American or what; New York is, after all, so Europeanized, and so many of one's friends are European, that the distinction between you as an American and the European blurs. Also Europe has become so much more Americanized. No, I no longer see that Jamesian distinction. I mean, I see it in James, and I could see it even in 1946, but I don't see it any more. I don't feel any more this antithesis of Young America, Old Europe. I think that's really gone. For better or worse, I'm not sure. Maybe for worse.

INTERVIEWER: What about the novel you're writing while you're here—have you been working on it a long time?

McCARTHY: Oh, years! Let me think, I began it around the time of the first Stevenson campaign. Then I abandoned it and wrote the books on Italy, and *A Charmed Life*, and *Memories of a Catholic Girlhood*. When did I begin this thing again? A year ago last spring, I guess. Part of it came out in *Partisan Review*. The one called "Dotty Makes an Honest Woman of Herself."

INTERVIEWER: Is it unfair to ask you what it will be about?

McCARTHY: No, it's very easy. It's called *The Group*, and it's about eight Vassar girls. It starts with the inauguration of Roosevelt, and—well, at first it was going to carry them up to the present time, but then I decided to stop at the inauguration of Eisenhower. It was conceived as a kind of mock-chronicle novel. It's a novel about the idea of progress, really. The idea of progress seen in the female sphere, the feminine sphere. You know, home economics, architecture, domestic technology, contraception, child-bearing; the study of technology in the home, in the play-pen, in the bed. It's supposed to be the history of the loss of faith in progress, in the idea of progress, during that twenty-year period.

INTERVIEWER: Are these eight Vassar girls patterned more or less after ones you knew when you were there in college?

MCCARTHY: Some of them are drawn pretty much from life, and some of them are rather composite. I've tried to keep myself out of this book. Oh, and all their mothers are in it. That's the part I almost like the best.

INTERVIEWER: Just the mothers, not the fathers?

MCCARTHY: Not the fathers. The fathers vaguely figure, offstage and so on, but the mothers are really monumentally present!

INTERVIEWER: Does it matter to you at all where you write?

MCCARTHY: Oh, a nice peaceful place with some good light.

INTERVIEWER: Do you work regularly, every morning, say?

MCCARTHY: Normally; right now I haven't been. Normally I work from about nine tò two, and sometimes much longer—if it's going well, sometimes from nine to seven.

INTERVIEWER: Typewriter?

MCCARTHY: Typewriter, yes. This always has to get into a *Paris Review* interview! I very rarely go out to lunch. That's a rule. I've been accepting lunch dates recently—*why* didn't I remember that? My excuse—the excuse I've been forgetting—is simply that I don't go out to lunch! And in general, I don't. That was the best rule I ever made.

INTERVIEWER: Once you've published part of a novel separately, in a magazine or short-story collection, do you do much work on it afterwards, before it is published in the novel itself?

MCCARTHY: It depends. With this novel, I have.

INTERVIEWER: Speaking not of a novel, but of your autobiography, I remember that you published parts of *Memories of a Catholic Girlhood* as one section in *Cast a Cold Eye*. You changed the story about your nickname a great deal, reducing it to just a small incident in *Catholic Girlhood*.

McCARTHY: I couldn't *bear* that one! It had appeared years ago in *Mademoiselle*, and when I put it in *Cast a Cold Eye*, I didn't realize how much I disliked it. When I came to put *Catholic Girlhood* together, I simply couldn't stand it, and when I was reading the book in proof, I decided to tear it out, to reduce it to a tiny tiny incident. As it stood, it was just impossible, much too rhetorical.

INTERVIEWER: When you publish chapters of a book separately on their own, do you think of them as chapters, or as independent short stories?

McCARTHY: As chapters, but if somebody, a magazine editor, thought they were what *Partisan Review* calls a "self-contained chapter," all right, but I've never tried to make them into separate units. If one happens to be, all right—if they want to publish it as such. The *New Yorker* has given me surprises: they've printed things that I would never have thought could stand by themselves. But *they* thought so.

INTERVIEWER: Did you, when you saw them in print?

McCARTHY: Surprisingly, yes.

INTERVIEWER: What about in your first novel, *The Company She Keeps?*

McCARTHY: Those chapters were written originally as short stories. About halfway through, I began to think of them as a kind of unified story. The same character kept reappearing, and so on. I decided finally to call it a novel, in that it does in a sense tell *a* story, one story. But the first chapters were written without any idea of there being a novel. It was when I was doing the one about the Yale man that I decided to put the heroine of the earlier stories in that story too. The story of the Yale man is not a bit autobiographical, but the heroine appears anyway, in order to make a unity for the book.

INTERVIEWER: Were you also interested simply in the problem of writing one story from various different points of view, in experimenting with the different voices?

McCARTHY: There were no voices in that. I don't think I was really very much interested in the technical side of it. It was the first piece of fiction I had ever written, I mean I'd never made any experiments before. I was too inexperienced to worry about technical problems.

INTERVIEWER: You hadn't written any fiction before then?

McCARTHY: No. Well, in college I had written the tiniest amount of fiction: very bad short stories, very unrealized short stories, for courses, and that was all. I once started a detective story to make money—but I couldn't get the murder to take place! At the end of three chapters I was still describing the characters and the milieu, so I thought, this is not going to work. No corpse! And that was all. Then I simply did *The Company She Keeps*, and was only interested in the technical side from the point of view of establishing the truth, of trying to re-create what happened. For instance, the art-gallery story was written in the first person because that's the way you write that kind of story—a study of a curious individual.

INTERVIEWER: You imply that most of the stories were distinctly autobiographical.

McCARTHY: They all are more or less, except the one about the Yale man.

INTERVIEWER: Is this distinction between autobiography and fiction clear in your mind before you begin writing a story, or does it become so as you write? Or is there no such distinction?

McCARTHY: Well, I think it depends on what you're doing. Let's be frank. Take "The Man in the Brooks Brothers Shirt"; in that case it was an attempt to describe something that really happened—though naturally you have to do a bit of name-changing and city-changing. And the first story, the one about the divorce: that was a stylization—there were no proper names in it or anything—but still, it was an attempt to be as exact as possible about something that had happened. The Yale man was based on a real person. John Chamberlain, actually, whom I didn't know very well. But there it was an attempt to make this real man a broad type. You know, to use John Chamberlain's boyish looks and a few of the features of his career, and then draw all sorts of other Yale men into it. Then the heroine was put in, in an imaginary love affair, which *had* to be because she had to be in the story. I always thought that was all very hard on John Chamberlain, who was married. But of course he knew it wasn't true, and he knew that I didn't know him very well, and that therefore in the story he was just a kind of good-looking clothes-hanger. Anything else that I've written later—I may make a mistake—has been on the whole a fiction. Though it may have autobiographical elements in it that I'm conscious of, it has been conceived as a fiction, even a thing like *The Oasis*, that's supposed to have all these real people in it. The whole story is a complete fiction. Nothing of the kind ever happened; after all, it happens in the future. But in general, with characters, I do try at least to be as exact as possible about the essence of a person, to find the key that works the person both in real life and in the fiction.

INTERVIEWER: Do you object to people playing the *roman à clef* game with your novels?

McCARTHY: I suppose I really ask for it, in a way. I *do* rather object to it at the same time, insofar as it deflects attention from what I'm trying to do in the novel. What I really do is take real plums and put them in an imaginary cake. If you're interested in the cake, you get rather annoyed with people saying what species the real plum was. In *The Groves of Academe*, for instance. I had taught at Bard College and at Sarah Lawrence, but I didn't want to make a composite of those two places: I really wanted to make a weird imaginary college of my own. I even took a trip to the Mennonite country in Pennsylvania to try to find a perfect location for it, which I found—now where was it? Somewhere near Ephrata—yes, it was Lititz, Pennsylvania, the home of the pretzel.

There's a very charming old-fashioned sort of academy, a girls' college there—I'd never heard of it before and can't remember the name. It had the perfect setting, I thought, for this imaginary college of mine. Anyway, I would get terribly annoyed if people said it had to do with Sarah Lawrence, which it had almost no resemblance to. It was quite a bit like Bard. Sarah Lawrence is a much more *borné* and dull place than Bard, or than my college. And of course I was even more annoyed if they said it was Bennington. There was not supposed to be anything there of Bennington at all!

INTERVIEWER: When were you at Bard?

McCARTHY: '45 to '46.

INTERVIEWER: And at Sarah Lawrence?

McCARTHY: I was there just for one term, the winter of '48.

INTERVIEWER: Did you enjoy teaching?

McCARTHY: I adored teaching at Bard, yes. But the students were so poor at Sarah Lawrence that I didn't much enjoy it there. I don't think anyone I knew who was teaching there then did. But at Bard it was very exciting. It was all quite mad, crazy. I had never taught before, and I was staying up till two in the morning every night trying to keep a little bit behind my class. Joke.

INTERVIEWER: Did they ask you to teach "Creative Writing"?

McCARTHY: I've always refused to teach creative writing. Oh, I had in addition to two courses, about seven or eight tutorials, and some of those tutees wanted to study creative writing. I think I finally weakened and let one boy who was utterly ungifted for it study creative writing because he was so incapable of studying anything else.

INTERVIEWER: But mostly it was these two courses.

McCARTHY: Yes, and then you had to keep up with all these students. I had one boy doing all the works of James T. Farrell and a girl who was studying Marcus Aurelius and Dante. That was fun. That one I did the work for. And one girl was doing a thesis on Richardson; that was just hopeless. I mean, I couldn't even try to keep up with teaching Russian novels, and, say, Jane Austen—who in my course came under the head of "Modern Novel"—*and* all the works of Richardson. So I could never tell, you know, whether she had read what she was supposed to have read, because I couldn't remember it! Everything was reversed! The student was in a position to see whether the professor was cheating, or had done her homework. Anyway, everybody ended up ill after this year—you know, various physical ailments. But it was exciting, it was fun. The students were fun. The bright ones were bright, and there wasn't much of a middle layer. They were either bright or they were just cretins. I must say, there are times when you welcome a B student.

I liked teaching because I loved this business of studying. I found it quite impossible to give a course unless I'd read the material the night before. I absolutely couldn't handle the material unless it was fresh in my mind. Unless you give canned lectures, it really has to be—though that leads, I think, to all sorts of very whimsical, perhaps, and capricious interpretations; that is, you see the whole book, say *Anna Karenina*, in terms that are perhaps dictated by the moment. One wonders afterwards whether one's interpretation of *Anna Karenina* that one had rammed down the throats of those poor students was really as true as it seemed to one at the time.

INTERVIEWER: Which books did you teach in the "Modern Novel"?

McCARTHY: Well, you had to call everything at Bard either modern or contemporary, or the students wouldn't register for it. Everyone thinks this a joke, but it was true. I originally was going to teach a whole course on critical theory, from Aristotle to T. S. Eliot or something, and only three students registered for it, but if it had been called "Contemporary Criticism," then I think we would have had a regular class. So we called this course "The Modern Novel," and it began with Jane Austen, I think, and went up, well, certainly to Henry James. That was when I taught novels in pairs. I taught *Emma* and *Madame Bovary* together. Then *The Princess Casamassima*, with the anarchist plot in it and everything, with *The Possessed*. *The Red and the Black* with *Great Expectations*. And *Fontamara* with something. I only taught novels I liked.

INTERVIEWER: Would it be roughly the same list, were you teaching the course now? Or do you have new favorites?

McCARTHY: Oh I don't know, I might even add something like *Dr. Zhivago* at the end. I would probably do some different Dickens. I've read an awful lot of Dickens over again since then. Now I think I'd teach *Our Mutual Friend* or *Little Dorritt*.

INTERVIEWER: Why did you start reading Dickens over again?

McCARTHY: I don't know, I got interested in Dickens at Bard, and then at Sarah Lawrence. Another stimulus was a book done by a man called Edgar Johnson, a biographer of Dickens. Anthony West had attacked it in the *New Yorker*, and this made me so angry that I reviewed the book, and that set off another kind of chain reaction. I really *passionately* admire Dickens.

INTERVIEWER: Could I go back for a moment to what you said about your early writing at college? I think you said that *The Company She Keeps* was the first fiction you ever wrote, but that was some years after you left Vassar, wasn't it?

McCARTHY: Oh, yes. You know, I had been terribly discouraged when I was at Vassar, and later, by being told that I was really a critical mind, and that I had no creative talent. Who knows? they may have been right. This was done in a generous spirit, I don't mean that it was harsh. Anyway, I hadn't found any way at all, when I was in college, of expressing anything in the form of short stories. We had a rebel literary magazine that Elizabeth Bishop and Eleanor Clark were on, and Muriel Rukeyser and I. I wrote, not fiction, but sort of strange things for this publication.

INTERVIEWER: A rebel magazine?

McCARTHY: There was an official literary magazine, which we were all against. Our magazine was anonymous. It was called *Con Spirito*. It caused a great sort of scandal. I don't know why—it was one of these perfectly innocent undertakings. But people said, "How awful, it's anonymous." The idea of anonymity was of course to keep the judgment clear, especially the editorial board's judgment—to make people read these things absolutely on their merits. Well anyway, *Con Spirito* lasted for only a few numbers. Elizabeth Bishop wrote a wonderful story for it which I still remember, called "Then Came the Poor." It was about a revolution, a fantasy that took place in modern bourgeois society, when the poor invade, and take over a house.

INTERVIEWER: When you left Vassar, what then?

MCCARTHY: Well, I went to New York, and I began reviewing for the *New Republic* and the *Nation*—right away. I wrote these little book reviews. Then there was a series about the critics. The *Nation* wanted a large-scale attack on critics and book-reviewers, chiefly those in the *Herald Tribune*, the *Times*, and the *Saturday Review*, and so on. I had been doing some rather harsh reviews, so they chose me as the person to do this. But I was so young, I think I was twenty-two, that they didn't *trust* me. So they got Margaret Marshall, who was the assistant literary editor then, to do it with me: actually we divided the work up and did separate pieces. But she was older and was supposed to be—I don't know—a restraining influence on me; anyway, someone more responsible. That series was a great sensation at the time, and it made people very mad. I continued just to do book reviews, maybe one other piece about the theater, something like the one on the literary critics. And then nothing more until *Partisan Review* started. That was when I tried to write the detective story—before *Partisan Review*. To be exact, *Partisan Review* had existed as a Stalinist magazine, and then it had died, gone to limbo. But after the Moscow trials, the PR boys, Rahv and Phillips, revived it, got a backer, merged with some other people—Dwight Macdonald and others—and started it again. As an anti-Stalinist magazine. I had been married to an actor, and was supposed to know something about the theater, so I began writing a theater column for them. I didn't have any other ambitions at all. Then I married Edmund Wilson, and after we'd been married about a week, he said, "I think you have a talent for writing fiction." And he put me in a little room. He didn't literally lock the door, but he said, "Stay in there!" And I did. I just sat down, and it just came. It was the first story I had ever written, really: the first story in *The Company She Keeps*. Robert Penn Warren published it in the *Southern Review*. And I found myself writing fiction to my great surprise.

INTERVIEWER: This was when you became involved in politics, wasn't it?

McCARTHY: No. Earlier. In 1936, at the time of the Moscow trials. That changed absolutely everything. I got swept into the whole Trotskyite movement. But by accident. I was at a party. I knew Jim Farrell—I'd reviewed one of his books, I think it was *Studs Lonigan*—in any case, I knew Jim Farrell, and I was asked to a party given by his publisher for Art Young, the old *Masses* cartoonist. There were a lot of Communists at this party. Anyway, Farrell went around asking people whether they thought Trotsky was entitled to a hearing and to the right of asylum. I said yes, and that was all. The next thing I discovered I was on the letterhead of something calling itself the American Committee for the Defense of Leon Trotsky. I was furious, of course, at this use of my name. Not that my name had any consequence, but still, it was mine. Just as I was about to make some sort of protest, I began to get all sorts of calls from Stalinists, telling me to get off the committee. I began to see that other people were falling off the committee, like Freda Kirchwey—she was the first to go, I think—and this cowardice impressed me so unfavorably that naturally I didn't say anything about my name having got on there by accident, or at least without my realizing. So I stayed.

I began to know all the people on the committee. We'd attend meetings. It was a completely different world. Serious, you know. Anyway, that's how I got to know the PR boys. They hadn't yet revived the *Partisan Review*, but they were both on the Trotsky committee, at least Philip was. We—the committee, that is— used to meet in Farrell's apartment. I remember once when we met on St. Valentine's Day and I thought, Oh, this is so strange, because I'm the only person in this room who realizes that it's Valentine's Day. It was true! I had a lot of rather rich Stalinist friends, and I was always on the defensive with them, about the Moscow Trial question, Trotsky, and so on. So I had to inform myself, really, in order to conduct the argument. I found that I was reading more and more, getting more and more involved in this business. At the same time I got a job at Covici Friede, a rather left-wing publishing house now out of business, also full of Stalinists. I began to see Philip Rahv again because Covici Friede needed some readers' opinions on Russian books, and I remembered that he read Russian, so he came around to the office, and we began to see each other. When *Partisan Review* was revived I appeared as a sort of fifth wheel—there may have been more than that—but in any case as a kind of appendage of *Partisan Review*.

INTERVIEWER: Then you hadn't really been interested in politics before the Moscow trials?

McCARTHY: No, not really. My first husband had worked at the Theater Union, which was a radical group downtown that put on proletarian plays, and there were lots of Communists in that. Very few Socialists. And so I knew all these people; I knew that kind of person. But I wasn't very sympathetic to them. We used to see each other, and there were a lot of jokes. I even marched in May Day parades. Things like that. But it was all . . . fun. It was all done in that spirit. And I remained, as the *Partisan Review* boys said, absolutely bourgeois throughout. They always said to me very sternly, "You're really a throwback. You're really a twenties figure."

INTERVIEWER: How did you react to that?

McCARTHY: Well, I suppose I was wounded. I was a sort of gay, good-time girl, from their point of view. And they were men of the thirties. Very serious. That's why my position was so insecure on *Partisan Review*; it wasn't exactly insecure, but . . . lowly. I mean, in *fact*. And that was why they let me write about the theater, because they thought the theater was of absolutely no consequence.

INTERVIEWER: How did the outbreak of the war affect your political opinion? The *Partisan Review* group split apart, didn't it?

McCARTHY: At the beginning of the war we were all isolationists, the whole group. Then I think the summer after the fall of France—certainly before Pearl Harbor—Philip Rahv wrote an article in which he said in a measured sentence, "In a certain sense, this is our war." The rest of us were deeply shocked by this, because we regarded it as a useless imperialist war. You couldn't beat Fascism that way: "Fight the enemy at home," and so on. In other words, we reacted to the war rather in the manner as if it had been World War I. This was after Munich, after the so-called "phony war." There was some reason for having certain doubts about the war, at least about the efficacy of the war. So when Philip wrote this article, a long controversy began on *Partisan Review*. It split between those who supported the war, and those who didn't. I was among those who didn't— Edmund Wilson also, though for slightly different reasons. Dwight Macdonald and Clement Greenberg split off, and Dwight founded his own magazine, *Politics*, which started out as a Trotskyite magazine, and then became a libertarian, semi-anarchist one. Meyer Schapiro was in this group, and I forget who else. Edmund was really an unreconstructed isolationist. The others were either Marxist or libertarian. Of course there was a split in the Trotskyite movement at that period.

Toward the end of the war, I began to realize that there was something hypocritical about my position—that I was really supporting the war. I'd go to a movie—there was a marvelous documentary called *Desert Victory* about the British victory over Rommel's Africa Corps—and I'd find myself weeping madly when Montgomery's bagpipers went through to El Alamein. In other words, cheering the war, and on the other hand, being absolutely against Bundles for Britain, against Lend Lease—this was after

Lend Lease, of course—against every practical thing. And suddenly, I remember—it must have been the summer of '45 that I first said this aloud—I remember it was on the Cape, at Truro. There were a lot of friends, Chiaromonte, Lionel Abel, Dwight, et cetera, at my house—by this time I was divorced from Edmund, or separated, anyway. And I said, "You know, I think I, and all of us, are really *for* the war." This was the first time this had been said aloud by me. Dwight indignantly denied it. "I'm *not* for the war!" he said. But he was. Then I decided I wanted to give a blood transfusion. And I practically had to get cleared! Now no one was making me do this, but I felt I had to go and get cleared by my friends first. Was it wrong of me to support the war effort by giving a blood transfusion? It was agreed that it was all right. All this *fuss!* So I gave a blood transfusion, just one. Some other people were doing it too, I believe, independently, at the same time, people of more or less this tendency. That is the end of that story.

Years later, I realized I really thought that Philip had been right, and that the rest of us had been wrong. Of course we didn't know about the concentration camps: the death camps hadn't started at the beginning. All that news came in fairly late. But once this news was in, it became clear—at least to me, and I still believe it—that the only way to have stopped it was in a military way. That only the military defeat of Hitler could stop this, and it had to be stopped. But it took a long, long time to come to this view. You're always afraid of making the same mistake over again. But the trouble is you can always correct an earlier mistake like our taking the attitude to World War II as if it were World War I, but if you ever try to project the correction of a mistake into the future, you may make a different one. That is, many people now are talking about World War III as if it were World War II.

INTERVIEWER: What I don't see, though, is how all this left you once the war was over.

MCCARTHY: Actually, as I remember, after the war was the

very best period, politically, that I've been through. At that time, it seemed to me there was a lot of hope around. The war was over! Certain—perhaps—mistakes had been recognized. The bomb had been dropped on Hiroshima, and there was a kind of general repentance of this fact. This was before the hydrogen bomb; and we never even dreamed that the Russians were going to get the atomic bomb. The political scene looked free. This was not only true for us—it seemed a good moment. At least there was still the hope of small libertarian movements. People like Dwight and Chiaromonte and I used to talk about it a great deal, and even Koestler was writing at that period about the possibility of founding oases—that's where I took the title of that book from. It seemed possible still, utopian but possible, to change the world on a small scale. Everyone was trying to live in a very principled way, but with quite a lot of energy, the energy that peace had brought, really. This was the period of the Marshall Plan, too. It was a good period. Then of course the Russians got the atom bomb, and the hydrogen bomb came. That was the end of *any* hope, or at least any hope that I can see of anything being done except in a massive way.

INTERVIEWER: How do you characterize your political opinion now?

McCARTHY: Dissident!

INTERVIEWER: All the way round?

McCARTHY: Yes! No, I still believe in what I believed in then —I still believe in a kind of libertarian socialism, a decentralized socialism. But I don't see any possibility of achieving it. That is, within the span that I can see, which would be, say, to the end of my son's generation, your generation. It really seems to me sometimes that the only hope is space. That is to say, perhaps the most energetic—in a bad sense—elements will move on to a new world in space. The problems of mass society will be transported into space, leaving behind this world as a kind of Europe, which then eventually tourists will visit. The Old World. I'm only half joking. I don't think that the problem of social equality has ever been solved. As soon as it looks as if it were going to be solved, or even as if it were going to be confronted,—say, as at the end of the eighteenth century—there's a mass move to a new continent which defers this solution. After '48, after the failure of the '48 revolutions in Europe, hope for an egalitarian Europe really died, and the '48-ers, many of them, went to California in the Gold Rush as '49-ers. My great-grandfather, from central Europe, was one of them. The Gold Rush, the Frontier was a substitute sort of equality. Think of Chaplin's film. And yet once the concept of equality had entered the world, life becomes intolerable without it; yet life continues without its being realized. So it may be that there will be another displacement, another migration. The problem, the solution, or the confrontation, will again be postponed.

INTERVIEWER: Do you find that your critical work, whether it's political or literary, creates any problems in relation to your work as a novelist?

MCCARTHY: No, except that you have the perpetual problem, if somebody asks you to do a review, whether to interrupt what you're writing—if you're writing a novel—to do the review. You have to weigh whether the subject interests you enough, or whether you're tired at that moment, emotionally played out by the fiction you're writing. Whether it would be a good thing to stop and concentrate on something else. I just agreed to and did a review of Camus' collected fiction and journalism. That *was* in some way connected with my own work, with the question of the novel in general. I thought, yes, I will do this because I want to read all of Camus and decide what I think about him finally. (Actually, I ended up almost as baffled as when I started.) But in general, I don't take a review unless it's something like that. Or unless Anthony West attacks Dickens. You know. Either it has to be some sort of thing that I want very much to take sides on, or something I'd like to study a bit, that I want to find out about anyway. Or where there may, in the case of study, be some reference—very indirect—back to my own work.

INTERVIEWER: This is quite a change from the time when you wrote criticism and never even thought of writing fiction. But now you consider yourself a novelist? Or don't you bother with these distinctions?

McCARTHY: Well, I suppose I consider myself a novelist. Yes. Still, whatever way I write was really, I suppose, formed critically. That is, I learned to write reviews and criticism and then write novels so that however I wrote, it was formed that way. George Eliot, you know, began by translating Strauss, began by writing about German philosophy—though her philosophic passages are not at all good in *Middlemarch*. Nevertheless, I *think* that this kind of training really makes one more interested in the subject than in the style. Her work certainly doesn't suffer from any kind of stylistic frippery. There's certainly no voluminous drapery around. There is a kind of concision in it, at her best—that passage where she's describing the character of Lydgate—which shows, I think, the critical and philosophic training. I've never liked the conventional conception of "style." What's confusing is that style usually means some form of fancy writing—when people say, oh yes, so and so's such a "wonderful stylist." But if one means by style the voice, the irreducible and always recognizable and alive thing, then of course style is really everything. It's what you find in Stendhal, it's what you find in Pasternak. The same thing you find in a poet—the sound of, say, Donne's voice. In a sense, you can't go further in an analysis of Donne than to be able to place this voice, in the sense that you recognize Don Giovanni by the voice of Don Giovanni.

INTERVIEWER: In speaking of your own writing, anyway, you attribute its "style" to your earlier critical work—then you don't feel the influence of other writers of fiction?

McCARTHY: I don't think I have any influences. I think my first story, the first one in *The Company She Keeps*, definitely shows the Jamesian influence—James is so terribly catching. But beyond that, I can't find any influence. That is, I can't as a detached person—as detached as I can be—look at my work and see where it came from from the point of view of literary sources.

INTERVIEWER: There must be certain writers, though, that you are *drawn* to more than others.

McCARTHY: Oh, yes! But I don't think I write like them. The writer I really like best is Tolstoi, and I *know* I don't write like Tolstoi. I wish I did! Perhaps the best English prose is Thomas Nash. I don't write at all like Thomas Nash.

INTERVIEWER: It would seem also, from hints you give us in your books, that you like Roman writers as well.

McCARTHY: I did when I was young, very much. At least, I adored Catullus, and Juvenal; those were the two I really passionately loved. And Caesar, when I was a girl. But you couldn't say that I had been influenced by *Catullus!* No! And Stendhal I like very, very much. Again, I would be happy to write like Stendhal, but I don't. There are certain sentences in Stendhal that come to mind as how to do it if one could. I can't. A certain kind of clarity and brevity—the author's attitude summed up in a sentence, and done so simply, done without patronizing. Some sort of joy.

INTERVIEWER: It's a dangerous game to play, the influence one.

McCARTHY: Well in some cases it's easy to see, and people themselves acknowledge it, and are interested in it, as people are interested in their genealogy. I simply can't find my ancestors. I was talking to somebody about John Updike, and he's another one I would say I can't find any sources for.

INTERVIEWER: Do you like his writing?

McCARTHY: Yes. I've not quite finished *Rabbit, Run*—I must get it back from the person I lent it to and finish it. I thought it was very good, and so stupidly reviewed. I'd read *Poorhouse Fair*, which I thought was really remarkable. Perhaps it suffered from the point-of-view problem, the whole virtuosity of doing it through the eyes of this old man sitting on the veranda of the poorhouse, through his eyes with their refraction, very old eyes, and so on. I think, in a way, this trick prevents him saying a good deal in the book. Nevertheless, it's quite a remarkable book. But anyway, I nearly didn't read *Rabbit, Run* because I thought, Oh my God! from reading those reviews. The reviewers seemed to be under the impression that the hero was a terrible character. It's incredible! No, I think it's the most interesting American novel I've read in quite a long time.

INTERVIEWER: What about others? Did you like *Henderson the Rain King?*

McCARTHY: Well, yes, the first part of *Henderson* I think is marvelous. The vitality! I still think it's an amusing novel right through the lions, almost like a French eighteenth-century novel, or *conte*, very charming. But it doesn't have this tremendous blast of vitality that the first part has, and it doesn't have the density.

INTERVIEWER: What other recent American novels have you been interested by?

McCARTHY: Well, name one. There really aren't any! I mean, are there? I can't think of any. I don't like Salinger, not at all. That last thing isn't a novel anyway, whatever it is. I don't like it. Not at all. It suffers from this terrible sort of metropolitan sentimentality and it's *so* narcissistic. And to me, also, it seemed so false, so calculated. Combining the plain man with an absolutely megalomaniac egoism. I simply can't stand it.

INTERVIEWER: What do you think of women writers, or do you think the category "woman writer" should not be made?

McCARTHY: Some women writers make it. I mean, there's a certain kind of woman writer who's a capital W, capital W. Virginia Woolf certainly was one, and Katherine Mansfield was one, and Elizabeth Bowen is one. Katherine Anne Porter? Don't think she really is—I mean, her writing is certainly very feminine, but I would say that there wasn't this "WW" business in Katherine Anne Porter. Who else? There's Eudora Welty, who's certainly not a "Woman Writer." Though she's become one lately.

INTERVIEWER: What is it that happens to make this change?

McCARTHY: I think they become interested in décor. You

notice the change in Elizabeth Bowen. Her early work is much more masculine. Her later work has much more drapery in it. Who else? Jane Austen was never a "Woman Writer," I don't think. The cult of Jane Austen pretends that she was, but I don't think she was. George Eliot *certainly* wasn't, and George Eliot is the kind of woman writer I admire. I was going to write a piece at some point about this called "Sense and Sensibility," dividing women writers into these two. I *am* for the ones who represent sense, and so was Jane Austen.

INTERVIEWER: Getting away from novels for a moment, I'd like to ask you about *Memories of a Catholic Girlhood* if I might. Will you write any more autobiography?

MCCARTHY: I was just reading—oh God, actually I *was* just starting to read Simone de Beauvoir's second volume, *La Force de l'Age*, and she announces in the preface that she can't write about her later self with the same candor that she wrote about her girlhood.

INTERVIEWER: You feel that too?

MCCARTHY: On this one point I agree with her. One has to be really old, I think, really quite an old person—and by that time I don't know what sort of shape one's memory would be in.

INTERVIEWER: You don't agree with her on other points?

MCCARTHY: I had an interview with *L'Express* the other day, and I gave Simone de Beauvoir the works. Let's not do it twice. I think she's pathetic, that's all. This book is supposed to be better, more interesting anyway, than the first one because it's about the thirties, and everyone wants to read about the thirties. And her love affair with Sartre, which is just about the whole substance of this book, is supposed to be very touching. The book *is* more interesting than the first one. But I think she's odious. A mind totally bourgeois turned inside out.

INTERVIEWER: I have something else to ask, apropos of *Memories of a Catholic Girlhood*. There are certain points, important points and moments in your novels, where you deepen or enlarge the description of the predicament in which a character may be by reference to a liturgical or ecclesiastical or theological parallel or equivalence. What I want to know is, is this simply a strict use of analogy, a technical literary device, or does it indicate any conviction that these are valid and important ways of judging a human being?

McCarthy: I suppose it's a reference to a way of thinking about a human being. But I think at their worst they're rather just literary references. That is, slightly show-off literary references. I have a terrible compulsion to make them—really a dreadful compulsion. The first sentence of *The Stones of Florence* begins, "How can you stand it? This is the first thing, and the last thing, the eschatological question that the visitor leaves echoing in the air behind him." Something of that sort. Well, everybody was after me to take out that word. I left it out when I published that chapter in the *New Yorker*, but I put it back in the book. No, I do have this great compulsion to make those references. I think I do it as a sort of secret signal, a sort of looking over the heads of the readers who don't recognize them to the readers who do understand them.

Interviewer: If these references *are* only literary ones, secret signals, then they are blasphemous.

McCarthy: Yes, I see what you mean. I suppose they are. Yes, they are secret jokes, they are blasphemies. But—I think I said something of this in the introduction of *Catholic Girlhood*—I think that religion offers to Americans (I mean the Roman Catholic religion) very often the only history and philosophy they ever get. A reference to it somehow opens up that historical vista. In that sense it is a device for deepening the passage.

Interviewer: Could we go back to your novels for a moment? I'd like to ask you about how you begin on them. Do you start with the characters, the situation, the plot? What comes first? Perhaps that's too hard a question, too general.

McCarthy: Very hard, and I'm awfully specific. I can really only think in specific terms, at least about myself. *The Groves of Academe* started with the plot. The plot and this figure: there can't be the plot without this figure of the impossible individual, the unemployable professor and his campaign for justice. Justice, both in quotes, you know, and serious in a way. What *is* justice for the unemployable person? That was conceived from the beginning as a plot: the whole idea of the reversal at the end, when Mulcahy is triumphant and the President is about to lose his job or quit, when the worm turns and is triumphant. I didn't see exactly what would happen in between; the more minute details weren't worked out. But I did see that there would be his campaign for reinstatement and then his secret would be discovered. In this case that he had *not* been a Communist. A *Charmed Life* began with a short story; the first chapter was written as a short story. When I conceived the idea of its being a novel, I think about all I knew was that the heroine would have to die in the end. Everybody objected to that ending, and said that it was terrible to have her killed in an automobile accident in the last paragraph— utterly unprepared for, and so on. But the one thing I knew absolutely certainly was that the heroine had to die in the end. At first I was going to have her have an abortion, and have her die in the abortion. But that seemed to me so trite. Then I conceived the idea of having her drive on the correct side of the road and get killed, because in this weird place everyone is always on the wrong side of the road. But all that is really implicit in the first chapter.

INTERVIEWER: So the charge that readers are unprepared for the last paragraph you feel is unfair?

McCARTHY: There may be something wrong with the novel, I don't know. But it was always supposed to have a fairy tale element in it. New Leeds is *haunted!* Therefore nobody should be surprised if something unexpected happens, or something catastrophic, for the place is also pregnant with catastrophe. But it may be that the treatment in between was too realistic, so that the reader was led to expect a realistic continuation of everything going on in a rather moderate way. It was, to some extent, a symbolic story. The novel is supposed to be about doubt. All the

characters in different ways represent doubt, whether it is philosophical or ontological doubt as in the case of the strange painter
who questions everything—"Why don't I murder my grandmother?" and so on. Or the girl's rather nineteenth-century self-
doubt, doubt of the truth, of what she perceives. In any case,
everyone is supposed to represent one or another form of doubt.
When the girl finally admits to herself that she's pregnant, and
also recognizes that she must do something about it, in other
words, that she has to put up a real stake—and she does put up
a real stake—at that moment she becomes mortal. All the other
characters are immortal. They have dozens of terrible accidents,
and they're all crippled in one way or another, and yet they have
this marvelous power of survival. All those drunks and human
odds and ends. Anyway, the girl makes the decision—which from
the point of view of conventional morality is a wicked decision—
to have an abortion, to kill life. Once she makes this decision, she
becomes mortal, and doesn't belong to the charmed circle any
more. As soon as she makes it, she gets killed—to get killed is
simply a symbol of the fact that she's mortal.

INTERVIEWER: You say that her decision makes her mortal. But
her decision has also included someone else, the painter.

McCARTHY: Yes, yes. I see what you mean. I hadn't thought of
that, that when she asks somebody to help her it implies some
sort of social bond, some sort of mutual bond between people in
society, while the rest of these people are still a community of
isolates.

INTERVIEWER: His joining her in this mortal, social bond, that
doesn't make him mortal as well? He is still a part of the charmed
circle?

McCARTHY: He's too sweet to be mortal! Well, he's a comic
figure, and I have this belief that all comic characters are immortal. They're eternal. I believe this is Bergson's theory too. He
has something, I'm told, about comic characters being *figé*. Like
Mr. and Mrs. Micawber: they all have to go on forever and be
invulnerable. Almost all Dickens' characters have this peculiar

existence of eternity, except the heroes, except Pip, or Nicholas Nickleby, or David Copperfield.

INTERVIEWER: What other characters in your novels do you consider—

McCARTHY: The comic ones? Who knows whether they're immortal! As far as I'm concerned, they're immortal!

INTERVIEWER: Then you haven't thought of this distinction between "mortal" and "immortal" in relation to characters in other of your novels besides *A Charmed Life?*

McCARTHY: I didn't think of this distinction until just recently, and not in connection with myself. It's just at this very moment—*now* talking with you—that I'm thinking of it in connection with myself. I would say that it is a law that applies to *all* novels: that the comic characters are *figé*, are immortal, and that the hero or heroine exists in time, because the hero or heroine is always in some sense equipped with purpose.

The man in *The Groves of Academe*. Well, he's immortal, yes. He is a comic villain, and villains too always—I think—partake in this comic immortality. I *think* so. I'm not sure that you couldn't find an example, though, of a villain it wasn't true of. In Dickens again. In the late novels, somebody like Bradley Headstone, the schoolmaster, he's a mixed case. He's certainly not a villain in the sense of, say, the villain in *Little Dorritt*, who belongs to the old-fashioned melodramatic immortal type of villain. Headstone is really half a hero, Steerforth is half a hero, and therefore they don't conform to this.

This all came to me last year, this distinction, when I was thinking about the novel. Not my novel: The Novel.

But maybe that's really part of the trouble I'm having with *my* novel! These girls are all essentially comic figures, and it's awfully hard to make anything happen to them. Maybe this is really the trouble! Maybe I'm going to find out something in this interview! That the whole problem is *time!* I mean for me, in this novel. The passage of time, to show development. I think maybe my trouble is that these girls are comic figures, and that therefore they really can't develop! You see what I mean? They're not all so terribly comic, but most of them are.

How're they ever going to progress through the twenty years between the inauguration of Roosevelt and the inauguration of Eisenhower? This has been the great problem, and here I haven't had a form for it. I mean, all I know is that they're supposed to be middle-aged at the end.

Yes, I think maybe that *is* the trouble. One possibility would be . . . I've been introducing them one by one, chapter by chapter. They all appear at the beginning, you know, like the beginning of an opera, or a musical comedy. And then I take them one by one, chapter by chapter. I have been bringing each one on a little later on in time. But perhaps I can make bigger and bigger jumps so that you could meet, say, the last one when she is already middle-aged. You see what I mean. Maybe this would solve the problem. One five years later, another eight years later, and so on. I could manage the time problem that way. This has been very fruitful! Thank you!

INTERVIEWER: I want to ask you about the problem of time in the novel. You have written that a novel's action cannot take place in the future. But you have said that the action described in *The Oasis* all takes place in the future.

MCCARTHY: *The Oasis* is not a novel. I don't classify it as such. It was terribly criticized, you know, on that ground; people objected, said it wasn't a novel. But I never meant it to be. It's a *conte*, a *conte philosophique*.

INTERVIEWER: And *A Charmed Life* you say has fairy-tale elements.

MCCARTHY: I'm not sure any of my books are novels. Maybe none of them are. Something happens in my writing—I don't mean it to—a sort of distortion, a sort of writing on the bias, seeing things with a sort of swerve and swoop. *A Charmed Life*, for instance. You know, at the beginning I make a sort of inventory of all the town characters, just telling who they are. Now I did this with the intention of describing, well, this nice, ordinary, old-fashioned New England town. But it ended up differently. Something is distorted, the description takes on a sort of extravagance—I don't know exactly how it happens. I know I don't mean it to happen.

INTERVIEWER: You say in one of your articles that perhaps the fault lies simply in the material which the modern world affords, that it itself lacks—

McCARTHY: Credibility? Yes. It's a difficulty I think all modern writers have.

INTERVIEWER: Other than the problem of arrangement of time, are there other specific technical difficulties about the novel you find yourself particularly concerned with?

McCARTHY: Well, the whole question of the point of view, which tortures everybody. It's the problem that everybody's been up against since Joyce, if not before. Of course James really began it, and Flaubert even. You find it as early as *Madame Bovary*. The problem of the point of view, and the voice: *style indirect libre*—the author's voice, by a kind of ventriloquism, disappearing in and completely limited by the voices of his characters. What it has meant is the complete banishment of the author. I would like to restore the author! I haven't tried yet, but I'd like to try after this book, which is as far as I can go in ventriloquism. I would like to try to restore the author. Because you find that if you obey this Jamesian injunction of "Dramatize, dramatize," and especially if you deal with comic characters, as in my case, there is so much you can't say because you're limited by these mentalities. It's just that a certain kind of intelligence—I'm not only speaking of myself, but of anybody, Saul Bellow, for example—is more or less absent from the novel, and has to be, in accordance with these laws which the novel has made for itself. I think one reason that everyone—at least I—welcomed *Dr. Zhivago* was that you had the author in the form of the hero. And this beautiful tenor voice, the hero's voice and the author's—this marvelous voice, and this clear sound of intelligence. The Russians have never gone through the whole development of the novel you find in

Joyce, Faulkner, et cetera, so that Pasternak was slightly unaware of the problem! But I think this technical development has become absolutely killing to the novel.

INTERVIEWER: You say that after this novel about the Vassar girls, you—

McCARTHY: I don't know what I'm going to do, but I want to try something that will introduce, at least back into my work, my own voice. And not in the disguise of a heroine. I'm awfully sick of my heroine. I don't mean in this novel: my heroine of the past. Because the sensibility in each novel got more and more localized with this heroine, who became an agent of perception, et cetera.

Let me make a jump now. The reason that I enjoyed doing those books on Italy, the Venice and Florence books, was that I was writing *in my own voice*. One book was in the first person, and one was completely objective, but it doesn't make any difference. I felt, you know, now I can talk freely! The books were written very fast, the Venice one faster. Even the Florence book, with masses of research in it, was written very fast, with a great deal of energy, with a kind of liberated energy. And without the peculiar kind of painstakingness that's involved in the dramatization that one does in a novel, that is, when nothing can come in that hasn't been perceived through a character. The technical difficulties are so great, in projecting yourself, in feigning an alien consciousness, that too much energy gets lost, I think, in the masquerade. And I think this is not only true of me.

INTERVIEWER: How did you come to write those books about Florence and Venice?

McCARTHY: By chance. I was in Paris, just about to go home to America, and somebody called up and asked if I would come and have a drink at the Ritz before lunch, that he wanted to ask me something. It was an intermediary from the Berniers, who edit *L'Oeil*. They were in Lausanne, and this man wanted to know whether I would write a book on Venice for them. I had been in Venice once for ten days, years ago, but it seemed somehow adventurous. And there were other reasons too. So I said yes. I went out to meet the Berniers in Lausanne. I had absolutely no money left, about twenty dollars, and I thought, what if all this is a terrible practical joke? You know. I'll get to Lausanne and there won't be any of these people! There'll be nobody! I ran into Jay Laughlin that night, and he said that his aunt was in Lausanne at the moment, so that if anything happened to me, I could call on her! But in any case, I went to Lausanne, and they were real, they were there. And we drove to Venice together.

I knew nothing about the subject—maybe I exaggerate my ignorance now—but I was *appalled*. I was afraid to ask any questions —whenever I'd ask a question Georges Bernier would shudder because it revealed such absolutely terrifying depths of ignorance. So I tried to be silent. I'd never heard before that there was more than one Tiepolo, or more than one Tintoretto, that there was a son. I vaguely knew Bellini, but didn't have any idea there were three Bellinis. Things like that. I couldn't have been expected to know Venetian history, but actually Venetian history is very easy to bone up on, and there isn't much. But the art history! And I considered myself a reasonably cultivated person! My art history was of the most fragmentary nature!

But it was fun, and then that led me into doing the Florence book. I didn't want to, at first. But everything in Venice, in Italy for that matter, really points to Florence, everything in the Renaissance anyway, like signposts on a road. Whenever you're near discovery, you're near Florence. So I felt that this was all incomplete; I thought I had to go to Florence. It was far from my mind to write a book. Then various events happened, and slowly I decided, All right, I would do the book on Florence. After that I went back to Venice and studied the Florentines in Venice, just for a few days. It was so strange to come back to Venice after being immersed in Florence. It looked so terrible! From an architectural point of view, so scrappy and nondescript, if you'd been living with the Florentine substance and monumentality, and intellectuality of architecture. At first coming back was a real shock. Oh, and

I discovered I liked history! And I thought, my God, maybe I've made a mistake. Maybe I should have been an historian.

INTERVIEWER: It would also appear that you discovered you loved Brunelleschi.

McCARTHY: Oh, yes! Yes! Also, I felt a great, great congeniality —I don't mean with Brunelleschi personally, I would flatter myself if I said that—but with the history of Florence, the Florentine temperament. I felt that through the medium of writing about this city I could set forth what I believed in, what I was for; that through this city, its history, its architects and painters—more its sculptors than its painters—it was possible for me to say what I believed in. And say it very affirmatively, even though this all ended in 1529, you know, long before the birth of Shakespeare.

INTERVIEWER: In reading the Florence book, I remember being very moved by the passage where you talk of Brunelleschi, about his "absolute integrity and essence," that solidity of his, both real and ideal. When you write about Brunelleschi, you write about this sureness, this "being-itself," and yet as a novelist—in *The Company She Keeps* for instance—you speak of something so very different, and you take almost as a theme this fragmented un-placeability of the human personality.

McCARTHY: But I was very young then. I think I'm really not interested in the quest for the self any more. Oh, I suppose everyone continues to be interested in the quest for the self, but what you feel when you're older, I think, is that—how to express this— that you really must *make* the self. It's absolutely useless to look for it, you won't find it, but it's possible in some sense to make it. I don't mean in the sense of making a mask, a Yeatsian mask. But you finally begin in some sense to make and to choose the self you want.

INTERVIEWER: Can you write novels about that?

McCARTHY: I never have. I never have, I've never even thought of it. That is, I've never thought of writing a developmental novel in which a self of some kind is discovered or is made, is forged, as they say. No. I suppose in a sense I don't know any more today than I did in 1941 about what my identity is. But I've stopped looking for it. I must say, I believe much more in truth now than I did. I do believe in the solidity of truth much more. Yes. I believe there is a truth, and that it's knowable.

Elisabeth Niebuhr

13. Ralph Ellison

Ralph Ellison was born in Oklahoma City on March 1, 1914, the older of two sons born to parents who moved to Oklahoma from South Carolina shortly after Oklahoma became a state. Except for one year in Indiana, he spent his childhood and youth in Oklahoma City and received his education in the public schools there.

Upon graduation from high school he won a state scholarship and attended Tuskegee Institute from 1933 to 1936. There he was a music major, and the trumpet was his instrument. Earlier he had studied musical composition in Oklahoma City.

Mr. Ellison came to New York City to study sculpture during a summer vacation from Tuskegee, but soon abandoned this and the idea of returning to college in order to concentrate on music and composition. He worked briefly with Dr. Wallingford Riegger. Finally he gave up music for writing and participation in the New York City Writer's Project. Since 1939 his short stories, essays, criticism, and articles have appeared in many American publications.

In 1945 Mr. Ellison was granted a Rosenwald Fellowship on which he began work on *Invisible Man*, which was published in 1952, and for which he received the National Book Award of that year.

During his life Ralph Ellison has had a variety of occupations—newsboy, when he was in grade school, dental assistant, receptionist, jazz trumpeter, lecturer on literature, and professional photographer. His principal hobby is experimental audio-electronics.

In 1955 Mr. Ellison was awarded the Prix de Rome Fellowship by the American Academy of Arts and Letters. In 1954 he lectured at the Salzburg, Austria, Seminar in American Studies. From 1957 to 1961 he was Visiting Lecturer in Literature at Bard College, and during the fall quarter, 1961, was Alexander White Visiting Professor at the University of Chicago. He is a Board member of P.E.N. and of the Institute of Jazz Studies.

(Later he goes into cataleptic state in coffee pot where proprietor
thinks he's drunk and props him up outside where he can see and hear
muggers rob white-man looking for prostitutes; then he is rolled by these
two and lies helpless; then by cripple , then by child. Around corner

I walked back to Harlem at top speed, never slackening my pace until

black faces began to dominate the streets. God, what had come over me?

What had happened to people, couldn't they see me? Didn't they know that

I was nothing like what they? First the eviction and now this.

One group as confused as the other! Had I become invisible? And then I

had a terrifying thought; Perhaps I was everything, or nothing , depending

upon who was looking at me at the moment! Hadn't I acted the role of

priest as quickly as I had played ? This was

most frightening, because I hadn't wanted to do either--or at least

part of me had I had gone along, and who knew what I would do

next! Perhaps someone would whisper that I was a bank

robber--a Dillinger or Robin Hood-- to find myself masked

and gun demanding all the banknotes a teller. And what

if someone took the notion that I was a moron? I might find myself arrested

for indecent exposure. This would have to stop now, today, I thought as I

passed a shooting gallery. I knew who I was, perhaps, but not what I was.

And what I appeared to be to others was liable to get me into serious

trouble. No doubt the police were looking for me this

very minute. But I wasn't sure; perhaps by now I

had come to look like anybody and everyone and not even could

look at a man and determine the quality of his voice. And yet I remembered,

stepping around a car, that had stopped too far into the intersection ,

that certain types of Negro did

many of our alto and contralto singers tended to be short dark girls....

Anyway, they couldn't look at me and tell what I'd say in a speech, anymore

than the cover of Leroy's diary and what he had to say inside. Be-

sides, I know what I would say myself. Lord, how simple life had

seemed on the campus where everyone had had his name and his role

Well, I was tired, perhaps that was the explanation. Perhaps I was

Manuscript page from Ralph Ellison's novel Invisible Man.

R. STARK

Ralph Ellison

When Invisible Man, *Ralph Ellison's first novel, received the National Book Award for 1952, the author in his acceptance speech noted with dismay and gratification the conferring of the award to what he called "an attempt at a major novel." His gratification was understandable, so too his dismay when one considers the amount of objectivity Mr. Ellison can display toward his own work. He felt the state of United States fiction to be so unhappy that it was an "attempt" rather than an achievement which received the important award.*

Many of us will disagree with Mr. Ellison's evaluation of his own work. Its crackling, brilliant, sometimes wild, but always controlled prose warrants this; so does the care and logic with which its form is revealed, and not least its theme: that of a young Negro who emerges from the South and—in the tradition

*of James's Hyacinth Robinson and Stendhal's Julien Sorel—moves
into the adventure of life at large.*

*In the summer of 1954, Mr. Ellison came abroad to travel and
lecture. His visit ended with Paris where for a very few weeks he
mingled with the American expatriate group to whom his work
was known and of much interest. The day before he left he talked
to us in the Café de la Mairie du VIe about art and the novel.*

*Ralph Ellison takes both art and the novel seriously. And the
Café de la Mairie has a tradition of seriousness behind it, for here
was written Djuna Barnes' spectacular novel,* Nightwood. *There
is a tradition, too, of speech and eloquence, for Miss Barnes' hero,
Dr. O'Connor, often drew a crowd of listeners to his mighty
rhetoric. So here gravity is in the air and rhetoric too. While Mr.
Ellison speaks, he rarely pauses, and although the strain of organ-
izing his thought is sometimes evident, his phraseology and the
quiet steady flow and development of ideas are overwhelming.
To listen to him is rather like sitting in the back of a huge hall and
feeling the lecturer's faraway eyes staring directly into your own.
The highly emphatic, almost professorial intonations, startle with
their distance, self-confidence, and warm undertones of humor.*

ELLISON: Let me say right now that my book is not an autobiographical work.

INTERVIEWERS: You weren't thrown out of school like the boy in
your novel?

ELLISON: No. Though, like him, I went from one job to another.

INTERVIEWERS: Why did you give up music and begin writing?

ELLISON: I didn't give up music, but I became interested in
writing through incessant reading. In 1935 I discovered Eliot's
The Waste Land which moved and intrigued me but defied my
powers of analysis—such as they were—and I wondered why I had
never read anything of equal intensity and sensibility by an American Negro writer. Later on, in New York, I read a poem by
Richard Wright, who, as luck would have it, came to town the
next week. He was editing a magazine called *New Challenge* and

asked me to try a book review of E. Waters Turpin's *These Low Grounds*. On the basis of this review Wright suggested that I try a short story, which I did. I tried to use my knowledge of riding freight trains. He liked the story well enough to accept it and it got as far as the galley proofs when it was bumped from the issue because there was too much material. Just after that the magazine failed.

INTERVIEWERS: But you went on writing—

ELLISON: With difficulty, because this was the Recession of 1937. I went to Dayton, Ohio, where my brother and I hunted and sold game to earn a living. At night I practiced writing and studied Joyce, Dostoevski, Stein, and Hemingway. Especially Hemingway; I read him to learn his sentence structure and how to organize a story. I guess many young writers were doing this, but I also used his description of hunting when I went into the fields the next day. I had been hunting since I was eleven, but no one had broken down the process of wing-shooting for me, and it was from reading Hemingway that I learned to lead a bird. When he describes something in print, believe him; believe him even when he describes the process of art in terms of baseball or boxing; he's been there.

INTERVIEWERS: Were you affected by the social realism of the period?

ELLISON: I was seeking to learn and social realism was a highly regarded theory, though I didn't think too much of the so-called proletarian fiction even when I was most impressed by Marxism. I was intrigued by Malraux, who at that time was being claimed by the Communists. I noticed, however, that whenever the heroes of *Man's Fate* regarded their condition during moments of heightened self-consciousness, their thinking was something other than Marxist. Actually they were more profoundly intellectual than their real-life counterparts. Of course, Malraux was more of a humanist than most of the Marxist writers of that period—and also much more of an artist. He was the artist-revolutionary rather than a politician when he wrote *Man's Fate*, and the book lives not because of a political position embraced at the time but because of its larger concern with the tragic struggle of humanity. Most of the social realists of the period were concerned less with tragedy than with injustice. I wasn't, and am not, *primarily* concerned with injustice, but with art.

INTERVIEWERS: Then you consider your novel a purely literary work as opposed to one in the tradition of social protest.

ELLISON: Now, mind, I recognize no dichotomy between art and protest. Dostoevski's *Notes from Underground* is, among other things, a protest against the limitations of nineteenth-century rationalism; *Don Quixote, Man's Fate, Oedipus Rex, The Trial* —all these embody protest, even against the limitation of human life itself. If social protest is antithetical to art, what then shall we make of Goya, Dickens, and Twain? One hears a lot of complaints about the so-called "protest novel," especially when written by Negroes; but it seems to me that the critics could more accurately complain about the lack of craftsmanship and the provincialism which is typical of such works.

INTERVIEWERS: But isn't it going to be difficult for the Negro writer to escape provincialism when his literature is concerned with a minority?

ELLISON: All novels are about certain minorities: the individual is a minority. The universal in the novel—and isn't that what we're all clamoring for these days?—is reached only through the depiction of the specific man in a specific circumstance.

INTERVIEWERS: But still, how is the Negro writer, in terms of what is expected of him by critics and readers, going to escape his particular need for social protest and reach the "universal" you speak of?

ELLISON: If the Negro, or any other writer, is going to do what is expected of him, he's lost the battle before he takes the field. I suspect that all the agony that goes into writing is borne precisely because the writer longs for acceptance—but it must be acceptance on his own terms. Perhaps, though, this thing cuts both ways: the Negro novelist draws his blackness too tightly around him when he sits down to write—that's what the anti-protest critics believe—but perhaps the white reader draws his whiteness around himself when he sits down to read. He doesn't want to identify himself with Negro characters in terms of our immediate racial and social situation, though on the deeper human level identification can become compelling when the situation is revealed artistically. The white reader doesn't want to get too close, not even in an imaginary re-creation of society. Negro writers have felt this, and it has led to much of our failure.

Too many books by Negro writers are addressed to a white audience. By doing this the authors run the risk of limiting themselves to the audience's presumptions of what a Negro is or should be; the tendency is to become involved in polemics, to plead the Negro's humanity. You know, many white people question that humanity, but I don't think that Negroes can afford to indulge in such a false issue. For us the question should be, what are the specific *forms* of that humanity, and what in our background is worth preserving or abandoning. The clue to this can be found in folklore, which offers the first drawings of any group's character. It preserves mainly those situations which have repeated themselves again and again in the history of any given group. It describes those rites, manners, customs, and so forth, which insure the good life, or destroy it; and it describes those boundaries of feeling, thought, and action which that particular group has found to be the limitation of the human condition. It projects this wisdom in symbols which express the group's will to survive; it embodies those values by which the group lives and dies. These drawings may be crude but they are nonetheless profound in that they represent the group's attempt to humanize the world. It's no accident that great literature, the product of individual artists, is erected upon this humble base. The hero of Dostoevski's *Notes from Underground* and the hero of Gogol's "The Overcoat" appear in their rudimentary forms far back in Russian folklore. French literature has never ceased exploring the nature of the Frenchman. Or take Picasso—

INTERVIEWERS: How does Picasso fit into all this?

ELLISON: Why, he's the greatest wrestler with forms and techniques of them all. Just the same, he's never abandoned the old symbolic forms of Spanish art: the guitar, the bull, daggers, women, shawls, veils, mirrors. Such symbols serve a dual function: they allow the artist to speak of complex experiences and to annihilate time with simple lines and curves; and they allow the viewer an orientation, both emotional and associative, which goes so deep that a total culture may resound in a simple rhythm, an image. It has been said that Escudero could recapitulate the history and spirit of the Spanish dance with a simple arabesque of his fingers.

INTERVIEWERS: But these are examples from homogeneous cultures. How representative of the American nation would you say Negro folklore is?

ELLISON: The history of the American Negro is a most intimate part of American history. Through the very process of slavery came the building of the United States. Negro folklore, evolving within a larger culture which regarded it as inferior, was an especially courageous expression. It announced the Negro's willingness to trust his own experience, his own sensibilities as to the definition of reality, rather than allow his masters to define these crucial matters for him. His experience is that of America and the West, and is as rich a body of experience as one would find anywhere. We can view it narrowly as something exotic, folksy, or "low-down," or we may identify ourselves with it and recognize it as an important segment of the larger American experience— not lying at the bottom of it, but intertwined, diffused in its very texture. I can't take this lightly or be impressed by those who cannot see its importance; it is important to *me*. One ironic witness to the beauty and the universality of this art is the fact that the descendants of the very men who enslaved us can now sing the spirituals and find in the singing an exaltation of their own humanity. Just take a look at some of the slave songs, blues, folk ballads; their possibilities for the writer are infinitely suggestive. Some of them have named human situations so well that a whole corps of writers could not exhaust their universality. For instance, here's an old slave verse:

Ole Aunt Dinah, she's just like me
She work so hard she want to be free
But ole Aunt Dinah's gittin' kinda ole
She's afraid to go to Canada on account of the cold.

Ole Uncle Jack, now he's a mighty "good nigger"
You tell him that you want to be free for a fac'
Next thing you know they done stripped the skin off your back.

Now ole Uncle Ned, he want to be free
He found his way north by the moss on the tree
He cross that river floating in a tub
The patateroller* give him a mighty close rub.

It's crude, but in it you have three universal attitudes toward the problem of freedom. You can refine it and sketch in the psychological subtleties and historical and philosophical allusions, action and whatnot, but I don't think its basic definition can be exhausted. Perhaps some genius could do as much with it as Mann has done with the Joseph story.

INTERVIEWERS: Can you give us an example of the use of folklore in your own novel?

ELLISON: Well, there are certain themes, symbols, and images which are based on folk material. For example, there is the old saying among Negroes: If you're black, stay back; if you're brown, stick around; if you're white, you're right. And there is the joke Negroes tell on themselves about their being so black they can't be seen in the dark. In my book this sort of thing was merged with the meanings which blackness and light have long had in Western mythology: evil and goodness, ignorance and knowledge, and so on. In my novel the narrator's development is one through blackness to light; that is, from ignorance to enlightenment:

---

* Patroller.

invisibility to visibility. He leaves the South and goes North; this, as you will notice in reading Negro folk tales, is always the road to freedom—the movement upward. You have the same thing again when he leaves his underground cave for the open.

It took me a long time to learn how to adapt such examples of myth into my work—also ritual. The use of ritual is equally a vital part of the creative process. I learned a few things from Eliot, Joyce and Hemingway, but not how to adapt them. When I started writing, I knew that in both *The Waste Land* and *Ulysses* ancient myth and ritual were used to give form and significance to the material; but it took me a few years to realize that the myths and rites which we find functioning in our everyday lives could be used in the same way. In my first attempt at a novel—which I was unable to complete—I began by trying to manipulate the simple structural unities of *beginning, middle,* and *end,* but when I attempted to deal with the psychological strata— the images, symbols, and emotional configurations—of the experience at hand, I discovered that the unities were simply cool points of stability on which one could suspend the narrative line—but beneath the surface of apparently rational human relationships there seethed a chaos before which I was helpless. People rationalize what they shun or are incapable of dealing with; these superstitions and their rationalizations become ritual as they govern behavior. The rituals become social forms, and it is one of the functions of the artist to recognize them and raise them to the level of art.

I don't know whether I'm getting this over or not. Let's put it this way: Take the "Battle Royal" passage in my novel, where the boys are blindfolded and forced to fight each other for the amusement of the white observers. This is a vital part of behavior pattern in the South, which both Negroes and whites thoughtlessly accept. It is a ritual in preservation of caste lines, a keeping of taboo to appease the gods and ward off bad luck. It is also the initiation ritual to which all greenhorns are subjected. This passage states what Negroes will see I did not have to invent; the patterns were already there in society so that all I had to do was present them in a broader context of meaning. In any society there are many rituals of situation which, for the most part, go unquestioned. They can be simple or elaborate, but they are the connective tissue between the work of art and the audience.

INTERVIEWERS: Do you think a reader unacquainted with this folklore can properly understand your work?

ELLISON: Yes, I think so. It's like jazz; there's no inherent problem which prohibits understanding but the assumptions brought to it. We don't all dig Shakespeare uniformly, or even "Little Red Riding Hood." The understanding of art depends finally upon one's willingness to extend one's humanity and one's knowledge of human life. I noticed, incidentally, that the Germans, having no special caste assumptions concerning American Negroes, dealt with my work simply as a novel. I think the Americans will come to view it that way in twenty years—if it's around that long.

INTERVIEWERS: Don't you think it will be?

ELLISON: I doubt it. It's not an important novel. I failed of eloquence and many of the immediate issues are rapidly fading away. If it does last, it will be simply because there are things going on in its depth that are of more permanent interest than on its surface. I hope so, anyway.

INTERVIEWERS: Have the critics given you any constructive help in your writing, or changed in any way your aims in fiction?

ELLISON: No, except that I have a better idea of how the critics react, of what they see and fail to see, of how their sense of life differs with mine and mine with theirs. In some instances they were nice for the wrong reasons. In the U.S.—and I don't want this to sound like an apology for my own failures—some reviewers did not see what was before them because of this nonsense about protest.

INTERVIEWERS: Did the critics change your view of yourself as a writer?

ELLISON: I can't say that they did. I've been seeing by my own candle too long for that. The critics did give me a sharper sense of a larger audience, yes; and some convinced me that they were willing to judge me in terms of my writing rather than in terms of my racial identity. But there is one widely syndicated critical bankrupt who made liberal noises during the thirties and has been frightened ever since. He attacked my book as a "literary race riot." By and large, the critics and readers gave me an affirmed sense of my identity as a writer. You might know this within yourself, but to have it affirmed by others is of utmost importance. Writing is, after all, a form of communication.

INTERVIEWERS: When did you begin *Invisible Man?*

ELLISON: In the summer of 1945. I had returned from the sea, ill, with advice to get some rest. Part of my illness was due, no doubt, to the fact that I had not been able to write a novel for which I'd received a Rosenwald Fellowship the previous winter. So on a farm in Vermont where I was reading *The Hero* by Lord Ragland and speculating on the nature of Negro leadership in the U.S., I wrote the first paragraph of *Invisible Man,* and was soon involved in the struggle of creating the novel.

INTERVIEWERS: How long did it take you to write it?

ELLISON: Five years with one year out for a short novel which was unsatisfactory, ill-conceived, and never submitted for publication.

INTERVIEWERS: Did you have everything thought out before you began to write *Invisible Man?*

ELLISON: The symbols and their connections were known to me. I began it with a chart of the three-part division. It was a conceptual frame with most of the ideas and some incidents indicated. The three parts represent the narrator's movement from, using Kenneth Burke's terms, purpose to passion to perception. These three major sections are built up of smaller units of three which mark the course of the action and which depend for their development upon what I hoped was a consistent and developing motivation. However, you'll note that the maximum insight on the hero's part isn't reached until the final section. After all, it's a novel about innocence and human error, a struggle through illusion to reality. Each section begins with a sheet of paper; each piece of paper is exchanged for another and contains a definition of his identity, or the social role he is to play as defined for him by others. But all say essentially the same thing: "Keep this nigger boy running." Before he could have some voice in his own destiny he had to discard these old identities and illusions; his enlightenment couldn't come until then. Once he recognizes the hole of darkness into which these papers put him, he has to burn them. That's the plan and the intention; whether I achieved this is something else.

INTERVIEWERS: Would you say that the search for identity is primarily an American theme?

ELLISON: It is *the* American theme. The nature of our society is such that we are prevented from knowing who we are. It is still a young society, and this is an integral part of its development.

INTERVIEWERS: A common criticism of "first novels" is that the central incident is either omitted or weak. *Invisible Man* seems to suffer here; shouldn't we have been present at the scenes which are the dividing lines in the book—namely, when the Brotherhood organization moves the narrator downtown, then back uptown?

ELLISON: I think you missed the point. The major flaw in the hero's character is his unquestioning willingness to do what is required of him by others as a way to success, and this was the specific form of his "innocence." He goes where he is told to go; he does what he is told to do; he does not even choose his Brotherhood name. It is chosen for him and he accepts it. He has accepted party discipline and thus cannot be present at the scene since it is not the will of the Brotherhood leaders. What is important is not the scene but his failure to question their decision. There is also the fact that no single person can be everywhere at once, nor can a single consciousness be aware of all the nuances of a large social action. What happens uptown while he is downtown is part of his darkness, both symbolic and actual. No; I don't feel that any vital scenes have been left out.

INTERVIEWERS: Why did you find it necessary to shift styles throughout the book; particularly in the Prologue and Epilogue?

ELLISON: The Prologue was written afterwards, really—in terms of a shift in the hero's point of view. I wanted to throw the reader off balance—make him accept certain non-naturalistic effects. It was really a memoir written underground, and I wanted a foreshadowing through which I hoped the reader would view the actions which took place in the main body of the book. For another thing, the styles of life presented are different. In the South, where he was trying to fit into a traditional pattern and where his sense of certainty had not yet been challenged, I felt a more naturalistic treatment was adequate. The college trustee's speech to the students is really an echo of a certain kind of Southern rhetoric and I enjoyed trying to re-create it. As the hero passes from the South to the North, from the relatively stable to the swiftly changing, his sense of certainty is lost and the style becomes expressionistic. Later on during his fall from grace in the Brotherhood it becomes somewhat surrealistic. The styles try to express both his state of consciousness and the state of society. The Epilogue was necessary to complete the action begun when he set out to write his memoirs.

INTERVIEWERS: After four hundred pages you still felt the Epilogue was necessary?

ELLISON: Yes. Look at it this way. The book is a series of reversals. It is the portrait of the artist as a rabble-rouser, thus the various mediums of expression. In the Epilogue the hero discovers what he had not discovered throughout the book: you have to make your own decisions; you have to think for yourself. The hero comes up from underground because the act of writing and thinking necessitated it. He could not stay down there.

INTERVIEWERS: You say that the book is "a series of reversals." It seemed to us that this was a weakness, that it was built on a series of provocative situations which were canceled by the calling up of conventional emotions.

ELLISON: I don't quite see what you mean.

INTERVIEWERS: Well, for one thing, you begin with a provocative situation of the American Negro's status in society. The responsibility for this is that of the white American citizen; that's where the guilt lies. Then you cancel it by introducing the Communist Party, or the Brotherhood, so that the reader tends to say to himself, "Ah, they're the guilty ones. They're the ones who mistreat him; not us."

ELLISON: I think that's a case of misreading. And I didn't identify the Brotherhood as the C.P., but since you do I'll remind you that they too are white. The hero's invisibility is not a matter of being seen, but a refusal to run the risk of his own humanity, which involves guilt. This is not an attack upon white society! It is what the hero refuses to do in each section which leads to further action. He must assert and achieve his own humanity; he cannot run with the pack and do this—this is the reason for all the reversals. The Epilogue is the most final reversal of all; therefore it is a necessary statement.

INTERVIEWERS: And the love affairs—or almost-love-affairs—

ELLISON: [*Laughing*] I'm glad you put it that way. The point is that when thrown into a situation which he thinks he wants, the hero is sometimes thrown at a loss; he doesn't know how to act. After he had made this speech about the Place of the Woman in Our Society, for example, and was approached by one of the women in the audience, he thought she wanted to talk about the Brotherhood and found that she wanted to talk about brother-*and-sisterhood*. Look, didn't you find the book at all *funny*? I felt that such a man as this character would have been incapable of a love affair; it would have been inconsistent with his personality.

INTERVIEWERS: Do you have any difficulty controlling your characters? E. M. Forster says that he sometimes finds a character running away with him.

ELLISON: No, because I find that a sense of the ritual understructure of the fiction helps to guide the creation of characters. Action is the thing. We are what we do and do not do. The problem for me is to get from A to B to C. My anxiety about transitions greatly prolonged the writing of my book. The naturalists stick to case histories and sociology and are willing to compete with the camera and the tape recorder. I despise concreteness in writing, but when reality is deranged in fiction, one must worry about the seams.

INTERVIEWERS: Do you have difficulty turning real characters into fiction?

ELLISON: Real characters are just a limitation. It's like turning your own life into fiction: you have to be hindered by chronology and fact. A number of the characters just jumped out, like Rinehart and Ras.

INTERVIEWERS: Isn't Ras based on Marcus Garvey? *

ELLISON: No. In 1950 my wife and I were staying at a vacation spot where we met some white liberals who thought the best way to be friendly was to tell us what it was like to be Negro. I got mad at hearing this from people who otherwise seemed very intelligent. I had already sketched Ras, but the passion of his statement came out after I went upstairs that night feeling that we needed to have this thing out once and for all and get it done with; then we could go on living like people and individuals. No conscious reference to Garvey is intended.

INTERVIEWERS: What about Rinehart? Is he related to Rinehart in the blues tradition, or Django Rheinhardt, the jazz musician?

ELLISON: There is a peculiar set of circumstances connected with my choice of that name. My old Oklahoma friend, Jimmy Rushing, the blues singer, used to sing one with a refrain that went:

> *Rinehart, Rinehart,*
> *It's so lonesome up here*
> *On Beacon Hill,*

which haunted me, and as I was thinking of a character who was a master of disguise, of coincidence, this name with its suggestion of inner and outer came to my mind. Later I learned that it was a call used by Harvard students when they prepared to riot, a call

---

* Marcus Garvey: Negro nationalist and founder of a "Back to Africa" movement in the United States during the early 1900s.

to chaos. Which is very interesting, because it is not long after Rinehart appears in my novel that the riot breaks out in Harlem. Rinehart is my name for the personification of chaos. He is also intended to represent America and change. He has lived so long with chaos that he knows how to manipulate it. It is the old theme of *The Confidence Man*. He is a figure in a country with no solid past or stable class lines; therefore he is able to move about easily from one to the other. . . .

You know, I'm still thinking of your question about the use of Negro experience as material for fiction. One function of serious literature is to deal with the moral core of a given society. Well, in the United States the Negro and his status have always stood for that moral concern. He symbolizes among other things the human and social possibility of equality. This is the moral question raised in our two great nineteenth-century novels, *Moby Dick* and *Huckleberry Finn*. The very center of Twain's book revolves finally around the boy's relations with Nigger Jim and the question of what Huck should do about getting Jim free after the two scoundrels had sold him. There is a magic here worth conjuring, and that reaches to the very nerve of the American consciousness—so why should I abandon it? Our so-called race problem has now lined up with the world problems of colonialism and the struggle of the West to gain the allegiance of the remaining non-white people who have thus far remained outside the Communist sphere; thus its possibilities for art have increased rather than lessened. Looking at the novelist as manipulator and depicter of moral problems, I ask myself how much of the achievement of democratic ideals in the U.S. has been affected by the steady pressure of Negroes and those whites who were sensitive to the implications of our condition; and I know that without that pressure the position of our country before the world would be much more serious than it is even now. Here is part of the social dynamics of a great society. Perhaps the discomfort about protest in books by Negro authors comes because since the nineteenth century American literature has avoided profound moral searching. It was too painful and besides there were specific problems of language and form to which the writers could address themselves. They did wonderful things, but perhaps they left the real problems untouched. There are exceptions, of course, like Faulkner who has been working the great moral theme all along, taking it up where Mark Twain put it down.

I feel that with my decision to devote myself to the novel I took on one of the responsibilities inherited by those who practice the craft in the U.S.: that of describing for all that fragment of the huge diverse American experience which I know best, and which offers me the possibility of contributing not only to the growth of the literature but to the shaping of the culture as I should like it to be. The American novel is in this sense a conquest of the frontier; as it describes our experience, it creates it.

ALFRED CHESTER
VILMA HOWARD

14. Robert Lowell

Robert Lowell was born in Boston on March 1, 1917, great-grand-nephew of James Russell Lowell. He first attended St. Mark's School, and then Harvard, which he left after two years for Kenyon in order to study poetry, criticism, and the classics under John Crowe Ransom. He then attended Louisiana State University and afterward worked for a short while with a New York publisher. During World War II he was a conscientious objector and served a prison sentence.

In 1947 and 1948 Mr. Lowell was Consultant in Poetry at the Library of Congress. He has held a Guggenheim fellowship and an Institute of Arts and Letters grant. He has lectured in poetry and creative writing at the State University of Iowa, the Kenyon School of English, and the Salzburg Seminar in American Studies in Austria; he has also taught at Boston University. In 1959 he was awarded a fellowship by the Ford Foundation to work as a poet-librettist in association with the Metropolitan Opera and the New York City Opera companies.

His first book of poems was *Land of Unlikeness*, published in 1944. Most of these poems were included in his second volume, *Lord Weary's Castle* (1946). In 1951 he published a third volume of poetry, *The Mills of the Kavanaughs*, and in 1959 *Life Studies*, consisting of new poems and an autobiographical fragment. He received the Pulitzer Prize for poetry in 1947 for *Lord Weary's Castle*.

Mr. Lowell is married to the writer Elizabeth Hardwick and has one child, a daughter, Harriet.

THE VOYAGE

I

For the child playing with its globe and stamps,
the planet equals its rapacity--
how grand the world in the light of the lamps,
how small in the blue day of maturity!

One morning we set sail, giddy with brave
predjudices, judgements, ingenuity--
we swing with the velvet swell of the wave,
our infinite is rocked by the fixed sea.

Some wish to fly a cheapness they detest,
others their crades' terror--others stand
sky-watching the great arc of a woman's breast,
reptilian Circe with her junk and wand.

Not to be changed to reptiles, such men craze
themselves with spaces, light, the burning sky;
cold toughens them, they bronze in the sun's blaze,
and dry the sores of their debauchery.

But the true voyagers are those who move
simply to move--balloons; their heart
is a sick motor thumping in one groove,
their irrational scream is, "Let's depart!"

Oh conscripts lusting for the first fire of the guns,
our sciences have never learned to tag
your dreams--unfathomable, enormous, vague
hopes grease the gears of these automatons.

Manuscript page from Robert Lowell's translation of Baudelaire's "Le Voyage."

HANS BECK

Robert Lowell

On one wall of Mr. Lowell's study was a large portrait of Ezra Pound, the tired, haughty outlines of the face concentrated as in the raised outlines of a ring seal in an enlargement. Also bearded, but on another wall, over the desk, James Russell Lowell looked down from a gray old-fashioned photograph on the apex of the triangle thus formed, where his great-grand-nephew sat and answered questions.

Mr. Lowell had been talking about the classes he teaches at Boston University.

Four floors below the study window, cars whined through the early spring rain on Marlborough Street toward the Boston Public Garden.

INTERVIEWER: What are you teaching now?

LOWELL: I'm teaching one of these poetry-writing classes and a course in the novel. The course in the novel is called Practical Criticism. It's a course I teach every year, but the material changes. It could be anything from Russian short stories to Baude-laire, a study of the New Critics, or just fiction. I do whatever I happen to be working on myself.

INTERVIEWER: Has your teaching over the last few years meant anything to you as a writer?

LOWELL: It's meant a lot to me as a human being, I think. But my teaching is part time and has neither the merits nor the burdens of real teaching. Teaching is entirely different from writing. You're always up to it, or more or less up to it; there's no question of it's clogging, of it's not coming. It's much less sub-jective, and it's a very pleasant pursuit in itself. In the kind of teaching I do, conversational classes, seminars, if the students are good, which they've been most of the time, it's extremely enter-taining. Now, I don't know what it has to do with writing. You review a lot of things that you like, and you read things that you haven't read or haven't read closely, and read them aloud, go into them much more carefully than you would otherwise; and that must teach you a good deal. But there's such a jump from teach-ing to writing.

INTERVIEWER: Well, do you think the academic life is liable to block up the writer-professor's sensitivity to his own intui-tions?

LOWELL: I think it's impossible to give a general answer. Al-most all the poets of my generation, all the best ones, teach. I only know one, Elizabeth Bishop, who doesn't. They do it for a livelihood, but they also do it because you can't write poetry all the time. They do it to extend themselves, and I think it's undoubtedly been a gain to them. Now the question is whether something else might be more of a gain. Certainly the danger of teaching is that it's much too close to what you're doing—close and not close. You can get expert at teaching and be crude in practice. The revision, the consciousness that tinkers with the poem—that has something to do with teaching and criticism. But the impulse that starts a poem and makes it of any impor-tance is distinct from teaching.

INTERVIEWER: And protected, you think, from whatever you bring to bear in the scrutiny of parts of poems and aspects of novels, etc.?

LOWELL: I think you have to tear it apart from that. Teaching may make the poetry even more different, less academic than it would be otherwise. I'm sure that writing isn't a craft, that is, something for which you learn the skills and go on turning out. It must come from some deep impulse, deep inspiration. That can't be taught, it can't be what you use in teaching. And you may go further afield looking for that than you would if you didn't teach. I don't know, really; the teaching probably makes you more cautious, more self-conscious, makes you write less. It may make you bolder when you do write.

INTERVIEWER: You think the last may be so?

LOWELL: The boldness is ambiguous. It's not only teaching, it's growing up in this age of criticism which we're all so conscious of, whether we like it or don't like it, or practice it or don't practice it. You think three times before you put a word down, and ten times about taking it out. And that's related to boldness; if you put words down they must do something, you're not going to put clichés. But then it's related to caution; you write much less.

INTERVIEWER: You yourself have written very little criticism, haven't you? You did once contribute to a study of Hopkins.

LOWELL: Yes, and I've done a few omnibus reviews. I do a review or two a year.

INTERVIEWER: You did a wonderful one of Richards' poems.

LOWELL: I felt there was an occasion for that, and I had something to say about it. Sometimes I wish I did more, but I'm very anxious in criticism not to do the standard analytical essay. I'd like my essay to be much sloppier and more intuitive. But my friends are critics, and most of them poet-critics. When I was twenty and learning to write, Allen Tate, Eliot, Blackmur, and Winters, and all those people were very much news. You waited for their essays, and when a good critical essay came out it had the excitement of a new imaginative work.

INTERVIEWER: Which is really not the case with any of the critics writing today, do you think?

LOWELL: The good critics are almost all the old ones. The most brilliant critic of my generation, I think, was Jarrell, and he in a way connects with that older generation. But he's writing less criticism now than he used to.

INTERVIEWER: In your schooling at St. Mark's and Harvard— we can talk about Kenyon in a minute—were there teachers or friends who had an influence on your writing, not so much by the example of their own writing as by personal supervision or direction—by suggesting certain reading, for instance?

LOWELL: Well, my school had been given a Carnegie set of art books, and I had a friend, Frank Parker, who had great talent as a painter but who'd never done it systematically. We began reading the books and histories of art, looking at reproductions, tracing the Last Supper on tracing paper, studying dynamic symmetry, learning about Cézanne, and so on. I had no practical interest in painting, but that study seemed rather close to poetry. And from there I began. I think I read Elizabeth Drew or some such book on modern poetry. It had free verse in it, and that seemed very simple to do.

INTERVIEWER: What class were you in then?

LOWELL: It was my last year. I'd wanted to be a football player very much, and got my letter but didn't make the team. Well, that was satisfying but crushing too. I read a good deal, but had never written. So this was a recoil from that. Then I had some luck in that Richard Eberhart was teaching there.

INTERVIEWER: I'd thought he'd been a student there with you.

LOWELL: No, he was a young man about thirty. I never had him in class, but I used to go to him. He'd read aloud and we'd talk, he was very pleasant that way. He'd smoke honey-scented tobacco, and read Baudelaire and Shakespeare and Hopkins—it made the thing living—and he'd read his own poems. I wrote very badly at first, but he was encouraging and enthusiastic. That probably was decisive, that there was someone there whom I admired who was engaged in writing poetry.

INTERVIEWER: I heard that a very early draft of "The Drunken Fisherman" appeared in the St. Mark's magazine.

LOWELL: No, it was the Kenyon college magazine that published it. The poem was very different then. I'd been reading Winters, whose model was Robert Bridges, and what I wanted was a rather distant, quiet, classical poem without any symbolism. It was in four-foot couplets as smooth as I could write them. The *Kenyon Review* had published a poem of mine and then they'd stopped. This was the one time they said, if you'd submitted this we'd have taken it.

INTERVIEWER: Then you were submitting other poems to the Review?

LOWELL: Yes, and that poem was rather different from anything else I did. I was also reading Hart Crane and Thomas and Tate and Empson's *Seven Types of Ambiguity*; and each poem was more difficult than the one before, and had more ambiguities. Ransom, editing the *Kenyon Review*, was impressed, but didn't want to publish them. He felt they were forbidding and clotted.

INTERVIEWER: But finally he did come through.

LOWELL: Well, after I'd graduated. I published when I was a junior, then for about three years no magazine would take anything I did. I'd get sort of pleasant letters—"One poem in this group interests us, if you can get seven more." At that time it took me about a year to do two or three poems. Gradually I just stopped, and really sort of gave it up. I seemed to have reached a great impasse. The kind of poem I thought was interesting and would work on became so cluttered and overdone that it wasn't really poetry.

INTERVIEWER: I was struck on reading *Land of Unlikeness* by the difference between the poems you rejected for *Lord Weary's Castle* and the few poems and passages that you took over into the new book.

LOWELL: I think I took almost a third, but almost all of what I took was rewritten. But I wonder what struck you?

INTERVIEWER: One thing was that almost all the rejected poems seemed to me to be those that Tate, who in his introduction spoke about two kinds of poetry in the book, said were the more strictly religious and strictly symbolic poems, as against the poems he said were perhaps more powerful because more experienced or relying more on your sense of history. What you took seemed really superior to what you left behind.

LOWELL: Yes, I took out several that were paraphrases of early Christian poems, and I rejected one rather dry abstraction, then whatever seemed to me to have a messy violence. All the poems have religious imagery, I think, but the ones I took were more concrete. That's what the book was moving toward: less symbolic imagery. And as I say, I tried to take some of the less fierce poems. There seemed to be too much twisting and disgust in the first book.

INTERVIEWER: I wondered how wide your reading had been at the time. I wondered, when I read in Tate's introduction that the stanza in one of your poems was based on the stanza in "The Virginian Voyages," whether someone had pointed out Drayton's poem to you.

LOWELL: Tate and I started to make an anthology together. It was a very interesting year I spent with Tate and his wife. He's a poet who writes in spurts, and he had about a third of a book. I was going to do a biography of Jonathan Edwards and he was going to write a novel, and our wives were going to write novels. Well, the wives just went humming away. "I've just finished three pages," they'd say at the end of the day; and their books mounted up. But ours never did, though one morning Allen wrote four pages to his novel, very brilliant. We were in a little study together separated by a screen. I was heaping up books on Jonathan Edwards and taking notes, and getting more and more numb on the subject, looking at old leather-bound volumes on freedom of the will and so on, and feeling less and less a calling. And there we stuck. And then we decided to make an anthology together. We both liked rather formal, difficult poems, and we were reading particularly the Sixteenth and Seventeenth centuries. In the evening we'd read aloud, and we started a card catalogue of what we'd make for the anthology. And then we started writing. It seems to me we took old models like Drayton's Ode—Tate wrote a poem called "The Young Proconsuls of the Air" in that stanza. I think there's a trick to formal poetry. Most poetry is very formal, but when a modern poet is formal he gets more attention for it than old poets did. Somehow we've tried to make it look difficult. For example, Shelley can just rattle off terza rima by the page, and it's very smooth, doesn't seem an obstruction to him—you sometimes wish it were more difficult. Well, someone does that today and in modern style it looks as though he's wrestling with every line and may be pushed into confusion, as though he's having a real struggle with form and content. Marks of that are in the finished poem. And I think both Tate and I felt that we wanted our formal patterns to seem a hardship and something that we couldn't rattle off easily.

INTERVIEWER: But in *Lord Weary's Castle* there were poems moving toward a sort of narrative calm, almost a prose calm— "Katherine's Dream," for example, or the two poems on texts by Edwards, or "The Ghost"—and then, on the other hand, poems in which the form was insisted upon and maybe shown off, and where the things that were characteristic of your poetry at that time—the kind of enjambments, the rhyming, the meters, of course—seem willed and forced, so that you have a terrific log jam of stresses, meanings, strains.

LOWELL: I know one contrast I've felt, and it takes different forms at different times. The ideal modern form seems to be the novel and certain short stories. Maybe Tolstoi would be the perfect example—his work is imagistic, it deals with all experience, and there seems to be no conflict of the form and content. So one thing is to get into poetry that kind of human richness in rather simple descriptive language. Then there's another side of poetry: compression, something highly rhythmical and perhaps wrenched into a small space. I've always been fascinated by both these things. But getting it all on one page in a few stanzas, getting it all done in as little space as possible, revising and revising so that each word and rhythm though not perfect is pondered and wrestled with—you can't do that in prose very well, you'd never get your book written. "Katherine's Dream" was a real dream. I found that I shaped it a bit, and cut it, and allegorized it, but still it was a dream someone had had. It was material that ordinarily, I think, would go into prose, yet it would have had to be much longer or part of something much longer.

INTERVIEWER: I think you can either look for forms, you can do specific reading for them, or the forms can be demanded by what you want to say. And when the material in poetry seems under almost unbearable pressure you wonder whether the form hasn't cookie-cut what the poet wanted to say. But you chose the couplet, didn't you, and some of your freest passages are in couplets.

LOWELL: The couplet I've used is very much like the couplet Browning uses in "My Last Duchess," in *Sordello,* run-on with its rhymes buried. I've always, when I've used it, tried to give the impression that I had as much freedom in choosing the rhyme word as I had in any of the other words. Yet they were almost all true rhymes, and maybe half the time there'd be a pause after the rhyme. I wanted something as fluid as prose; you wouldn't notice the form, yet looking back you'd find that great obstacles had been climbed. And the couplet is pleasant in this way—once you've got your two lines to rhyme, then that's done and you can go on to the next. You're not stuck with the whole stanza to round out and build to a climax. A couplet can be a couplet or can be split and left as one line, or it can go on for a hundred lines; any sort of compression or expansion is possible. And that's not so in a stanza. I think a couplet's much less lyrical than a stanza, closer to prose. Yet it's an honest form, its difficulties are in the open. It really is pretty hard to rhyme each line with the one that follows it.

INTERVIEWER: Did the change of style in *Life Studies* have something to do with working away from that compression and pressure by way of, say, the kind of prose clarity of "Katherine's Dream"?

LOWELL: Yes. By the time I came to *Life Studies* I'd been writing my autobiography and also writing poems that broke meter. I'd been doing a lot of reading aloud. I went on a trip to the West Coast and read at least once a day and sometimes twice for fourteen days, and more and more I found that I was simplifying my poems. If I had a Latin quotation I'd translate it into English. If adding a couple of syllables in a line made it clearer I'd add them, and I'd make little changes just impromptu as I read. That seemed to improve the reading.

INTERVIEWER: Can you think of a place where you added a a syllable or two to an otherwise regular line?

LOWELL: It was usually articles and prepositions that I added, very slight little changes, and I didn't change the printed text. It was just done for the moment.

INTERVIEWER: Why did you do this? Just because you thought the most important thing was to get the poem over?

LOWELL: To get it over, yes. And I began to have a certain disrespect for the tight forms. If you could make it easier by adding syllables, why not? And then when I was writing *Life Studies*, a good number of the poems were started in very strict meter, and I found that, more than the rhymes, the regular beat was what I didn't want. I have a long poem in there about my father, called "Commander Lowell," which actually is largely in couplets, but I originally wrote perfectly strict four-foot couplets. Well, with that form it's hard not to have echoes of Marvell. That regularity just seemed to ruin the honesty of sentiment, and became rhetorical; it said, "I'm a poem"—though it was a great help when I was revising having this original skeleton. I could keep the couplets where I wanted them and drop them where I didn't; there'd be a form to come back to.

INTERVIEWER: Had you originally intended to handle all that material in prose?

LOWELL: Yes. I found it got awfully tedious working out transitions and putting in things that didn't seem very important but were necessary to the prose continuity. Also, I found it hard to revise. Cutting it down into small bits, I could work on it much more carefully and make fast transitions. But there's another point about this mysterious business of prose and poetry, form and content, and the reasons for breaking forms. I don't think there's any very satisfactory answer. I seesaw back and forth between something highly metrical and something highly free; there isn't any one way to write. But it seems to me we've gotten into a sort of Alexandrian age. Poets of my generation and particularly younger ones have gotten terribly proficient at these forms. They write a very musical, difficult poem with tremendous skill, perhaps there's never been such skill. Yet the writing seems divorced from culture somehow. It's become too much something specialized that can't handle much experience. It's become a craft, purely a craft, and there must be some breakthrough back into life. Prose is in many ways better off than poetry. It's quite hard to think of a young poet who has the vitality, say, of Salinger or Saul Bellow. Yet prose tends to be very diffuse. The novel is really a much more difficult form than it seems; few people have the wind to write anything that long. Even a short story demands almost poetic perfection. Yet on the whole prose is less cut off from life than poetry is. Now, some of this Alexandrian poetry is very brilliant, you would not have it changed at all. But I thought it was getting increasingly stifling. I couldn't get my experience into tight metrical forms.

INTERVIEWER: So you felt this about your own poetry, your own technique, not just about the general condition of poetry?

LOWELL: Yes, I felt that the meter plastered difficulties and mannerisms on what I was trying to say to such an extent that it terribly hampered me.

INTERVIEWER: This then explains, in part anyway, your admiration for Elizabeth Bishop's poetry. I know that you've said the qualities and the abundance of its descriptive language reminded you of the Russian novel more than anything else.

LOWELL: Any number of people are guilty of writing a complicated poem that has a certain amount of symbolism in it and really difficult meaning, a wonderful poem to teach. Then you unwind it and you feel that the intelligence, the experience, whatever goes into it, is skin-deep. In Elizabeth Bishop's "Man-Moth" a whole new world is gotten out and you don't know what will come after any one line. It's exploring. And it's as original as Kafka. She's gotten a world, not just a way of writing. She seldom writes a poem that doesn't have that exploratory quality; yet it's very firm, it's not like beat poetry, it's all controlled.

INTERVIEWER: What about Snodgrass? What you were trying to do in *Life Studies* must have something to do with your admiration for his work.

LOWELL: He did these things before I did, though he's younger than I am and had been my student. He may have influenced me, though people have suggested the opposite. He spent ten years at the University of Iowa, going to writing classes, being an instructor; rather unworldly, making little money, and specializing in talking to other people writing poetry, obsessed you might say with minute technical problems and rather provincial experience—and then he wrote about just that. I mean, the poems are about his child, his divorce, and Iowa City, and his child is a Dr. Spock child—all handled in expert little stanzas. I believe that's a new kind of poetry. Other poems that are direct that way are slack and have no vibrance. His experience wouldn't be so interesting and valid if it weren't for the whimsy, the music, the balance, everything revised and placed and pondered. All that gives light to those poems on agonizing subjects comes from the craft.

INTERVIEWER: And yet his best poems are all on the verge of being slight and even sentimental.

LOWELL: I think a lot of the best poetry is. Laforgue—it's hard to think of a more delightful poet, and his prose is wonderful too. Well, it's on the verge of being sentimental, and if he hadn't dared to be sentimental he wouldn't have been a poet. I mean, his inspiration was that. There's some way of distinguishing between false sentimentality, which is blowing up a subject and giving emotions that you don't feel, and using whimsical, minute, tender, small emotions that most people don't feel but which Laforgue and Snodgrass do. So that I'd say he had pathos and fragility—but then that's a large subject too. He has fragility along the edges and a main artery of power going through the center.

INTERVIEWER: Some people were disappointed with *Life Studies* just because earlier you had written a kind of heroic poetry, an American version of heroic poetry, of which there had been none recently except your own. Is there any chance that you will go back to that?

LOWELL: I don't think that a personal history can go on forever, unless you're Walt Whitman and have a way with you. I feel I've done enough personal poetry. That doesn't mean I won't do more of it, but I don't want to do more now. I feel I haven't gotten down all my experience, or perhaps even the most important part, but I've said all I really have much inspiration to say, and more would just dilute. So that you need something more impersonal, and other things being equal it's better to get your emotions out in a Macbeth than in a confession. Macbeth must have tons of Shakespeare in him. We don't know where, nothing in Shakespeare's life was remotely like Macbeth, yet he somehow gives the feeling of going to the core of Shakespeare. You have much more freedom that way than you do when you write an autobiographical poem.

INTERVIEWER: These poems, I gather from what you said earlier, did take as much working over as the earlier ones.

LOWELL: They were just as hard to write. They're not always factually true. There's a good deal of tinkering with fact. You leave out a lot, and emphasize this and not that. Your actual experience is a complete flux. I've invented facts and changed things, and the whole balance of the poem was something invented. So there's a lot of artistry, I hope, in the poems. Yet there's this thing: if a poem is autobiographical—and this is true of any kind of autobiographical writing and of historical writing— you want the reader to say, this is true. In something like Macaulay's *History of England* you think you're really getting William III. That's as good as a good plot in a novel. And so there was always that standard of truth which you wouldn't ordinarily have in poetry—the reader was to believe he was getting the *real* Robert Lowell.

INTERVIEWER: I wanted to ask you about this business of taking over passages from earlier poems and rewriting them and putting them in new contexts. I'm thinking of the passage at the end of the "Cistercians in Germany," in *Land of Unlikeness*, which you rewrote into those wonderful lines that end "At the Indian Killer's Grave." I know that Hart Crane rewrote early scraps a great deal and used most of the rewrites. But doesn't doing this imply a theory of poetry that would talk much more about craft than about experience?

LOWELL: I don't know, it's such a miracle if you get lines that are halfway right; it's not just a technical problem. The lines must mean a good deal to you. All your poems are in a sense one poem, and there's always the struggle of getting something that balances and comes out right, in which all parts are good, and that has experience that you value. And so if you have a few lines that shine in a poem or are beginning to shine, and they fail and get covered over and drowned, maybe their real form is in another poem. Maybe you've mistaken the real inspiration in the original poem and they belong in something else entirely. I don't think that violates experience. The "Cistercians" wasn't very close to me, but the last lines seemed felt; I dropped the Cistercians and put a Boston graveyard in.

INTERVIEWER: But in Crane's "Ode to an Urn," a poem about a personal friend, there are lines which originally applied to something very different, and therefore, in one version or the other, at least can't be called personal.

LOWELL: I think we always bring over some unexplained obscurities by shifting lines. Something that was clear in the original just seems odd and unexplained in the final poem. That can be quite bad, of course; but you always want—and I think Chekhov talks about this—the detail that you can't explain. It's just there. It seems right to you, but you don't have to have it; you could have something else entirely. Now if everything's like that you'd just have chaos, but a few unexplained difficult things—they seem to be the life-blood of variety—they may work. What may have seemed a little odd, a little difficult in the original poem, gets a little more difficult in a new way in the new poem. And that's purely accidental, yet you may gain more than you lose—a new suggestiveness and magic.

INTERVIEWER: Do you revise a very great deal?

LOWELL: Endlessly.

INTERVIEWER: You often use an idiom or a very common phrase either for the sake of irony or to bear more meaning than it's customarily asked to bear—do these come late in the game, do you have to look around for them?

LOWELL: They come later because they don't prove much in themselves, and they often replace something that's much more formal and worked-up. Some of my later poetry does have this quality that the earlier doesn't: several lines can be almost what you'd say in conversation. And maybe talking with a friend or with my wife I'd say, "This doesn't sound quite right," and sort of reach in the air as I talked and change a few words. In that way the new style is easier to write; I sometimes fumble out a natural sequence of lines that will work. But a whole poem won't come that way; my seemingly relaxed poems are just about as hard as the very worked-up ones.

INTERVIEWER: That rightness and familiarity, though, is in "Between the Porch and the Altar" in several passages which are in couplets.

LOWELL: When I am writing in meter I find the simple lines never come right away. Nothing does. I don't believe I've ever written a poem in meter where I've kept a single one of the original lines. Usually when I was writing my old poems I'd write them out in blank verse and then put in the rhymes. And of course I'd change the rhymes a lot. The most I could hope for at first was that the rhymed version wouldn't be much inferior to the blank verse. Then the real work would begin, to make it something much better than the original out of the difficulties of the meter.

INTERVIEWER: Have you ever gone as far as Yeats and written out a prose argument and then set down the rhymes?

LOWELL: With some of the later poems I've written out prose versions, then cut the prose down and abbreviated it. A rapidly written prose draft of the poem doesn't seem to do much good, too little pain has gone into it; but one really worked on is bound to have phrases that are invaluable. And it's a nice technical problem: how can you keep phrases and get them into meter?

INTERVIEWER: Do you usually send off your work to friends before publishing it?

LOWELL: I do it less now. I always used to do it, to Jarrell and one or two other people. Last year I did a lot of reading with Stanley Kunitz.

INTERVIEWER: At the time you were writing the poems for *Lord Weary's Castle*, did it make a difference to you whether the poet to whom you were sending your work was Catholic?

LOWELL: I don't think I ever sent any poems to a Catholic. The person I was closest to then was Allen Tate, who wasn't a Catholic at the time; and then later it became Jarrell, who wasn't at all Catholic. My two close Catholic writer friends are prose writers, J. F. Powers and Flannery O'Connor, and they weren't interested in the technical problems of poems.

INTERVIEWER: So you feel that the religion is the business of the poem that it's in and not at all the business of the Church or the religious person.

LOWELL: It shouldn't be. I mean, a religion ought to have objective validity. But by the time it gets into a poem it's so mixed up with technical and imaginative problems that the theologian, the priest, the serious religious person isn't of too much use. The poem is too strange for him to feel at home and make any suggestions.

INTERVIEWER: What does this make of the religious poem as a religious exercise?

LOWELL: Well, it at least makes this: that the poem tries to be a poem and not a piece of artless religious testimony. There is a drawback. It seems to me that with any poem, but maybe particularly a religious one where there are common interests, the opinion of intelligent people who are not poets ought to be useful. There's an independence to this not getting advice from religious people and outsiders, but also there's a narrowness. Then there is a question whether my poems are religious, or whether they just use religious imagery. I haven't really any idea. My last poems don't use religious imagery, they don't use symbolism. In many ways they seem to me more religious than the early ones, which are full of symbols and references to Christ and God. I'm sure the symbols and the Catholic framework didn't make the poems religious experiences. Yet I don't feel my experience changed very much. It seems to me it's clearer to me now than it was then, but it's very much the same sort of thing that went into the religious poems—the same sort of struggle, light and darkness, the flux of experience. The morality seems much the same. But the symbolism is gone; you couldn't possibly say what creed I believed in. I've wondered myself often. Yet what made the earlier poems valuable seems to be some recording of experience, and that seems to be what makes the later ones.

INTERVIEWER: So you end up saying that the poem does have some integrity and can have some beauty apart from the beliefs expressed in the poem.

LOWELL: I think it can only have integrity apart from the beliefs; that no political position, religious position, position of generosity, or what have you, can make a poem good. It's all to the good if a poem *can* use politics, or theology, or gardening, or anything that has its own validity aside from poetry. But these things will never *per se* make a poem.

INTERVIEWER: The difficult question is whether when the beliefs expressed in a poem are obnoxious the poem as a whole can be considered to be beautiful—the problem of the *Pisan Cantos*.

LOWELL: The *Pisan Cantos* are very uneven, aren't they? If you took what most people would agree are maybe the best hundred passages, would the beliefs in those passages be obnoxious? I think you'd get a very mixed answer. You could make quite a good case for Pound's good humor about his imprisonment, his absence of self-pity, his observant eye, his memories of literary friends, for all kinds of generous qualities and open qualities and lyrical qualities that anyone would think were good. And even when he does something like the death of Mussolini, in the passage that opens the *Pisan Cantos*, people debate about it. I've talked to Italians who were partisans, and who said that this is the only poem on Mussolini that's any good. Pound's quite wily often: Mussolini hung up like an ox—his brutal appearance. I don't know whether you could say the beliefs there are wrong or not. And there are other poems that come to mind: in Eliot, the Jew spelled with a small j in "Gerontion," is that anti-Semitism or not? Eliot's not anti-Semitic in any sense, but there's certainly a dislike of Jews in those early poems. Does he gain in the fierceness of writing his Jew with a small j? He says you write what you have to write and in criticism you can say what you think you should believe in. Very ugly emotions perhaps make a poem.

INTERVIEWER: You were on the Bollingen Committee at the

time the award was made to Pound. What did you think of the
great ruckus?

LOWELL: I thought it was a very simple problem of voting for
the best book of the year; and it seemed to me Pound's was. I
thought the *Pisan Cantos* was the best writing Pound had ever
done, though it included some of his worst. It is a very mixed
book: that was the question. But the consequences of not giving
the best book of the year a prize for extraneous reasons, even
terrible ones in a sense—I think that's the death of art. Then you
have Pasternak suppressed and everything becomes stifling. Particularly in a strong country like ours you've got to award things
objectively and not let the beliefs you'd like a man to have govern
your choice. It was very close after the war, and anyone must feel
that the poetry award was a trifling thing compared with the
concentration camps. I actually think they were very distant from
Pound. He had no political effect whatsoever and was quite
eccentric and impractical. Pound's social credit, his Fascism, all
these various things, were a tremendous gain to him; he'd be a
very Parnassan poet without them. Even if they're bad beliefs—
and some were bad, some weren't, and some were just terrible,
of course—they made him more human and more to do with life,
more to do with the times. They served him. Taking what interested him in these things gave a kind of realism and life to his
poetry that it wouldn't have had otherwise.

INTERVIEWER: Did you become a translator to suit your own
needs or because you wanted to get certain poems, most of them
not before translated, into English? Or was it a matter of both,
as I suppose it usually is, and as it was for Pound?

LOWELL: I think both. It always seemed to me that nothing
very close to the poems I've translated existed in English; and on
the other hand, there was some kind of closeness, I felt a kinship.
I felt some sort of closeness to the Rilke and Rimbaud poems
I've translated, yet they were doing things I couldn't do. They
were both a continuation of my own bias and a release from
myself.

INTERVIEWER: How did you come to translate Propertius—in fact, how did you come to have such a great interest in Roman history and Latin literature?

LOWELL: At Harvard my second year I took almost entirely English courses—the easiest sort of path. I think that would have been a disaster. But before going to Kenyon I talked to Ford Madox Ford and Ransom, and Ransom said you've just got to take philosophy and logic, which I did. The other thing he suggested was classics. Ford was rather flippant about it, said of course you've got to learn classics, you'll just cut yourself off from humanity if you don't. I think it's always given me some sort of yardstick for English. And then the literature was amazing, particularly the Greek; there's nothing like Greek in English at all. Our plays aren't formally at all like Aeschylus and Sophocles. Their whole inspiration was unbelievably different, and so different that you could hardly think of even the attempt to imitate them, great as their prestige was. That something like *Antigone* or *Oedipus* or the great Achilles moments in the *Iliad* would be at the core of a literature is incredible for anyone brought up in an English culture—Greek wildness and sophistication all different, the women different, everything. Latin's of course much closer. English is a half-Latin language, and we've done our best to absorb the Latin literature. But a Roman poet is much less intellectual than the Englishman, much less abstract. He's nearer nature somehow—somewhat what we feel about a Frenchman but more so still. And yet he's very sophisticated. He has his way of doing things, though the number of forms he explored is quite limited. The amount he could take from the Greeks and yet change is an extraordinary piece of firm discipline. Also, you take almost any really good Roman poet—Juvenal, or Vergil, or Propertius, Catullus—he's much more raw and direct than anything in English, and yet he has this blocklike formality. The Roman frankness interests me. Until recently our literature hasn't been as raw as the Roman, translations had to have stars. And their history has a terrible human frankness that isn't customary with us—corrosive attacks on the establishment, comments on politics and the decay of morals, all felt terribly strongly, by poets as well as historians. The English writer who reads the classics is working at one thing, and his eye is on something else that can't be done. We will always have the Latin and Greek classics, and they'll never be absorbed. There's something very restful about that.

INTERVIEWER: But, more specifically, how did Latin poetry—your study of it, your translations—affect your measure of English poetry?

LOWELL: My favorite English poetry was the difficult Elizabethan plays and the Metaphysicals, then the nineteenth century, which I was aquiver about and disliked but which was closer to my writing than anything else. The Latin seemed very different from either of these. I immediately saw how Shelley wasn't like Horace and Vergil or Aeschylus—and the Latin was a mature poetry, a realistic poetry, which didn't have the contortions of the Metaphysicals. What a frail, bony, electric person Marvell is compared with Horace!

INTERVIEWER: What about your adaptation of Propertius?

LOWELL: I got him through Pound. When I read him in Latin I found a kind of Propertius you don't get in Pound at all. Pound's Propertius is a rather Ovidian figure with a great deal of Pound's fluency and humor and irony. The actual Propertius is a very excited, tense poet, rather desperate; his line is much more like parts of Marlowe's *Faustus*. And he's of all the Roman poets the most like a desperate Christian. His experiences, his love affair with Cynthia, are absolutely rending, destroying. He's like a fallen Christian.

INTERVIEWER: Have you done any other translations of Latin poems?

LOWELL: I did a monologue that started as a translation of Vergil and then was completely rewritten, and there are buried translations in several other poems. There's a poem called "To Speak of Woe That Is in Marriage" in my last book that started as a translation of Catullus. I don't know what traces are left, but it couldn't have been written without the Catullus.

INTERVIEWER: You've translated Pasternak. Do you know Russian?

LOWELL: No, I have rewritten other English translations, and seldom even checked with Russian experts. I want to get a book of translations together. I read in the originals, except for Russian, but I have felt quite free to alter things, and I don't know that Pasternak would look less close than the Italian, which I have studied closely. Before I publish, I want to check with a Russian expert.

INTERVIEWER: Can I get you back to Harvard for a minute? Is it true you tried out for the Harvard *Advocate*, did all the dirty work for your candidacy, and then were turned down?

LOWELL: I nailed a carpet down. I forget who the editor was then, but he was a man who wrote on Frost. At that time people who wrote on Frost were quite different from the ones who write on him now; they tended to be conservative, out of touch. I wasn't a very good writer then, perhaps I should have been turned down. I was trying to write like William Carlos Williams, very simple, free verse, imagistic poems. I had a little group I was very proud of which was set up in galleys; when I left Harvard it was turned down.

INTERVIEWER: Did you know any poets at the time?

LOWELL: I had a friend, Harry Brown, who writes dialogue for movies and has been in Hollywood for years. He was a terribly promising poet. He came to Harvard with a long correspondence with Harriet Monroe and was much more advanced than anyone else. He could write in the style of Auden or Webster or Eliot or Crane. He'd never graduated from high school, and wasn't a student, but he was the person I felt closest to. My other friends weren't writers.

INTERVIEWER: Had you met any older poets—Frost, for instance, who must have been around?

LOWELL: I'd gone to call on Frost with a huge epic on the First Crusade, all written out in clumsy longhand on lined paper. He read a page of that and said, "You have no compression." Then he read me a very short poem of Collins, "How Sleep the Brave," and said, "That's not a great poem, but it's not too long." He was very kindly about it. You know his point about the voice coming into poetry: he took a very unusual example of that, the opening of *Hyperion*; the line about the Naiad, something about her pressing a cold finger to her cold lips, which wouldn't seem like a voice passage at all. And he said, "Now Keats comes alive here." That was a revelation to me; what had impressed me was the big Miltonic imitation in *Hyperion*. I don't know what I did with that, but I recoiled and realized that I was diffuse and monotonous.

INTERVIEWER: What decided you to leave Harvard and go to Kenyon?

LOWELL: I'd made the acquaintance of Merrill Moore, who'd been at Vanderbilt and a Fugitive. He said that I ought to study with a man who was a poet. He was very close to Ransom, and the plan was that I'd go to Vanderbilt; and I would have, but Ransom changed to Kenyon.

INTERVIEWER: I understand you left much against the wishes of your family.

LOWELL: Well, I was getting quite morose and solitary, and they sort of settled for this move. They'd rather have had me a genial social Harvard student, but at least I'd be working hard this way. It seemed to them a queer but orderly step.

INTERVIEWER: Did it help you that you had had intellectual and literary figures in your family?

LOWELL: I really didn't know I'd had them till I went to the South. To my family, James Russell Lowell was the ambassador to England, not a writer. Amy seemed a bit peculiar to them. When I began writing I think it would have been unimaginable to take either Amy or James Russell Lowell as models.

INTERVIEWER: Was it through Ransom that you met Tate?

LOWELL: I met them at more or less the same time, but actually stayed with Tate before I knew Ransom very well.

INTERVIEWER: And Ford Madox Ford was there at some time, wasn't he?

LOWELL: I met Ford at a cocktail party in Boston and went to dinner with him at the Athens Olympia. He was going to visit the Tates, and said, "Come and see me down there, we're all going to Tennessee." So I drove down. He hadn't arrived, so I got to know the Tates quite well before his appearance.

INTERVIEWER: Staying in a pup-tent.

LOWELL: It's a terrible piece of youthful callousness. They had one Negro woman who came in and helped, but Mrs. Tate was doing all the housekeeping. She had three guests and her own family, and was doing the cooking and writing a novel. And this young man arrived, quite ardent and eccentric. I think I suggested that maybe I'd stay with them. And they said, "We really haven't any room, you'd have to pitch a tent on the lawn." So I went to Sears, Roebuck and got a tent and rigged it on their lawn. The Tates were too polite to tell me that what they'd said had been just a figure of speech. I stayed two months in my tent and ate with the Tates.

INTERVIEWER: And you were showing him your work all the while.

LOWELL: Oh, I became converted to formalism and changed my style from brilliant free verse, all in two months. And everything was in rhyme, and it still wasn't any good. But that was a great incentive. I poured out poems and went to writers' conferences.

INTERVIEWER: What about Ford?

LOWELL: I saw him out there and took dictation from him for a while. That was hell, because I didn't know how to type. I'd take the dictation down in longhand, and he rather mumbled. I'd ask him what he'd said, and he'd say, "Oh, you have no sense of prose rhythm," and mumble some more. I'd get most of his words, then I'd have to improvise on the typewriter.

INTERVIEWER: So for part of Ford's opus we're indebted to you.

LOWELL: A handful of phrases in *The March of Literature*, on the Provençal poets.

INTERVIEWER: That was the summer before you entered Kenyon; but most of the poems in *Land of Unlikeness* were written after you'd graduated, weren't they?

LOWELL: Yes, they were almost all written in a year I spent with the Tates, though some of them were earlier poems rewritten. I think becoming a Catholic convert had a good deal to do with writing again. I was much more interested in being a Catholic than in being a writer. I read Catholic writers but had no intention of writing myself. But somehow, when I started again, I won't say the Catholicism gave me subject matter, but it gave me some kind of form, and I could begin a poem and build it to a climax. It was quite different from what I'd been doing earlier.

INTERVIEWER: Why, then, did you choose to print your work in the small liberal magazines whose religious and political positions were very different from yours? Have you ever submitted to the *New Yorker* or the *Atlantic Monthly?*

LOWELL: I think I may have given something to the *Atlantic* on Santayana; the *New Yorker* I haven't given anything. I think the *New Yorker* does some of the best prose in the country, in many ways much more interesting than the quarterlies and little magazines. But poems are lost in it; there's no table of contents, and some of their poetry is light verse. There's no particular continuity of excellence. There just seems no point in printing there. For a while the little magazines, whose religious-political positions *were* very different from mine, were the only magazines that would publish me, and I feel like staying with them. I like magazines like the *New Statesman*, the *Nation*, the *New Republic*—something a little bit off the track.

INTERVIEWER: Just because they are off the track?

LOWELL: I think so. A political position I don't necessarily agree with which is a little bit adverse seems to me just more attractive than a time-serving, conventional position. And they tend to have good reviews, those magazines. I think you write for a small audience, an ardent critical audience. And you know Graves says that poets ought to take in each other's washing because they're the only responsible audience. There's a danger to that—you get too specialized—but I pretty much agree that's the audience you do write for. If it gets further, that's all fine.

INTERVIEWER: There is, though, a certain inbred, in-group anemia to those magazines, at least to the literary quarterlies. For instance, it would have been almost inconceivable for *Partisan Review*, which is the best of them, I think, to give your last book a bad review or even a sharp review.

LOWELL: I think no magazine likes to slam one of its old contributors. *Partisan* has sometimes just not reviewed a book by someone they liked very much and their reviewer didn't. I know Shapiro has been attacked in *Partisan* and then published there, and other people have been unfavorably reviewed and made rather a point of sending them something afterwards. You want to feel there's a certain degree of poorer writing that wouldn't get published in the magazine your work appears in. The good small magazine may publish a lot of rather dry stuff, but at least it's serious, and if it's bad it's not bad by trying to be popular and put something over on the public. It's a wrenched personal ineptitude that will get published rather than a public slickness. I think that has something to do with good reviews coming out in the magazine. We were talking about *Partisan*'s not slamming one of its contributors, but *Partisan* has a pretty harsh, hard standard of reviewing, and they certainly wouldn't praise one of their contributors who'd gone to pot.

INTERVIEWER: What poets among your contemporaries do you most admire?

LOWELL: The two I've been closest to are Elizabeth Bishop—I spoke about her earlier—and Jarrell, and they're different. Jarrell's a great man of letters, a very informed man, and the best critic of my generation, the best professional poet. He's written the best war poems, and those poems are a tremendous product of our culture, I feel. Elizabeth Bishop's poems, as I said, are more personal, more something she did herself, and she's not a critic but has her own tastes, which may be very idiosyncratic. I enjoy her poems more than anybody else's. I like some of Shapiro very much, some of Roethke and Stanley Kunitz.

INTERVIEWER: What about Roethke, who tries to do just about everything you don't try to do?

LOWELL: We've read to each other and argued, and may be rather alike in temperament actually, but he wants a very musical poem and always would quarrel with my ear as I'd quarrel with his eye. He has love poems and childhood poems and startling surrealistic poems, rather simple experience done with a blaze of power. He rejoices in the rhetoric and the metrics, but there's something very disorderly working there. Sometimes it will smash a poem and sometimes it will make it. The things he knows about I feel I know nothing about, flowers and so on. What we share, I think, is the exultant moment, the blazing out. Whenever I've tried to do anything like his poems, I've felt helpless and realized his mastery.

INTERVIEWER: You were apparently a very close friend of Delmore Schwartz's.

LOWELL: Yes, and I think that I've never met anyone who has somehow as much seeped into me. It's a complicated personal thing to talk about. His reading was very varied, Marx and Freud and Russell, very catholic and not from a conservative position at all. He sort of grew up knowing those things and has a wonderful penetrating humorous way of talking about them. If he met T. S. Eliot his impressions of Eliot would be mixed up with his impressions of Freud and what he'd read about Eliot; all these things flowed back and forth in him. Most of my writer friends were more specialized and limited than Schwartz, most of them took against-the-grain positions which were also narrow. Schwartz was a revelation. He felt the poet who had experience was very much better than the poet with polish. Wordsworth would interest him much more than Keats—he wanted openness to direct experience. He said that if you got people talking in a poem you could do anything. And his own writing, *Coriolanus* and *Shenandoah*, is interesting for that.

INTERVIEWER: Isn't this much what you were saying about your own hopes for *Life Studies*?

LOWELL: Yes, but technically I think that Delmore and I are quite different. There have been very few poets I've been able to get very much from technically. Tate has been one of the closest to me. My early poems I think grew out of my admiration for his poems.

INTERVIEWER: What about poets in the past?

LOWELL: It's hard for me to imitate someone; I'm very self-conscious about it. That's an advantage perhaps—you don't become too imitative—but it's also a limitation. I tremble when I feel I'm being like someone else. If it's Rilke or Rimbaud or Propertius, you know the language is a big bar and that if you imitate you're doing something else. I've felt greater freedom that way. I think I've tried to write like some of the Elizabethans.

INTERVIEWER: And Crane? You said you had read a good deal of Crane.

LOWELL: Yes, but his difficult style is one I've never been able to do much with. He can be very obscure and yet write a much more inspired poem than I could by being obscure. There's a relationship between Crane and Tate, and for some reason Tate was much easier for me. I could see how Tate was done, though Tate has a rhythm that I've never been able to imitate. He's much more irregular than I am, and I don't know where the rhythm comes from, but I admire it very much. Crane said somewhere that he could write five or six good lines but Tate could write twelve that would hang together, and you'd see how the twelve were built. Tate was somehow more of a model: he had a lot of wildness and he had a lot of construction. And of course I knew him and never knew Crane. I think Crane is the great poet of that generation. He got out more than anybody else. Not only is it the tremendous power there, but he somehow got New York City; he was at the center of things in the way that no other poet was. All the chaos of his life missed getting sidetracked the way other poets' did, and he was less limited than any other poet of his generation. There was a fullness of experience; and without that, if you just had his mannerisms, and not his rather simple writing —which if done badly would be sentimental merely—or just his obscure writing, the whole thing would be merely verbal. It isn't with Crane. The push of the whole man is there. But his style never worked for me.

INTERVIEWER: But something of Crane does seem to have gotten into your work—or maybe it's just that sense of power thrashing about. I thought it had come from a close admiring reading of Crane.

LOWELL: Yes, some kind of wildness and power that appeals to me, I guess. But when I wrote difficult poems they weren't meant to be difficult, though I don't know that Crane meant his to be. I wanted to be loaded and rich, but I thought the poems were all perfectly logical. You can have a wonderful time explaining a great poem like "Voyages II," and it all can be explained, but in the end it's just a love poem with a great confusion of images that are emotionally clear; a prose paraphrase wouldn't give you any impression whatever of the poem. I couldn't do that kind of poem, I don't think; at least I've never been able to.

INTERVIEWER: You said that most of the writers you've known have been against the grain. What did you mean?

LOWELL: When I began writing most of the great writers were quite unpopular. They hadn't reached the universities yet, and their circulation was small. Even Eliot wasn't very popular then. But life seemed to be there. It seemed to be one of those periods when the lid was still being blown. The great period of blowing the lid was the time of Schönberg and Picasso and Joyce and the early Eliot, where a power came into the arts which we perhaps haven't had since. These people were all rather traditional, yet they were stifled by what was being done, and they almost wrecked things to do their great works—even rather minor but very good writers such as Williams or Marianne Moore. Their kind of protest and queerness has hardly been repeated. They're wonderful writers. You wouldn't see anyone as strange as Marianne Moore again, not for a long while. Conservative and Jamesian as she is, it was a terrible, private, and strange revolutionary poetry. There isn't the motive to do that now. Yet those were the classics, and it seems to me they were all against the grain, Marianne Moore as much as Crane. That's where life was for the small audience. It would be a tremendous subject to say whether the feelings were against the grain too, and whether they were purifying, nihilistic, or both.

INTERVIEWER: Have you had much contact with Eliot?

LOWELL: I may have seen him a score of times in my life, and he's always been very kind. Long before he published me he had some of my poems in his files. There's some kind of New England connection.

INTERVIEWER: Has he helpfully criticized your work?

LOWELL: Just very general criticism. With the first book of mine Faber did he had a lot of little questions about punctuation, but he never said he liked this or disliked that. Then he said something about the last book—"These are first-rate, I mean it"—something like that that was very understated and gratifying. I feel Eliot's less tied to form than a lot of people he's influenced, and there's a freedom of the twenties in his work that I find very sympathetic. Certainly he and Frost are the great New England poets. You hardly think of Stevens as New England, but you have to think of Eliot and Frost as deeply New England and puritanical. They're a continuation and a criticism of the tradition, and they're probably equally great poets. Frost somehow put life into a dead tradition. His kind of poetry must have seemed almost unpublishable, it was so strange and fresh when it was first written. But still it was old-fashioned poetry and really had nothing to do with modern writing—except that he is one of the greatest modern writers. Eliot was violently modern and unacceptable to the traditionalist. Now he's spoken of as a literary dictator, but he's handled his position with wonderful sharpness and grace, it seems to me. It's a narrow position and it's not one I hold particularly, but I think it's been held with extraordinary honesty and finish and development. Eliot has done what he said Shakespeare had done: all his poems are one poem, a form of continuity that has grown and snowballed.

INTERVIEWER: I remember Jarrell in reviewing *Mills of the Kavanaughs* said that Frost had been doing narrative poems with ease for years, and that nobody else had been able to catch up.

LOWELL: And what Jarrell said is true: nobody except Frost can do a sort of Chaucerian narrative poem that's organized and clear. Well, a lot of people do them, but the texture of their verse is so limp and uninspired. Frost does them with great power. Most of them were done early, in that *North of Boston* period. That was a miracle, because except for Robinson—and I think Frost is a very much greater poet than Robinson—no one was doing that in England or America.

INTERVIEWER: But you hadn't simply wanted to tell a story in *Mills of the Kavanaughs*.

LOWELL: No, I was writing an obscure, rather Elizabethan, dramatic and melodramatic poem. I don't know quite how to describe this business of direct experience. With Browning, for instance, for all his gifts—and there is almost nothing Browning couldn't use—you feel there's a glaze between what he writes and what really happened, you feel the people are made up. In Frost you feel that's just what the farmers and so on were like. It has the virtue of a photograph but all the finish of art. That's an extraordinary thing; almost no other poet can do that now.

INTERVIEWER: What do you suppose are the qualities that go into that ability?

LOWELL: I don't know. Prose writers have it much more, and quite a few prose writers have it. It's some kind of sympathy and observation of people. It's the deep, rather tragic poems that I value most. Perhaps it's been overdone with Frost, but there's an abundance and geniality about those poems that isn't tragic.

With this sense of rhythm and words and composition, and getting into his lines language that is very much like the language he speaks—which is also a work of art, much better than other people's ordinary speech and yet natural to him; he has that continuity with his ordinary self and his poetic self—he's made what with anyone else would be just flat. A very good prose writer can do this and make something of it. You get it quite often in Faulkner. Though he's an Elizabethan sort of character, rather unlike Frost, he can get this amazing immediacy and simplicity. When it comes to verse the form is so hard that all of that gets drained out. In a very conventional old-fashioned writer, or someone who's trying to be realistic but also dramatic and inspired, though he may remain a good poet, most of that directness and realism goes. It's hard for Eliot to be direct that way, though you get it in bits of the *Wasteland*, that marvelous Cockney section. And he can be himself; I feel Eliot's real all through the *Quartets*. He can be very intelligent or very simple there, and *he's* there, but there are no other people in the *Quartets*.

INTERVIEWER: Have many of your poems been taken from real people and real events?

LOWELL: I think, except when I've used myself or occasionally named actual people in poems, the characters are purely imaginary. I've tried to buttress them by putting images I've actually seen and in indirect ways getting things I've actually experienced into the poem. If I'm writing about a Canadian nun the poem may have a hundred little bits of things I've looked at, but she's not remotely anyone I've ever known. And I don't believe anybody would think my nun was quite a real person. She has a heart and she's alive, I hope, and she has a lot of color to her and drama, and has some things that Frost's characters don't, but she doesn't have their wonderful quality of life. His Witch of Coös is absolutely there. I've gathered from talking to him that most of the *North of Boston* poems came from actual people he knew shuffled and put together. But then it's all-important that Frost's plots are so extraordinary, so carefully worked out though it almost seems that they're not there. Like some things in Chekhov, the art is very well hidden.

INTERVIEWER: Don't you think a large part of it is getting the right details, symbolic or not, around which to wind the poem tight and tighter?

LOWELL: Some bit of scenery or something you've felt. Almost the whole problem of writing poetry is to bring it back to what you really feel, and that takes an awful lot of maneuvering. You may feel the doorknob more strongly than some big personal event, and the doorknob will open into something that you can use as your own. A lot of poetry seems to me very good in the tradition but just doesn't move me very much because it doesn't have personal vibrance to it. I probably exaggerate the value of it, but it's precious to me. Some little image, some detail you've noticed—you're writing about a little country shop, just describing it, and your poem ends up with an existentialist account of your experience. But it's the shop that started it off. You didn't know why it meant a lot to you. Often images and often the sense of the beginning and end of a poem are all you have—some journey to be gone through between those things; you know that, but you don't know the details. And that's marvelous; then you feel the poem will come out. It's a terrible struggle, because what you really feel hasn't got the form, it's not what you can put down in a poem. And the poem you're equipped to write concerns nothing that you care very much about or have much to say on. Then the great moment comes when there's enough resolution of your technical equipment, your way of constructing things, and what you can make a poem out of, to hit something you really want to say. You may not know you have it to say.

FREDERICK SEIDEL

For a complete list of books available from Penguin in the United States, write to Dept. DG, Penguin Books, 299 Murray Hill Parkway, East Rutherford, New Jersey 07073.

For a complete list of books available from Penguin in Canada, write to Penguin Books Canada Limited, 2801 John Street, Markham, Ontario L3R 1B4.

If you live in the British Isles, write to Dept. EP, Penguin Books Ltd, Harmondsworth, Middlesex.